EDDYSTONE
THE FINGER OF LIGHT

Mike Palmer

with a foreword by Pete Goss MBE

Seafarer Books

This edition published in 2005 by

Seafarer Books

102 Redwald Road

Rendlesham

Woodbridge

Suffolk IP12 2TE

First published in 1998
by Palmridge Publishing

Copyright © 2005 by Mike Palmer
All rights reserved

British Library Cataloguing in Publication Data
Eddystone : the finger of light
1. Eddystone Lighthouse (England) - History
I. Title
627.9'22'0916336
ISBN 0 9547062 0 X

Cover design by Louis Mackay
Front cover picture courtesy of Plymouth City Museum and Art Gallery
Rear cover picture courtesy of Robert Oskar Lenkiewicz

Printed and bound in Great Britain
by E. J. Rickard

ISBN 0 9547062 0 X

CONTENTS

FOREWORD

MAN'S relationship with the sea is a tenuous one, riddled with untold disasters. The sea will never be overcome and when the chips are down there is never any doubt as to who rules. Yet we cannot survive without it, for the fruits of the relationship far outweigh the price that has to be paid, and has been, since time immemorial.

In the face of these odds there have been many stories of sacrifice for fellow mankind. Such is the unwritten law of those who ply the sea. And yet there is a group of people who have perhaps done more to save lives at sea than any others. Theirs is a story of untold courage, sacrifice and engineering genius.

The lighthouse, its symbol, seen on many a postcard, is synonymous with selfless sacrifice in the interests of others. Yet sadly, to many of us, the fact that it has become a symbol de-personalises the lighthouse. It is taken for granted, it has always been there and always will.

Three hundred years ago the Eddystone Rock saw Man's first attempt to put a lighthouse on it. It didn't last long, but the fight was picked up again and again until the Eddystone Lighthouse, as we now know it, took its solitary stand, reaching out as a beacon of safety to all, regardless of creed.

That light – and I have often used it myself – carries the spirit of many. The more you learn about the sacrifice and selfless dedication over the years, the more you appreciate that it is not just a beacon of light but a beacon of humanity at its best; of characters like Smeaton, whose visionary design set the blue-print for lighthouse construction the world over; and Richard Hall, the 84-year-old keeper who looked up during his desperate attempts to save Rudyerd's burning lighthouse – and, gasping for breath, swallowed seven ounces of molten lead.

Mike Palmer, thanks to his interest in people, and seven years of meticulous research, has done us, and those he has written about, the service of bringing that beacon to life. He has managed, in telling the fascinating history of the Eddystone Light, to capture the people and their spirit.

It is a book that makes one marvel at the sacrifice and feel humble in the face of what that light represents. It is a book about individuals, what motivated them, and how they changed not only the Eddystone Rocks with the first wave-washed lighthouse in the British Isles, but also Plymouth itself. For without the light, Plymouth would not have developed into what it has become today.

Thank you, Mike, for shedding light on the world, the endeavours and the achievements of the Eddystone heroes – a light that is every bit as illuminating as the towers themselves. It is a story that needed to be told, particularly as the lighthouse keeper is no more.

PETE GOSS MBE

PREFACE

THE Eddystone Reef lies alone in the blue expanse of the English Channel, many miles from the coast of Devon and Cornwall. The array of sharp stone peaks protruding just above the ocean's surface has claimed many a brave sailor and ship through the centuries.

However, a little over 300 years ago a unique building was erected on the rocky outcrop to help unwary seafarers avoid danger. And so, as if turning the tide itself, the area was finally marked by a lighthouse in the profound hope of saving life and helping vessels steer a safer passage.

On the evening of 14 November 1698, 60 candles were lit in the lantern on top of the tiny tower, their small flickering flames offering a faint light to any seafarer who saw them. The Eddystone's fragile pillar had been precariously anchored to the blackened rocks of the feared and dreadful spot, to warn passing ships of the danger around it.

The remarkable success and achievement in building the structure brought a new chapter to the story of the infamous Eddystone – and because of its unique importance to shipping, the beacon would take its rightful place in the annals of maritime history.

Four lighthouses have been built on the notorious reef in the last three centuries, with the original lighthouse being completely rebuilt in 1699 after surviving just one winter.

The lightkeepers employed in the early towers found themselves very isolated and vulnerable. They were often cold and wet from the stirring tide around them as the sea water penetrated the interior of their flimsy structure. Sometimes the mighty waves would crash completely over the lighthouse to swamp everyone inside; often the men would feel their building shudder and shake as the elements took their toll, pounding at the thin walls which surrounded them. Mountainous storm-swept seas frequently overwhelmed the early Eddystone beacons, obliterating the rays of light and rendering the lighthouses useless. Throughout the changing seasons, weather and tide tested the buildings for any weakness and made their frames bend and vibrate from the forces upon them while, inside their confined and lonely workplace, the anxious keepers could only prepare themselves for an uncertain fate.

Jagged gneiss rock formations make up the long slender fingers of the Eddystone reef. The stony outcrop is within the approaches to Plymouth Sound, a safe haven for shipping. Before any lighthouse had been erected on the rocks, a dark and gloomy legend had been established regarding the place. Etched into the minds of all seamen who sailed on the Channel was the thought of the frightening menace. The area was regarded as that of "a lurking demon, ready to catch any unwary mariner" and the unpredictable villain would grasp at every luckless vessel that strayed too close. Then, while being held fast, the unfortunate ship would be cast into the beast's jaws and devoured with its razor-sharp teeth, leaving nothing but splinters of wood and debris on the ocean's darkened surface.

The destruction of ships and their crews on the reef continued to cause immense concern to all sailors plying along the coast of the South-West, but especially during a stormy gale at night when the monster was invisible.

It was a fact that the Eddystone's notorious reputation and position worried the local fisherman and inhabitants of Plymouth, a town which during the 17th century was an up-and-coming naval base and important commercial port. Lying but 14 miles from the nearest landfall, everyone realised the constant danger would affect the growth of Plymouth itself so they decided to rid the

Eddystone of its "evil demon". Eventually it was decided that a light beacon should be constructed there in an effort to safeguard all shipping movements.

The unique achievement was saluted on a cold winter's night 3 centuries ago, when an Englishman succeeded in building Britain's first "wave-washed rock lighthouse".

Until recently, it had been assumed that the original Eddystone lighthouse was in fact the world's first wave-washed rock lighthouse, but most scholars in the field of pharology now agree that the honour should go to a little-known Italian lighthouse built on the Shoal of Meloria at the southern approaches to Porto Pisano in 1157, by the Pisans.

Nevertheless, the presence of the first Eddystone lighthouse virtually ended all shipping disasters around the reef and each evening, as the lighthouse's candles sent their rays across a dark horizon, passing sailors would cheer the sight and their hearts warmed as they glimpsed the "finger of light", knowing that the faint rays offered them a safe passage.

Many brave and hardy men had built and manned the beacon and more would follow in subsequent years as different lighthouses were erected on the reef. All the workmen and lightkeepers who toiled in the remote and inhospitable environment experienced great danger and their tales of life at "the stone" are now folklore. Myths and legends handed down through the generations have enriched the aura of the Eddystone's colourful history, and the remarkable story continues today.

For men to be perched on top of a wave-washed rocky outcrop, isolated and cocooned from the busy outside world, was an unusual and rewarding existence. However, many on land could not imagine why those individuals wanted to endure such a lifestyle. Indeed, most thought it a very precarious occupation and it was generally accepted that those people were a special breed.

My book celebrates all of the Eddystone Lighthouses and everyone who has been involved in their history; I hope that the following text will offer the reader not just a factual account, but a human perspective on this remarkable story.

This work has also been written as a stepping stone to other technical publications and specific authoritative works on the subject. But hopefully it will also enable readers to gain a greater awareness of this particular lighthouse and the service that it represents. Although it is now of lesser importance, it was, to all seafarers of the time, the difference between life and death itself.

Throughout the last 300 years, intense progress has changed every aspect of society. Today, machine and computer dominate our daily environment, providing remarkable advances which contribute to people's lives, especially at work. Unfortunately, they also erode the very existence of long-established traditional employment. Such development has threatened the livelihood of every lighthouse keeper, so that in the near future no human will watch from his high tower, or live in such dramatic settings, but will instead be replaced by a robotic computerised electric generator which will produce the power for the light and thus aid modern seafarers.

> Yet, were I fain still to remain
> Watch in my tower to keep,
> And tend my light in the stormiest night
> That ever did move the deep.
> And if it stood, why then 'twere good,
> Amid their tremulous stirs,
> To count each stroke when the mad waves broke
> For cheers of mariners
>
> — JEAN INGELOW

This story will also focus on the wonderful and courageous people who have found a place in maritime history; from the builder of the first Eddystone lighthouse, Henry Winstanley, a very remarkable individual whose reputation has faded and is almost forgotten, to the extraordinary tale of the 84-year-old lightkeeper, Richard Hall, who died from swallowing molten lead weighing more than 7.5 oz while trying to put out a major fire that destroyed the Eddystone's third lighthouse in 1755.

This book also highlights the difficulties of building the first rock lighthouses on the Eddystone, the men having to endure untold danger amidst the unpredictable ocean. Using no power tool or modern appliance to assist in their efforts, they raised the structures by muscle power and bold determination alone.

Not just on the reef was each man's life in the balance, but during the passage to and from his workplace.

In plying back and forth between the relative safety of Plymouth and the rock, the workmen would often suffer a journey that in treacherous seas could take up to seven hours. The sea and the weather would be their master and arrival at the Eddystone was never a certainty.

On many occasions the men's small craft would not even be able to reach the rocky island, but was carried many miles away from the reef and out into the empty English Channel, where the changing sea conditions would push the builders' boat far along the desolate coastline of the South-West before they would eventually come ashore at some uninhabited cove, then wait until the strong winds had abated enough to allow them the opportunity to row and sail back to their workplace on the Eddystone.

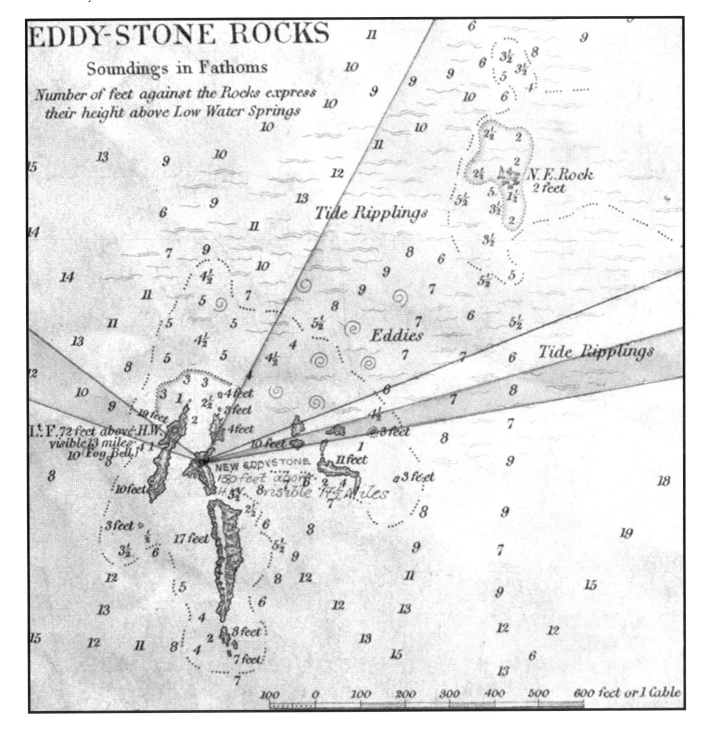

WINSTANLEY'S WONDER

THE WORLD'S first known land lighthouses were built around 330 BC, although the Greek poet Lesches suggested in 745 BC that a well-maintained fire beacon was located on the Troad in Sigaeum. It is acknowledged that the early structures were built by the Libyans and Cushites, tribespeople of ancient Egypt who used the buildings both as light beacons and as monasteries.

However, the most famous of all the ancient lighthouses was the Pharos, built at Alexandria in Egypt for King Ptolemaeus Philadelphus II, in about 260 BC.

It was a huge tower, constructed by the remarkable architect Sostrates, who had demonstrated incredible skills in his design.

His name is etched into the stone blocks of the walls to tell the world of his great talent. However, as he did not wish to offend his King, Sostrates inscribed "Ptolemaeus", the monarch's own name, onto the thick mortar which encased the building. This gave the appearance that the structure was dedicated to his leader, but in time of course the film of cement covering the stone would fall off, leaving the name of Sostrates and so identifying its clever builder.

Further details of the lighthouse are still coming to light, as a major archaeological survey is being undertaken to discover the truth about it. The important discovery has been made during recent work in Alexandria's great harbour and already the findings confirm the details known from ancient drawings. The Pharos appears to have been built of kedan stone and stood nearly 350 feet high, with many storeys that decreased in size towards the top of the tower. A fire burned continuously, showing a yellowish light at night and producing thick columns of smoke during the day, which provided the mariner with a truly functional and purpose-built lighthouse. The sea-mark was estimated to have been visible for 30 miles. The building was also documented by the Arabian geographer Edrisi (1099–1170) who told us the structure comprised well-jointed stonework united by lead overlays. However, the great Pharos was eventually destroyed, possibly by an earthquake, although some scholars believe that it was levelled during early Turkish wars with Egypt. Unfortunately, no records exist of the important landmark after the 13th century, but it was considered to be one of the Seven Wonders of the Ancient World and did exist for a remarkable 1500 years.

Another famous beacon, The Colossus Of Rhodes, was built in 300 BC by a pupil of the classical Greek sculptor Lysippus. The sea-mark was made from bronze and seems to have been a statue of Apollo which stood over 100 feet high, but not (as many had believed) with its legs astride the entrance to the main harbour of Rhodes. It now appears that the beautiful sculpture was actually on one outer pier head of the harbour. The site is being surveyed by archaeologists.

Many other early lighthouses have been documented throughout the world's oceans, including the Lanterna of Genoa, built in 1161, and others at Chrysorrhoas, Ostia, Puteoli, Ravenna and Messina. However, it is not until much later that we in Europe acknowledge what is generally thought to be the father of all modern lighthouses; that of the Tour de Cordouan in France, built between 1584 and 1611 by Louis de Foix, another outstanding architect. The wondrous lighthouse, erected on the mouth of the River Gironde and situated in the Gulf of Gascony, had existed as a simple fire beacon many centuries earlier, during the 1400s. Edward the Black Prince had replaced the primitive system by building an octagonal tower, with a "chauffeur" on top, basically an iron basket containing a coal fire, which provided a satisfactory light for the early ocean traders. It was only after the building had fallen into disrepair in the late 1500s that Louis de Foix was invited to rebuild the lighthouse. After completion of the new structure further developments and changes would continue; Louis XV insisted in 1727 that an iron lantern should replace the stone columns at the building's summit, giving the light better visibility. Oil lamps and reflectors were installed in 1782 and the chief engineer of Bordeaux, a man named Teulère, raised the lantern even more so the light could be seen further away.

The oldest remaining working lighthouse is that of La Coruña, in north-west Spain. Of Roman origins, the building has been extensively rebuilt throughout the centuries. The present tower is the result of major reconstruction work completed in 1791.

In Homer's *Iliad* we read his thoughts:

As to seamen o'er the waves is borne
The watch-fire's light, which, high among the
    hills,
Some shepherd kindles in his lonely field.

In England, sea beacons and light marks are known to have existed since Roman times. One can still be seen at Dover Castle, but it was not until the reign of Henry VIII and his Canterbury charter of 20 March 1512 that we recognise the beginnings of a genuine Lighthouse Service.

Until then the few lighthouses or simple beacons dotted about the English coastline were owned and operated by wealthy speculators who, at best, provided poor service – at a price – to mariners.

Henry VIII was born on 28 June 1491 at the Palace of Placentia in Greenwich. He reigned from 1509 to 1547 and had 46 ships and 13 small galleys built, purchased another 26 vessels and captured 13 more foreign prizes. His interest in naval matters resulted in the development of the Royal Navy and the construction of wooden warships to defend England from possible invasion by France and Spain. Henry VIII was very aware of the importance of his developing naval force and

had realised that the safety of the vessels was vital to any national success. He therefore focused his attention on the navigational difficulties encountered by all seafarers around our coastline and felt compelled to act.

His charter of 1512 was granted to a small body of respected mariners, a brotherhood who took their inspiration from religious and monastic ideas. The opportunity enabled them to forge greater links with the Crown itself

PORTRAIT OF HENRY VIII BY HANS HOLBEIN
BY KIND PERMISSION OF THE CORPORATION OF TRINITY HOUSE

and also helped establish a foundation to promote their ideology. The association would pray for the souls of sailors drowned at sea and perform certain devotional practices. Their moral efforts continued as a charitable organisation, building a school for destitute children and almshouses for old indigent mariners. Soon, with the help of Sir Thomas Spert, a Lighthouse Guild was born, initially in honour of the Holy Trinity and St Clement, but nonetheless the forerunner of today's Trinity House Lighthouse Service.

The seat of the Trinity House was in the fishing village of Deptford, on the Thames in London. Because of its position, Henry VIII built a dock there in 1513 and later added an arsenal which soon became one of the most important naval yards in the country.

The King's charter, addressing "The Brotherhood of Trinity House of Deptford Strond", although now lost, began as follows:

Know ye. That We of our especial grace, and on account of the sincere and entire love and likewise devotion which We bear and have towards the most glorious and undividable Trinity and also to St Clement the Confessor have granted and given License for Us and our Heirs, as much as in Us is, to our beloved Liege people and Subjects the shipmen or mariners of this our Realm of England, that they, or their heirs, to the Praise and Honour of the said most glorious and undividable Trinity and St Clement, may of new begin, erect, create, ordain, found, unite and establish a certain Guild or perpetual Fraternity of themselves and other persons whatsoever, as well men and women, of the parish of Deptford Strond, in our County of Kent.

The charter was confirmed by Edward VI in 1547, then by Queen Mary in 1553 and also by Queen Elizabeth I in 1558. Indeed the Crown would play a leading role in the business of lighthouses throughout the three centuries which followed.

Trinity House as a body had its origins in the 13th century when Stephen Langton, who was Archbishop of Canterbury from 1213 to 1228, founded "a band of Godly disposed men who do bind themselves together in the love of Lord Christ in the name of the Masters and Fellows of Trinity Guild, to succour from the dangers of the sea all who are beset upon the coast of England to feed them when they are hungered, and athirst, to bind up their wounds and to build and light proper beacons for the guidance of mariners".

As time unfolded and England prospered, the ocean around our coastline was recognised as an important gateway to the nation's growing success and gradually more respect

was afforded to the Trinity House Guild, then a fraternity made up of skilled seamen.

By 1514 Henry VIII incorporated the Trinity House Guild and installed Sir Thomas Spert as Master of the organisation, with an administration of four Wardens and eight Assistants who oversaw all daily proceedings. Membership was restricted to Captains or Masters of sea-going vessels and the requirement undoubtedly helped the elite organisation acquire high-ranking support including that of the monarch.

In 1547 the guild of mariners changed their name to the Corporation of Trinity House of Deptford Strond, and in 1573 the College of Heralds granted the Corporation their own coat of arms. They were then regarded as the sole authority for erecting sea beacons and aiding seafarers.

The coat of arms awarded to the maritime

THE TRINITY HOUSE COAT OF ARMS
THE AUTHOR'S COLLECTION

body consisted of an image of St George's Cross on a shield, with an Elizabethan galleon at each quarter, a crowned lion holding a sword, and a scrolled motto beneath it with the words "Trinitas in Unitate".

Acts of Parliament would soon give greater powers to the developing corporation and it was also the subject of a decree by Elizabeth:

And forasmuch as by destroying and taking away of certaine Steeples, Woods and other Marks, standing upon the mayne Shores adjoinying to the Sea Costes of thys Realme of England and Wales, being as Beakons and Markes of auncyent tyme accustomed for seafaring Men to save and kepe them and the shippes in their Charge from sundry Daungers thereto incident, in sailing from forrayne Partes towards this Realme of England and Wales, and specially to the Porte and Ryver of Thames, have by the lacke of suche Marks of late yeres ben myscaried perysshed and lost in the sea, to the great Detryment and Hurte of the Comon Weale, and the perysheng of no smale number of People; For Remedy wherein to be had, the Trinyte Howse at Deptforde Strond, shall and maye lawfully be vertue of this Acte from tyme to tyme, hereafter at theyre Wylles and Pleasures, and at their Costes make erecte and set up suche and so many Beakons Markes and Signes for the Sea, in such Place or Places of the Sea Shore and Uplandes near the Sea Costes or Forelands of the Sea, onely for Sea Markes, as to them shall seeme most meete needefull and reqisyte, whereby the Daungers maye be avoyded and escaped, and Shippes the better coome into their Portes without Peryll.

The dangerous reefs and extensive coastline of England were largely unmarked by beacons or light towers, especially on isolated wave-washed outcrops like the Eddystone Reef, so shipwrecks were a common occurrence around our shores.

Private individuals, nonetheless, were always keen to build a light tower on land and charge light dues to passing ships for the privilege. Most of the so-called lighthouses were no more than raised fires, some in constructed buildings, but most resembling large bonfires. Very few "lights" actually helped in guiding the anxious mariner at night, as they were haphazard affairs and solely erected for financial gain. Being a lucrative business to be involved in, many wealthy coastal landowners would often be found at court, hoping to catch the monarch's eye; for instance, Lord Grenville writes:

> Watch the moment when the King is in good temper to ask him for a lighthouse.

It was only by permission of the ruling monarch that a landowner could build his private "lighthouse", later paying a back-hander to the Crown for the favour. In time, however, Trinity House realised the many lucrative financial possibilities and, with the ruler's help, they monopolised the service by purchasing every worthwhile beacon in the country from its original owner. The infamous Eddystone Reef, 14 miles from the port of Plymouth, was considered to be one of the worst areas for shipping disasters, but no-one imagined it possible to put a sea-mark or beacon on it. No lighthouse (it was then thought) had been built on a rock out at sea and so the unmarked reef would remain just that and continue to cause immense difficulties to the unwary seaman. Most people felt nothing could be done to avert disasters there and so it was accepted that the "red rocks" would never be lit.

The Captain of the *Mayflower,* who took the Pilgrim Fathers to America, described it thus:

> This wicked reef of twenty three rust red granite rocks lying nine and a half miles south of Rame Head on the Devon mainland, great ragged stones around which the sea continuously eddies, a great danger to all ships hereabouts. For if any vessel makes too far to the south as likely as not she will be caught in the prevailing strong current and swept to her doom on these rocks.

The Eddystone may well have earned its name from the complexity and nature of the moving water about the reef, where tidal eddies cause great confusion to the ocean's currents surging around the rock mass itself.

In 1604, James I continued to empower the Corporation of Trinity House, in so much as they were then in control of pilotage and the licensing of pilots, as well as various safety issues, including harbour buoys and lights. With their new responsibilities came a stronger administration in the authority and the men were known as "Elder Brethren".

Oliver Cromwell, however, was not convinced of the Corporation's allegiance to him and dissolved their powers almost immediately, but as soon as Charles II was restored to the throne in 1660 the King undid the damage and Trinity House was back in its former position.

Samuel Pepys, who held high office in 1661, began to take a keen interest in maritime affairs and especially in the administration of Trinity House. His involvement continued to shape the Corporation and he was soon serving as one of the Elder Brethren in 1672; he went on to be the Corporation's Master in 1685.

In 1664 the first known proposal for lighting the Eddystone was presented to Trinity House. It came from Sir John Corytown of Newton Ferrers near Plymouth, "for the right to keep his lighthouses at the Lizard, Falmouth, Torbay, Rame Head and other beneficial places", but his proposal was rejected as unpractical.

SAMUEL PEPYS
THE AUTHOR'S COLLECTION

Research of local interest confirms that the ancient chapel of St Michael on Rame Head was an important sea beacon long before the lighting of the Eddystone. The site is known to have been first licensed for worship in 1397 and later records reveal that a watchman was employed to light a beacon there in 1488. It was a valuable vantage point of significant importance to the port of Plymouth and a duty of the watchman was to signal news to the townspeople of all approaching vessels. The chapel and its "light" rose to high prominence in 1588 when it was the first lookout to raise the alarm about the approaching Spanish Armada.

Another petition for a lighthouse, from Corytown and a Henry Brouncker of Plymouth, was sent to the Admiralty in 1665, which resulted in a curt reply – "could hardly be accomplished, though it was desirable"– and the proposal was rejected.

After the restoration of Charles II, many more people were asking to build their own private lighthouses and it has to be said that the proposals came mainly from Cavaliers who had lost their lands and liberty under the Cromwellian usurpation and were desperate to gain the Monarch's approval, hoping to recoup their losses by obtaining one of the potentially valuable lighthouse patents.

It is obvious, too, that many of the favoured proprietors who had been given permission to build their light towers showed little interest in helping the seafarer; sadly, many of the projects were not honourable, but simply a means to a profitable end. It would be nearly 30 years before another plan was submitted for a building on the Eddystone.

In 1691 a new plan was put to Trinity House. The initial reaction from the fraternity was surprisingly positive, so much so that by the following year the petition had been sent to the Admiralty for their approval.

The man responsible for putting forward the proposition was William Whitfield, who was said to have lived in Plymouth. In his initial correspondence with Trinity House, he wrote that his proposal was "to secure The Eddy stones from continuing to be obnoxious to navigation", which confused the Brethren as they asked in a reply if he meant "setting a lighthouse upon the rocks".

Whitfield appears to have been a wealthy and successful individual who had previously married an heiress, the second daughter of Baron Giffin Braybrook. The family were considered to be in the top tier of British society and their standing in Royal circles was undisputed; indeed Braybrook's home would in a few short years become the Royal Palace of Audley End in Essex.

Whitfield's association with the Braybrook family was undoubtedly instrumental in his eventually successful petition to the naval authorities which resulted in the monarchs, William and Mary, signing a patent roll on 22 June 1694, allowing Trinity House to erect a lighthouse on the Eddystone. For the first time, also, the patent would allow an official charge to be made to merchants and ships that passed the light, their captains paying a fee of 1d per ton for the privilege. The revenue would be used to compensate the builder for his effort and for the construction costs incurred by him. The system of funding the project by levying charges was also designed to generate regular finance for the continuing maintenance and wellbeing of the lighthouse.

Whitfield's guarantor in his contract with Trinity House was his father-in-law Lord Braybrook. Braybrook himself owned the lease of the Eddystone, although he had no further input into the project, allowing Whitfield overall control of the venture.

The William and Mary charter reads:

> Now know yee that Wee doe give and grant the Master Wardens and Assistants of the Trinity House, Authority that they may demand, collect and take of the Merchants and Owners of Shipps, Hoys and Barks which shall passe by the said Light House intended to bee erected on the said Eddystone the Duty of One penny per tunn outward bound and alsoe one penny per tunn inward excepting Coasters from whom wee doe give Authority to take twelve pence for each Voyage passing by the said Light House or beacon and noe more...

The steady interest in privately owned lighthouses grew more rapidly, and an upsurge in ownership ensued. It was even more obvious that an association with the Crown through Trinity House offered kudos, not to mention a beneficial bonus. So, for the influential few, the coastal landowners and wealthy individuals, putting forward their lighthouse building schemes was a chance not to be missed, especially when you considered the new legally binding financial incentive of collecting the light dues; that law alone ensured the speedy transformation of the lighthouse service.

However, even though in 1694 the newly agreed Eddystone project had been finalised, there were many who doubted that Whitfield's venture would succeed. Several high-ranking members of the Admiralty were concerned that the proposal would fail and many brethren of Trinity House shared the view. More importantly, they did not feel comfortable with a partnership involving any outside party or wealthy individual. But still more worrying to the members of Trinity House was the question of their own financial input to the scheme. With the possibility of escalating construction charges not being met by the private individual concerned, would the burden fall on the Corporation to meet the costs in completing the construction of the lighthouse? And what if the beacon were built, only to be destroyed at a later date? Would they again have to foot the bill? It was something that the members needed to clarify before too many new lighthouses were agreed to, so as not to cause financial embarrassment to the authority. Anyway, most believed that the role of Trinity House was simply to oversee the management of a fully functional lighthouse and not to put up money to help private speculators secure their own profitable ventures.

Lord Braybrook may well have been a wealthy man and friend to the King, but it was Whitfield that Trinity House would be dealing with – and so, after many hours of debate, a solution was offered. Although Whitfield had already been given the go-ahead to erect his lighthouse, the new contract required an amendment to it, a legally binding clause that excluded the authority from any financial risk or attachment to the project, so that the monetary requirements fell solely on Whitfield and his associates. The agreement would also apply to every lighthouse patent that Trinity House granted to other proprietors.

The change to the original document concerned many of Whitfield's supporters, but he still believed the venture would be successful and profitable.

The Eddystone lease had been offered to William Whitfield by Trinity House for 55 years. The contract, when broken down, gave him sole responsibility for the construction of the lighthouse, but only with the authority's approval of the building's design. He would also have to maintain the light to their high standards, but in so doing would be allowed to collect and keep all of the shipping dues from the vessels passing his new lighthouse – for the first five years, at any rate. After that and for the remaining 50 years of the agreement, an even share from any profit realised would be split between the two parties.

Whitfield was in no doubt that his plan to build on the Eddystone offered a rare opportunity to make a name for himself and impress his father-in-law. On signing the amended lease agreement with Trinity House, Whitfield began his search for someone to build the lighthouse. All he required was an architect and engineer capable of delivering an acceptable structure plan to Trinity House. He originally asked Christopher Wren, who had been known to him while he was engaged on restoration work at Lord Braybrook's house in Audley End. Wren, he assumed, would accept the challenge without hesitation, but to Whitfield's surprise, the busy architect turned him down, citing a more important calling, that of rebuilding the damaged St Paul's Cathedral after the Great Fire of London. The unexpected setback nearly resulted in the whole venture collapsing there and then as it seemed no other suitable engineer existed.

Whitfield was frustrated by his initial failure, but realised the enormity of the quest before him. Not wanting to face humiliation in the eyes of his father-in-law, Whitfield persevered with the project and met his small team to discuss the setback. It was the group's task to find an architect capable of building the first lighthouse on the Eddystone.

In the 17th century, Plymouth was still a small but growing town. The Duchy of Cornwall had become the new owners of the important harbour of Sutton, after King Charles II refused the Plymouth Corporation a continuation of ownership due to their record in the Civil War – i.e. their support for the wrong side! The King's Western Squadron was moored at the port's Cattewater but in 1696 it moved its base to the Hamoaze, where the town of Dock provided better maintenance facilities for the fleet. Indeed, Dock would soon eclipse Plymouth itself and expand rapidly, having a population of 3,000 inhabitants by 1733. It became the largest town in Devon during the Napoleonic Wars, with an estimated 24,000 people. Dock's special maritime importance was soon recognised. It was a superior naval dockyard and had a quality workforce in abundance. Further expansion of the facility continued as the Admiralty realised its effective and strategic prominence. A naval hospital with 1,200 beds was built there. However, as the years slipped by the original name of Dock was replaced and the area became known as Stonehouse.

The King's Naval Dockyard was developed in subsequent years, which resulted in more shipping movements in the Channel. It was an inevitable consequence therefore that the unlit Eddystone reef would become an even bigger threat to seamen plying back and forth from the Plymouth port.

Through the pages of maritime history the danger of the Eddystone is well documented.

In 1478, the chronicler William of Worcester mentioned the reef in his *Itinerary*; in the 1500s Robert Newman also wrote about it in a work called *The Rutter Of The Sea*; while by 1586 Camden had referred to the area in his *Britannia* as Scopulos Infamis or the "infamous rocks".

Whitfield's initial failure in finding a builder quickly was very frustrating, but especially so when unfortunate ships were still sinking at the Eddystone. Most Plymothians did not believe any lighthouse would ever be built there and they felt the venture was doomed from the start. The area of water was known for its difficult tidal patterns, being feared by the town's most skilled seamen. It just seemed out of the question that any structure could ever be erected on the tiny stony outcrop which lay many miles from the English mainland.

However, Whitfield and his associates continued to search for someone skilled enough to build their own private pharos, but it was proving to be difficult. Meanwhile, Lord Braybrook was eager to see his son-in-law's efforts come to fruition and suggested that someone else, also employed at Audley End, might just fit the bill and come to the group's rescue. Henry Winstanley had been employed on the estate for many years, like his father before him. Henry Winstanley Sr had worked for James the second Earl of Suffolk during the 1650s as bailiff and steward. His young son Henry had been a constant visitor to the house and had helped his father on many occasions. Winstanley Jr was on the payroll as the estate's Clerk of Works, a position he also held at Royal Newmarket. His duties at Audley End had enabled him to work as an understudy to the Surveyor General, Christopher Wren, while extensive restoration took place. The experience was to prove invaluable to Winstanley, who had been involved with much of the work. His skills and talent had been rightfully acknowledged by everyone at the house, including Braybrook himself, who suggested Winstanley for the new lighthouse project. Winstanley had seen many changes to the property during the years and Charles II was in the process of buying it from Lord Suffolk for £50,000. The house would soon become the New Palace for the King to hold court in and preside over the country's fate. (The conveyance of the house and estate to the crown was executed on 8 May 1669.)

Winstanley was a skilled craftsman and fine engraver. He was well known in Royal circles and it appears he was liked by everyone associated with the household; but was he up to the challenge? Could he possibly build Britain's first wave-washed lighthouse at the Eddystone?

Discussions between Whitfield, Winstanley and Braybrook continued during 1695/96 until an agreement was reached. Winstanley was offered the position of Resident Architect, but at a price.

He would put £4,000 of his own money into the scheme to offset the team's financial burden, then more cash at a later date, which he did and continued to do.

Winstanley's initial responsibility was in drawing and designing the lighthouse. It had to be accepted by all of the group's other

members, but more importantly the structure needed to be strong, for it would have to withstand the ocean's constant crashing upon it and the light had to be high enough for mariners to see from a distance.

The swirling waters around the dangerous Eddystone Rocks offered the builders an even greater challenge, but at least the problem was something Whitfield had local knowledge of, having lived in Devon.

Unfortunately, Winstanley had no experience at all in lighthouse building, although, coincidentally, the Eddystone had recently been on his mind due to the fact that he had lost money on two ships which had been wrecked there. However, it is also

HENRY WINSTANLEY – A SELF-PORTRAIT
COURTESY OF THE THE SAFFRON WALDEN MUSEUM

possible he was able to gain information from a relative in Kent, an Edmund Winstanley who had held cornets in the Parliamentary Army during 1646 and 1647. He, too, had been interested in lighthouses and owned a patent for the Dungeness Lighthouse in 1636. It is therefore a strong possibility that some useful advice was available to Winstanley from his relation.

Winstanley's completed drawings were taken by Whitfield to Trinity House in London for consideration. He was certain that his talented architect had provided the necessary examples of work to impress the authority and so secure the Eddystone contract.

On 10 June 1696, approval was given by the Brethren of Trinity House for Winstanley's structural design – and so, for Whitfield and his new-found builder, the first hurdle had been jumped. Immediately, the two men made their way to Plymouth, where their adventure would truly begin.

Winstanley was born in Saffron Walden, Essex, on 31 March 1644. He had two brothers, Robert, born on 14 March 1646 and Charles on 10 June 1649. He also had five sisters – Ann, born on 4 February 1652; Elizabeth, who was named after her mother, arrived on 19 July 1654, then Susannah on 27 February 1656, Arabella on 25 August 1661 and Dorothy on 11 November 1666.

Winstanley seems to have been a remarkable individual, both talented and modest. He was a lively person with a wonderful sense of humour and his character and personality endeared him to all who knew him. His abilities were many, but he was primarily an inventor and a showman, but also a painter, illusionist, designer, pamphleteer and entrepreneur. However, it was as one of this country's finest engravers that he came to the attention of the wealthy gentry. His important work included a set of plates of the Palace at Audley End, as well as many other renowned English buildings including the Tudor House at Rycote in Oxfordshire.

In one of Winstanley's advertisements of his talent, we read the following:

All Noble men and Gentlemen that please to have their Mansion Houses designed on Copper Plates to be printed for composing a volume of ye Prospects of Ye Principall Houses of England may have them done by Mr Hen. Winstanley by way of subscription, that is to say, subscribing to pay five pounds at the delivery of a fair Coppy of Their respective houses as large as This Plate; or tenn pounds for one as large as Royall paper will contain.

Winstanley was still unknown to the population of Plymouth, but in a very short time everyone there wanted to meet him. Luckily, we do know quite a bit about the remarkable man and are able to document his life accurately. He was married to Elizabeth Taylor and they had a son called William, born in 1695. Winstanley's wife does appear to have been well suited to her extraordinary husband. The couple lived in the small village of Littlebury, Essex, where they were well-known figures.

Winstanley had grown up in the close-knit community and his father was also well respected, through his work at Audley End and in the village, where he became church warden in 1680.

Winstanley was by all accounts a very happy and wealthy individual who had already achieved great success by the time he had been offered the challenge to build the Eddystone Lighthouse in 1695/96.

The new role was one that his enthusiastic nature enjoyed and it is clear that the popular man felt comfortable among the lords and ladies of the time. We know too that his mechanical interests developed while employed at the Earl of Suffolk's home, and at the age of 34 he built an astronomical clock for the parish church for a fee of £8.

An entry in the church records by his father, then the church warden, on 21 January 1678, read: "To my son Harry Winstanley for paynting and contryving ye dyall and motion in ye church clock = £8.00.00". Unfortunately, the device with its orbital moons painted on the face was to break down quite soon after installation and could not be repaired. Still, his reputation wasn't tarnished by the one slight embarrassment and he continued to invent even more technical objects.

In his youth, Winstanley travelled through Europe, visiting France, Germany and Italy along the way. He was able to speak fluent French and possibly German and the visits to foreign parts enabled him to amass an immense wealth of knowledge.

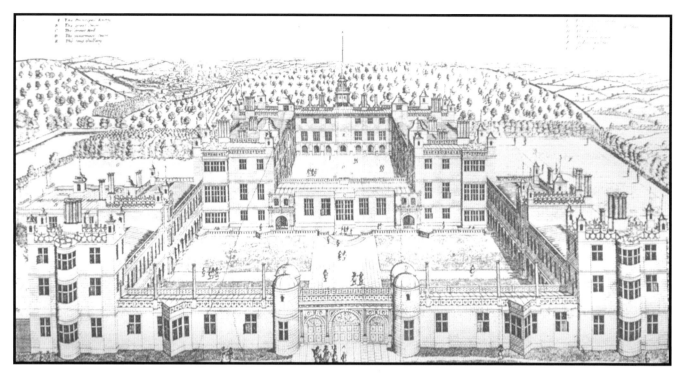

THE PALACE OF AUDLEY END
BY KIND PERMISSION OF ENGLISH HERITAGE

By 1695, he was a respected and wealthy businessman. He was just 50 and appeared to be at the height of his success, with many investments and other interests to occupy his time.

He owned and operated a famous "theme park" in London called the Water Gardens, where hydraulic devices were disguised as playing mermaids, gods and goddesses which spouted water. A dragon belched fireballs and a barrel dispensed a variety of drinks. The business remained open until 1714 and was visited by thousands. His own house too, was a lively and lucrative family attraction. Both venues were very successful, having caught the imagination of London's society and the general public.

For a small entrance fee, visitors were shown around the building, where every type of invention and amusement gadget was on display, from mechanical chairs that trapped you in their arms, to trick shoes nailed to the floor and even a garden seat which would catapult you into a nearby stream.

The fun house at Littlebury was a product of Winstanley's fertile mind and quirky character, which enabled him to express his enthusiastic nature and endearing personality.

His business activities included a financial interest in five trading vessels – and because of that, he followed a path that ultimately would gain him a unique honour in British maritime history. It would also lead to his very tragic and premature death.

During the stormy winter of 1695/96 two of the merchant ships, the *Snowdrop* and the *Constant,* foundered on the Eddystone and

WINSTANLEY'S LITTLEBURY HOME
BY KIND PERMISSION OF ENGLISH HERITAGE

were wrecked. News of the disaster reached Winstanley while he was with friends at a pub in London some weeks later and it so angered him that he was even more determined to succeed in the task which lay before him. Winstanley and Whitfield left soon afterwards for the Devon town of Plymouth, hoping to discover the truth about the Eddystone's reputation. A visit to the site would be their first task, enabling them to consider all the difficulties which might obstruct their plans.

It was June 1696 and Winstanley, 52, started work. We know he was in talks with naval sea captains and the local townspeople, which enabled him to gain further knowledge of what he was up against. The meetings made him plainly aware of the urgent need to erect a sea-mark on the reef mass. So, with the support of Whitfield behind him, Winstanley set out to achieve the impossible, something no-one else had managed since the beginning of time – to build a lighthouse on the Eddystone.

Undaunted by his seemingly impossible task, Winstanley began to undertake the most adventurous marine construction job of all time.

Unfortunately, he had very little technical information available to him about wave-washed lighthouses and so his efforts were to be based on his own experiences and talents. Undoubtedly, he was not prepared for what was to follow and with virtually no understanding of wind resistance or tidal science, the venture would be difficult. However, he embarked on his enormous project regardless, learning new skills as he went along.

His original building design was that of a very tiny naive, flimsy and inadequate-looking structure which resembled a rather quaint tower.

It was to have a solid stone base attached to the surface of the rock, which would support a second storey of more stonework and timber, containing the living room cum store. On the third floor, made entirely of timber, would be the service room and lantern house.

Winstanley's initial structure, his first attempt at lighthouse building, was to prove useless, but nonetheless the reef would soon have a genuine lighthouse on it.

Designing his building was one thing but building it would be another. The main obstacles to his courageous attempt were the elements. The whole project could fail, without a stone or timber being placed on the Eddystone, just because of the weather.

The constant problem of changing weather overshadowed the team's effort at the outset, especially when they looked from the heights of Plymouth Hoe across the sea to the speck of rock they intended to build upon; was it possible to work there or too much of a challenge for any man?

Finding the right people for the unique adventure would also cause them much frustration as who, besides Winstanley himself, would want to risk his life in such an uncertain quest? And what type of man could possibly undertake the construction in such a vulnerable and dangerous location?

Through sheer determination and enthusiasm the project's associates slowly overcame their fears, quickly learning the fundamental sciences involved. Several of the townspeople also supported Winstanley's efforts and offered him help, although the majority of the locals, it has to be said, thought he was mad to attempt the work. Getting to and from the rocks still remained a real problem and would continue to dog their initial efforts. The skill required by a boatman to carry workers back and forth to the reef mass was such that it deterred the very best local coxswains from joining the Eddystone project, resulting in greater frustration for the small team.

With the weather's uncertainty and the sea's uncompromising nature, every journey would prove a nightmare for the crew and workers. Even during good sea conditions, the passage to "the stone" would take the boat's crew many hours of hard sailing and rowing, a distance of 14 miles – and in open sea any misfortune could easily happen.

Nevertheless, Winstanley persisted in his efforts to secure a talented boatman by offering an impressive sum of money for the man who would take him to the Eddystone. Winstanley had spoken to most of the Plymouth fishermen based around the old Barbican, where they frequented the many ale houses that lined the backstreets of the quayside. He had little success. But eventually, through his association with them, a respected seaman came forward and offered his service. He was a well-liked fisherman named James Bound, who immediately convinced Winstanley of his expertise. Bound was hired and proved at once to be the right choice, being brave and hard-working. He was to play a very important role in the project and would become a good friend to Winstanley and an enthusiastic team member for the next seven years.

Besides his new-found boatman, a team of granite quarry workers were also encouraged to join the venture; at last a workforce had been found and everything seemed to be taking shape.

Winstanley believed his original promise to the town's mayor and gathered audience – "to build a lighthouse upon the reef for the Plymouth people" – was even more achievable. He was also much more confident with his new friends who supported him, plus an endless stream of admirers who loved his charm and endearing character.

His optimism was short-lived when he discovered the truth behind the stories of the dreaded Eddystone. Not only could it take up to nine hours to reach the reef itself, but there was no certainty that his small boat could tie up to the stony outcrop, allowing the passengers to clamber onto the slippery seaweed- coated surface. James Bound was unquestionably a superb seaman who could navigate his boat within the treacherous narrows of the sharp stones, but it was still a risky business and Winstanley had yet to land on the jagged rocks.

Finally, the weather eased, so Winstanley and Bound made another journey to the Eddystone. This time it was possible to put the boat gently alongside a flat rock edge for a moment, giving Winstanley time to climb onto the stony mass. He was overcome with excitement and stood for the first time on the slippery Eddystone surface, proving it was possible to land there. Elated by his modest success, he returned to Plymouth confident that the lighthouse would soon be built.

The quarrymen or "tinners" employed by Winstanley were of incredible strength and stamina, but still no-one could say whether they could endure the untold dangers or completely new working practices, while clinging to wet rocks and swinging a pick-axe.

Would the sea rise over the workforce without warning, drowning them all – and could precise holes be dug into the hard red gneiss rock to use as anchor points for the lighthouse?

So many questions were still unanswered, but Winstanley was confident and the foundation cutting was about to begin on the reef.

He had already completed the laborious task of drawing the base plan of the tower on the rock's surface, and with all the seaweed cleared from the reef, the quarrymen would be able to scrape and chisel the tower's outline into the surface. After many unforeseen difficulties and modified working practices, the tinners managed to carve the stone into flat platforms so the foundations could be secured more easily to the rock's surface.

THE BASE OF WINSTANLEY'S TOWER 1698
THE AUTHOR'S COLLECTION

Although the summer's weather had been good, there were many occasions when, after starting out from Plymouth, Winstanley and his men failed even to reach their destination and instead found their journey ending at some Cornish port or cove like Looe or Fowey, due to constant changes in weather and tides. Courageously they persevered although they were always wet and cold from the constant sea spray which fell over them. But the workers carried on chipping small fragments off the hard uncooperative rock.

In that first year only twelve holes were completed, but a learning curve had been climbed by every member of the team, as each day new challenges were tackled and overcome.

By the following summer, in 1697, their work was much more productive and Winstanley's leadership skills and character had gained him immense respect within his team. The men liked him greatly because of his enthusiasm and energy.

A sense of pride cemented the small group of men and everyone had a strong belief in why they were there – "to build a lighthouse for the safety of seafarers".

During the summer of 1697 the masons had secured twelve iron rods, 3.5 inches in diameter, into the holes, cementing them in lead. They were also able to build a pillar to encase the uprights, measuring 14 feet in diameter and 12 feet high.

England was at war with France and her king, Louis XIV, so the fact that Winstanley and his men were 14 miles from the British mainland and in open water made being captured from the rocks by French sailors a serious possibility.

Press gangs were always looking for men to serve in the fleet and both French and British navies would take anyone who was useful.

The Admiralty, aware of the threat to the lighthouse project, had already acted at the request of Winstanley and entrusted a warship, HMS *Terrible*, to look after the builders. Construction of the lighthouse was an important issue to those in power, being recognised as a very strong asset to this country's shipping growth and an important navigational aid to our own naval forces, particularly for the squadron moored off the strategic area of Plymouth, so its completion was a necessity.

However, during one morning in June 1697, the escort ship *Terrible*, commanded by Captain Timothy Bridge, went missing from her anchorage near the Eddystone, which left Winstanley and his men unprotected. The area was shrouded in blankets of thick fog throughout the day and white banks of cloud drifted across the sea.

With the Eddystone's isolation compounded by the weather, a passing French privateer took her opportunity to pounce on the unsuspecting builders. Cannon shots rang from the enemy vessel and the lighthouse was almost wrecked by the French gun crew, who then landed in several small boats, totally overwhelming Winstanley and his men. Outnumbered by the French seamen, Winstanley and his builders fought desperately from their damaged pillar until they were finally overpowered and captured.

The captain of the French privateer believed he had secured a valuable prize for his King and so set sail at once for France with Winstanley and some of his uninjured men on board, leaving the others marooned at the Eddystone. However, the optimistic captain was to be disappointed on his arrival home, for his King was displeased with the capture of the English lighthouse builders and screamed that "although he was at war with England, he was not at war with humanity". Louis, of course, was fully aware that the lighthouse would benefit all seafarers on the Channel, including his own, and it would be an important sea-mark should he decide to invade England's western shores. The unforeseen situation annoyed him greatly and so the unlucky opportunist captain was placed in irons and the court's ministers reprimanded. Meanwhile, in England, the authorities acted swiftly in seeking the release of Winstanley and in a short time the Admiralty petitioned Louis for the builder's immediate release, in return for an exchange of prisoners of war.

Louis appears to have been generous, as he did not wish to provoke England or her navy. It is reported that he demanded to see Winstanley and apologised personally. He even invited the builder to have further meetings with him and his maritime officials.

Their respect for one another quickly grew and the relationship was such that the King, also falling for Winstanley's charm, tried unsuccessfully to persuade the Briton to work for him, offering 2,000 Louis d'or per annum if he would serve him and, of course, France.

News of Winstanley's capture was in all the newspapers and his fate the talk of England; people everywhere asked if they would ever hear of him again.

From the diarist Narcissus Luttrell we read:

TUESDAY 29TH JUNE 1697.
A French privateer has seiz'd Mr Winstanley ye Engineer, together with his workmen as they were erecting a Lightt House on the Edystone Rock off Plymouth and carried him to France, destroy'd his work, but left his men behind them.

SATURDAY 3RD JULY 1697.
The Lords of ye Admiralty have sent to France to have Mr Winstanley ye Engineer (who was taken off ye Edystone Rock near Plymouth) exchanged according to ye cartel.

TUESDAY 13TH JULY 1697.
Mr Winstanley, ye Engineer, who was carried off to France, is come back, being exchanged according to ye cartel.

Two weeks of speculation and drama filled the papers and then Winstanley was back. Everyone rejoiced at his release and the embarrassment of the Navy was over, although those officers at fault, based at HM Naval Headquarters in Plymouth, were duly chastised in a Dispatch addressed to the Commissioner, St Loe. It stated:

Resolved that Commissioner St Loe be directed to give an account of how it happened, that workmen on the Eddystone, were so ill protected as that the Engineer was taken and carried to France by a small French Challope.

The Admiralty had made every effort to seek the release of Winstanley by communicating with the French authorities demanding his return. Unbeknown to them at the time, it was not necessary, as plans for the builders' return had already been made.

Less than two weeks after his capture, Winstanley was to be found once again working on his Eddystone tower, overseeing the building and telling everyone of his adventures. He was a national hero and the eyes of the whole country were on him and his work.

With the third working summer under way, public awareness of the lighthouse grew, as did each layer of stone and timber.

The building was, in clear weather, just about visible from the coastline and so attracted much attention from the local people, who were becoming increasingly excited by the real probability of having their first Eddystone lighthouse. As the building work neared completion, the grey skies of winter approached and Winstanley and his men were keen to leave the Eddystone Rocks. Another season had been completed, just one more to go before their final triumph. Many visitors continued to arrive in Plymouth to view the tower, gathering on the bleak cold cliff top of Plymouth Hoe to peer at the tiny speck on the horizon. Everybody was anxiously waiting for their first glimpse of the beacon's light.

From Winstanley's own *Narrative of the Building* comes the following description:

The Light-house was begun to be built in the year 1696 and was four Years in Building; not for ye Greatness of ye Work, but for ye Difficulty and Danger of getting backward and forward to the Place, nothing being or could be left safe there for ye first 2 Years, but what was most thoroughly affixed to ye rock, or ye work at very extraordinary charge and tho' nothing could be attempted to be done but in ye Summer Season, yet ye weather then at times would prove so bad yt for 10 or 14 days together ye Sea would be so Raging about these Rocks, caused by out Winds and ye running of ye ground Seas coming from ye main Ocean, that altho' ye weather should seem and be most Calm in other Places; yet here it would mount and fly more than 200 foot, as has been so found since there was lodgement upon ye Place, and therefore all our Mercy of ye Seas and no Power was able to come near to make good, or help any thing as I have often experienced with my Work men in a boat in great danger; only having ye satisfaction to see my Work imperfectly at times as ye Seas fell from it, and at a mile or two distance, and this at ye time of ye year and no Wind or appearance of bad weather; Yet trusting in God's assistance for his blessing on this

THE OPENING CEREMONY OF WINSTANLEY'S LIGHTHOUSE 1698, PAINTED BY PETER MONAMY
By KIND PERMISSION OF THE CORPORATION OF TRINITY HOUSE

undertaking, being for a general good and receiving most unexpressable Deliverances I proceeded as following. The first summer was spent in making twelve holes in ye Rock and fast'ning twelve great Irons to hold ye Work yt was to be done afterwards, the Rock being so hard, and ye time so short and ye many Journeys lost yt there could be no landing at all, and many times glad to land at our return at places yt if weather permitted would take up ye next day to get to Plymouth again. The next summer was spent in making a solid body or kind of round pillar, 12 feet high and 14 feet diameter: and then we had more time to work and a little better landing, having some small shelter from the Work, and something to hold by; but we had great trouble to carry off and land so many materials, and be forced to secure all things, aforesaid every night and time we left work or return them again in the boats. The third Year the aforesaid Pillar or Work was made good at the Foundation from the rock to 16 feet Diameter and all the Work was raised, which to the Vane was 80 foot, being all finished, with the Lanthorn and all the Roomes that was then in it. We ventured to lodge there soon after Midsummer for greater dispatch of ye Work, but ye first night ye weather came bad and so continued, that it was eleven days before any Boat could come near us again and not being acquainted with the hight of the Seas rising, we were almost all ye time neer drowned with wet, and all our Provisions in as bad a condition tho' we work'd night and day as much as possible to make shelter for ourselves. In

this storm we lost some of our Materials, altho' we did what we could to save them. But the Boat then returning we all left the House to be refreshed on shore, and as soon as ye Weather did permit, we returned again, and finished all, and put up the light on the 14th November 1698.

In a twist of fate, Winstanley was unable to celebrate his success on dry land, as due to deteriorating weather he became marooned at his lighthouse for the next six weeks. He continues:

> Which being so late in the Year, it was three days before Christmas before we had a relief to get ashore again and were almost at the last extremity for want of Provisions, but by good Providence then two Boats came with Provisions, and ye Family that was to take care of the Light and so ended this year's Work.

So, after immense trouble and effort, the lighthouse was finished and, on 14 November 1698, Winstanley succeeded in producing a miracle and climbed into the tiny lantern to light 60 tallow candles.

News of the great achievement travelled fast – and from every vantage point, people came to glimpse the breathtaking sight which many had thought impossible: the lighthouse on the Eddystone, shining faintly in the distance. (Whether the evening air was good enough for the crowds to view the rays of the lighthouse is uncertain; however a celebratory

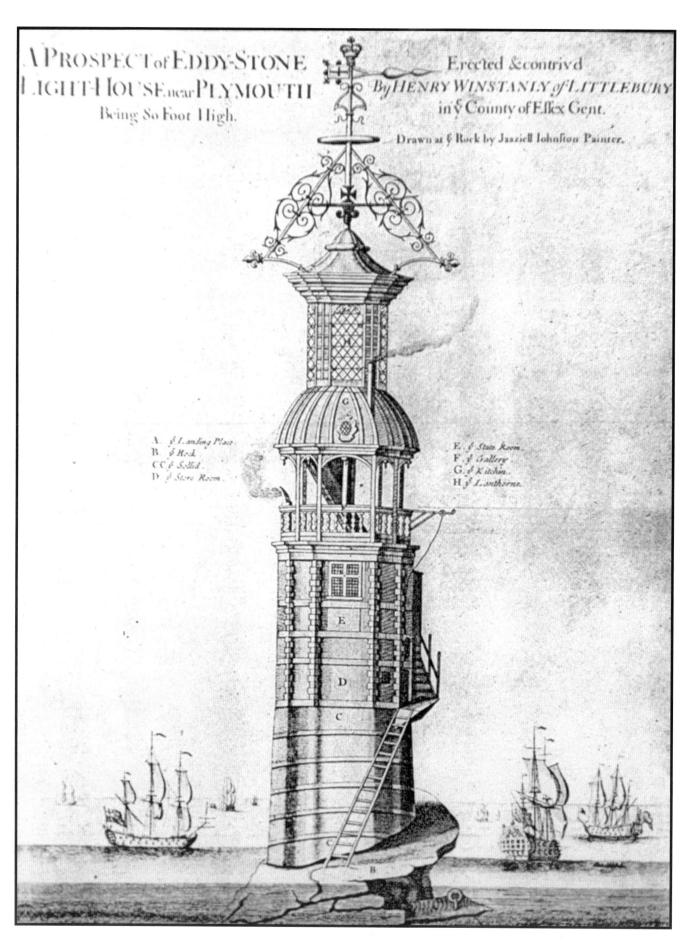

THE EDDYSTONE LIGHTHOUSE BY J JOHNSTON, 1698

BY KIND PERMISSION OF THE CORPORATION OF TRINITY HOUSE

party was enjoyed by the lease owner, Whitfield, and the local dignitaries of Plymouth).

A new chapter had begun in the story of the Eddystone and people wondered how long the structure would survive with the coming winter storms.

Early in the spring of 1699, Winstanley returned to the Eddystone and inspected the lighthouse, but on reaching the tower found his beacon in a poor condition. He realised that major repairs were urgently needed to the framework, as most of the cement around its base had been washed away. Immediate work in redesigning the tower was also necessary, and it would have to be stronger; in short the lighthouse must be completely rebuilt.

Winstanley stopped showing his light and went about increasing the base diameter to 24 feet, with the height being raised another two feet.

Iron bands would be placed at the bottom of the lighthouse to give added strength and a better superstructure would be incorporated to support it. Winstanley wrote:

> The fourth year finding in ye Winter the effects the sea had on this House and Burying the Lanthorn at times altho' more than 60 Foot high, early in the Spring I encompassed the aforesaid Building with a new Work of four foot thickness from ye foundation, making all solid near 20 foot high, and taking down the upper part of the first Building and enlarging every part in its proportion. I raised it 40 foot higher than it was at first, and made it as it now appears, and yet the Sea in time of Storms flies in appearance, 100 foot above ye Vane and at times doth cover half the side of the House and the Lanthorn as if it were under Water.

The hard work was nonetheless completed with remarkable speed and the redesigned building was completed exactly four years after Winstanley had first embarked on his venture. Now he believed that the stronger lighthouse would last forever and stand the test of time. Everything seemed to be going well. Even when Winstanley had left Plymouth, his team were able to continue to carry out all the necessary functions of

WINSTANLEY'S FIRST TOWER AS SEEN IN 1698
THE AUTHOR'S COLLECTION

THE NOTORIOUS NAVAL PRESS GANGS AT WORK
THE AUTHOR'S COLLECTION

servicing the lighthouse. Winstanley, however, would frequently visit his Eddystone light and repair any serious damage to the tower. His visits were happy occasions and he was normally accompanied by a small team of dedicated men, including his friend, the Eddystone coxswain James Bound.

The boat crew were a vital link between the lightkeepers at the rock and the support workers on shore and Bound was regarded as the Plymouth team's leader.

However, in April 1702 a calamity happened which was to cause much anxiety to all concerned, especially for the Eddystone keepers on duty at the rock 14 miles away.

James Bound had been forcibly taken from an ale house in the early evening by a press gang and shipped off with a group of other men in a naval boat to a destination unknown.

Bound had served Winstanley well from their first meeting and it was he who had made that first trip to the reef in 1696. The two men enjoyed each other's company from the start and they had developed a good

relationship, so it was particularly sad for Winstanley to receive such bad news concerning his friend's fate.

In Plymouth every effort had been made to locate the man and eventually it transpired he had been taken by a British naval press gang from the fighting vessel HMS *Rochester*, which lay at anchor in Plymouth Sound.

Unfortunate souls taken by the press gangs were unlikely to be seen again, and for the men of the Eddystone team the situation produced enormous problems. With no Bound at the helm, it seemed unlikely that any further trip to the Eddystone could be possible and so, with no stores being transported to the lightkeepers, a tragedy looked inevitable. It was still not easy to secure the services of a man willing to risk his life venturing to and from the isolated outcrop, even with its lighthouse, and only a few local sailors were capable of undertaking the dangerous passage.

Winstanley arrived in Plymouth from his Essex home to oversee the efforts of finding

Bound and immediately went to the Custom House to seek out the Trinity House agent, where he voiced his desperate plight.

The agent, who had known Winstanley for some time, wanted to help and understood the seriousness of the situation, but had little news to give the anxious builder. On 1 May 1702, the Trinity House agent wrote a letter of complaint to the Corporation and Admiralty concerning the boatman:

I need not say anything what the consequence will be if we have not people to tend upon't, and at this time ye occation is greeter yn ordinary, hear being workmen com from beyand London to repair ye damage the house sustained last winter. I hope the board will take it into their consideration that ye men may be protected to supply that house with what it shall want so as ye navigation may in no wise suffer. Mr Winstanley is under no small trouble to find his only man taken from him upon whome was all his dependance in landing at the house, where nobody els could or would venture. I have not more to ad save that I hope by ye returne of the poste to have a satisfactory answer so as that wee may proceed with savety to carry ye candles and things to the house which lye now reddy by ye waterside to goe off.

The Corporation wrote to J Burchett, secretary to the Lord High Admiral:

I am commanded by the gentlemen of this Corporation to lay before you the enclosed, from the person at Plimouth who hath the care of providing for the security and maintainance of the light-hous upon the Eddistone, so benificall, now in time of warr especially to her Majesty's cruising ships going in and out of that port in the night time. And on that consideration it is prayed that you would be pleased to move his Excellency the Lord High Admirall, to grant his order for the discharge of James Bound, whose business it is to attend with his boate upon that light.

James Bound was eventually discharged from HMS *Rochester* and continued to work for Winstanley in supplying the needs of the lighthouse for the next 17 months.

WINSTANLEY'S REDESIGNED LIGHTHOUSE 1699
THE AUTHOR'S COLLECTION

Winstanley's lighthouse was to change the course of maritime history. The dreaded Eddystone would no longer put fear into the hearts of passing sailors; instead the men would feel comforted by the sentinel's faint rays of light and rejoice in the knowledge that the strange-looking tower would also become a vital aid to their safety.

Winstanley had learned a great deal from his adventure and the whole experience had made him appreciate and respect the natural powers of weather and tide.

Although only a handful of sceptics still doubted the tower's strength, Winstanley wanted to be inside his lighthouse on the stormiest of nights and was often heard calling from the lantern gallery of the tower in

THE BARBICAN STEPS IN PLYMOUTH, WINSTANLEY'S PLACE OF DEPARTURE ON HIS FINAL JOURNEY 1703
THE AUTHOR'S COLLECTION

an air of triumph and defiance to "blow, winds", shouting at times in an attack of lyrical boldness to "revolt, sea; unchain yourselves, ye elements, and come and try my work".

His wish to be inside the lighthouse during a great storm was soon fulfilled, and during the winter of 1703 the remarkable man was to be found battling to save his tower and the lives of everyone in it from hurricane-force winds, the like of which this country had never seen.

In the early morning of 26 November 1703, Winstanley with several of his men prepared to sail to the Eddystone Lighthouse and relieve the lightkeepers of their duty.

Winstanley intended to stay in the tower for a few days, overseeing the repairs to the structure, then return to Plymouth, where he would catch the stagecoach for the journey to London and his Essex home, where he hoped to spend Christmas with his wife and family. Winstanley was 59 and still a strong man both in mind and body.

The sea on that morning showed a large rolling swell which pounded at the cliff base of the Hoe. After several weeks of severe gales the water was slowly abating.

For the boatmen and crew it would prove to be another dangerous trip, but one that had been taken many times before and in similar conditions.

In a twist of fate, James Bound was at the helm, although he voiced his reluctance to take Winstanley out to the lighthouse, due to the uncertain weather. However, Winstanley insisted and the party made for "the stone".

Large grey clouds hung heavy overhead as the anxious men sailed from the safety of Sutton Harbour under the high walls of the Citadel, into the dark and empty Sound and on towards the Eddystone.

The wet and miserable journey took the crew many hours. From the shore the men were seen in their tiny boat, alone in the ocean, disappearing into the gloom. On nearing the reef, the wind began to freshen and it became clear that they would have to hurry to reach the relative safety of the tower. Soon a ferocious storm was beating upon them and the waves were building high and

higher. No time could be lost as the tired men approached their anxious waiting colleagues. A rope was thrown towards the keepers and slowly the boat was pulled towards the tower.

Guide our barque among the waves,
Through the rocks our passage smooth,
Where the whirl pool frets and raves,
Let Thy love its anger soothe,
All our hope is placed in Thee:
Miserere Domine

— A A PROCTER

Winstanley and five of his men found much excitement inside the lighthouse, with the keepers eager to leave after having experienced many weeks of prolonged bad weather, marooned in their lonely tower.

They had been concerned about the safety of the tower and did not know if the relief party would be able to get out to them, especially in the worsening conditions. So, in much haste, Winstanley was informed of the repairs which had been completed during the previous weeks. An urgency surrounded the task of stowing the new stores and timbers in the store room. When the duties were complete, the outgoing keepers jumped into their waiting craft, happy to be in the capable hands of James Bound. Their passage home would be an uncertain one and the men's faces betrayed their fear.

Then he and the sea began their strife,
And worked with power and might;
Whatever the man reared up by day
The sea broke down by night.
He caught at ebb with bar and beam,
He sailed to shore at flow,
And at his side by that same tide
Came bar and beam also.
For ah! his looks that are so stout,
And his speeches brave and fair,
He may wait on wind, wait on the wave,
But he'll build no lighthouse there.

— JEAN INGELOW

The weather turned into a full storm and a sombre farewell was signalled as both groups of men realised the difficulties in which they found themselves. There would be little rest for the occupants of the lighthouse while the tempest rose outside. Winstanley and his men needed to secure everything movable in the shaking tower. For those in the open boat it was to be a journey of immense terror, fighting their way through the white phosphorous shrouds and foaming teeth of the ocean. They watched their lighthouse disappear from view in the darkness and wondered what might happen to the people in it, for a terrible night awaited the handful of men installed in the already damaged lighthouse and it was agreed that their plight appeared much worse than that of those escaping through the jaws of the tempest.

The severe sea conditions deteriorated rapidly about the Eddystone and Winstanley's wish to be in his lighthouse at the weather's most evil had surely been granted. It was to be the greatest storm in known history, which blew across all England; so wrote Daniel Defoe, who lived through the devastation and mayhem of that awful night of 26 November 1703.

Eerie darkness on the cold winter's evening created a threatening atmosphere as the mighty wind gathered even greater strength. The immense movement of air was frantic and people everywhere hid in the safety of their homes, hoping to survive. Those inside the Eddystone desperately tried to repair their disintegrating tower as crashing, mountainous waves demolished the structure piece by piece.

From Defoe's writing called *The Storm*, printed in 1704, the following extract is taken:

> The loss of The Edystone Lighthouse is a considerable damage; as 'tis very doubtful whether it will ever be attempted again, and as it was a great security to the sailors, many a good ship having been lost there in former times. And the lighthouse had not been long down when The Winchelsea, an homeward bound Virginia-man, was split upon the rock where that building stood, and most of her men were drowned.

The storm inflicted massive loss of life and untold damage. At least 500 large merchant ships were overwhelmed by the boiling ocean and more than 8,000 sailors lost their lives at sea.

Winstanley and his men were not able to contain the tempest as the waves battered at the breaking structure. No-one knows if Winstanley lit the candles of his lighthouse on that evening, but it's most likely he did.

Sadly, the doomed men were to endure several agonising hours of the thunderous power and noise of the ocean around them, their creation being savaged and torn to splinters. Escape was impossible and all inside were finally swept from their shattered building, the sea leaving no trace of them or of the lighthouse which had stood on the rock.

Of those final moments nothing is recorded, nor of the returning boatmen, save that no trace of the lighthouse, its builder or the other keepers was seen again.

The Eddystone Reef had finally claimed Winstanley. It became his tomb and resting place. At his home in Littlebury on that same night, a treasured wooden model of the Eddystone lighthouse was heard crashing to the floor.

It was a night that brought despair and destruction to every mortal in the land. The dawn revealed a devastated country. The loss of Winstanley was not immediately common knowledge but to local mariners it was clear there was no longer a lighthouse on the Eddystone.

The financial expenses incurred by Henry Winstanley during his adventure had reached £8,000 and by the time of his death it had recouped no more than £4,000.

However, he had always felt his endeavours were worthwhile, both in long-term profitability and architecturally as a great maritime achievement which naturally supported his other proposals and business interests.

An example of a project that summed up Winstanley's enthusiastic nature was a proposition of immense magnitude known as the Royal Fishery. This proposal offered to develop the whole fishing industry of the British Isles, with success being most beneficial to the entire country; the scheme was to provide guaranteed employment for 200,000 men.

More equally fantastic possibilities were being investigated by the remarkable man. Unfortunately, his loss was very much underestimated by the Parliamentary leaders and few state tributes were paid to him. On reflection, one must wonder what other great achievements would have enriched this nation if he had survived the disaster.

> Thou who in darkness walking dids't appear
> Upon the waves and Thy disciples cheer,
> Come, Lord, in lonesome days, when storms assail
> And earthly hopes and human succours fail;
> When all is dark may we behold Thee nigh
> And hear Thy voice, – Fear not, for it is I.
> Amen

Winstanley's death was a terrible loss, especially to seafarers in the Channel. Many of them had been at sea for some time and did not know of the terrible tragedy until their return to Plymouth, when, looking for the lighthouse, their peering eyes could find no trace of the guiding beacon which once stood proudly on the rocks of the Eddystone.

The only remains of any human activity to be found on the reef were a length of iron chain attached by revits to the stone, and a small lead clock weight discovered wedged in a small crevice.

From the *London Gazette* of 29 November to 2 December 1703, we read the final account of that terrible night:

PLYMOUTH. NOVEMBER 28TH 1703.

Yesterday we had a dreadful storm and three or four Merchant Ships were cast away. Nine were stranded, but many of the men were saved. Her Majesty's Ships, The Monk and The Mermaid were there in The Sound, the later rid out the storm but The Monk was driven near to shore and was obliged to cut all her masts by the board, which is all the Damage to shipping that has happened here. The Lighthouse upon The Edistone was blown down and two or three Persons who were in it were killed.

Soon, the writers of the day offered their thoughts on the Eddystone's demise. From a simile written by a Mr Gay for his work Irivia we read:

> To when fam'd Edyston's far shooting rays
> That led the sailor through the stormy way,
> Was from its rocky roots, by billows torn
> And the high turret in the whirlwind born.
> Boats bulg'd their sides against the craggy land,
> And pitchy ruins, blacken'd all his strand.

Centuries later, the poet Jean Ingelow would pen 75 verses of homage to Winstanley, including the following extract:

> And it fell out, fell out at last,
> That he would put to sea,
> To scan once more his lighthouse-tower
> On the rock o' destiny.
> And the winds woke, and the storm broke,
> And wrecks came plunging in;
> None in the town that night lay down
> Or sleep or rest to win.
> The great mad waves were rolling graves,
> And each flung up its dead;
> The seething flow was white below,
> And black the sky o'erhead.
> And when the dawn, the dull grey dawn,
> Broke on the trembling town,
> And men looked south to the harbour mouth,
> The lighthouse-tower was down!
> Down in the deep where he doth sleep
> Who made it shine afar,
> And then in the night that drowned its light
> Set, with his pilot star.
>
> — JEAN INGELOW

The loss of the lighthouse was a catastrophe, but so was that of Winstanley.

In my research for this book I had hoped to find descendants of this wonderful individual – but I was too late: the last of the Winstanleys died a few years ago in Manitoba. Florence Winstanley Jerrard moved to Winnipeg Island in 1918, having married John Jerrard, and was the only remaining descendant of the Newnham Winstanley line dating back to 1760.

In Plymouth City Museum is the Plymouth Salt. This fine piece of silverware was made by a local goldsmith, Peter Rowe, in 1698, in celebration of the first Eddystone lighthouse. The model of Winstanley's original structure was presented to him by the Plymouth mayor after the completion of his first tower. Salt

THE TRINITY HOUSE SALT
BY KIND PERMISSION OF THE CORPORATION OF TRINITY HOUSE

was then a scarce commodity and in wealthy families it was highly fashionable to own such an elaborate container.

A few "salts" survive from the 15th century and are extremely collectable objects; the Plymouth item is therefore of great value.

Winstanley's salt was to be seen at his house in Littlebury and in an account by some visitors in 1703 we read:

The curiosity is the model of the lighthouse that one sees out at sea a few miles from Plymouth, which is built of bricks in the garden, with all the measurements reduced to a small scale in height and circumference. One sees yet another model of the same lighthouse in one of the rooms of the house, wrought in silver and we are assured that this work had cost more than ninety pieces.

It would appear that after Winstanley's death his wife sold the salt to the Queen, as we know that written in the Lord Chamberlain's records of 24 June 1727 is a passage entitled "Account of plate brought from Leicester House and deld to Mr De Grave to be placed in the Queen's Apartment in St Jame's, The model of The Adistone Light-House in silver".

The salt mysteriously left its Royal address to become the property of a wealthy gentleman whose estate commanded a view of the Bristol Channel. He says the object made an elaborate centre-piece at his table. The new owners also allowed a copy to be made for Trinity House and the duplicate model was often used on special occasions at the Corporation's headquarters in Tower Hill, London, when illustrious seafarers gathered for their important meetings.

The small silver decoration was positioned on a big table in a place of honour to remind the lighthouse authority, the Brethren and others, of Winstanley's courage and fate, suggesting, as someone remarked at the time, that in things secular, as in things spiritual, the blood of martyrs is the seed of the world's progress.

The original silver model was later to find its way into the possession of the Morgan family of Tredegar. In a written account by C Octavus Morgan, published in the *Archaeological Journal* for 1878, vol xxxv, he states that the piece was given away by his father and was to be found in the possession of a Miss Rous of Courtyrala in Glamorganshire.

The disaster which destroyed Winstanley's lighthouse soon brought the sceptics into prominence once more, with forecasts that the reef would never be lit again.

WINSTANLEY'S COMPLETED AND REDESIGNED LIGHTHOUSE OF 1699, ARTIST UNKNOWN
BY KIND PERMISSION OF PLYMOUTH CITY MUSEUM & ART GALLERY

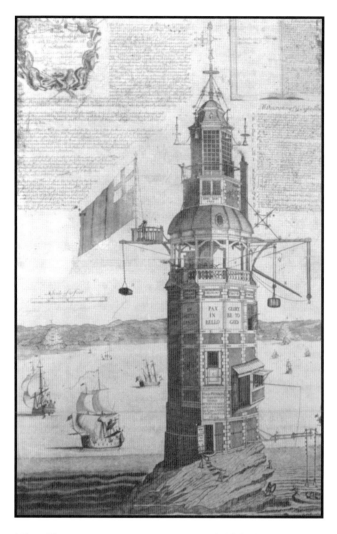

THE EDDYSTONE LIGHTHOUSE 1699–1703
BY KIND PERMISSION OF THE SAFFRON WALDON MUSEUM

Much debate did eventually take place regarding the tragedy of 27 November, both of the Great Storm itself and Winstanley's loss.

No sooner were the Eddystone Rocks laid bare, than once again ships were in peril. The first vessel to succumb to the barren reef did so the very day after the storm, as she was nearing the end of an horrendously rough passage from Virginia, laden with tobacco. Her captain, a local man eager to return home, desperately searched for the guiding rays of the lighthouse to steer a safe course into Plymouth Sound, but with no light to guide him, the town's registered merchant ship *Winchelsea* foundered on the rocks of the unlit Eddystone Reef, losing all but two of her crew. For five years, no ship had perished on the rocks – and yet, so soon after Winstanley's light had gone, it became clear that unwary

vessels, even those at home in the waters of the English Channel, would once again be in danger.

Winstanley's widow, who it seems was enjoying celebrity status after the death of her husband, sent a petition to the newly enthroned Queen Anne, asking that a state pension be paid to her, as she was now "in very mean circumstances". Although read by the monarch the correspondence was forwarded to Trinity House who endorsed the request.

However, no money was forthcoming to Mrs Winstanley and so in 1706 she sent another petition to the Queen. In 1707 a pension was finally awarded with a £200 grant from the Royal Bounty, and by a warrant of 25 June 1708, a further £100-a-year pension would be paid on the understanding that it was granted only while she remained a widow. Mrs Winstanley and her son William had lucrative business interests at the time – the London Water Garden and the Littlebury home were thriving attractions – but she felt the country owed her something for the death of her husband and believed that her pension was just. It was still being paid to her years after she married the French painter Tessier.

However, in her 2003 booklet on Winstanley, Alison Barnes suggests that the widow Elizabeth Winstanley in fact married a man she had probably known for 20 years, the famous ironsmith Jean Tijou, who built St Paul's Cathedral with Sir Christopher Wren. It appears that the Winstanleys had no children, and that Elizabeth died in 1721 and was buried at St Martin in the Fields, Middlesex.

From advertisements in the *Daily Courant* of Tuesday 22 April 1712 and of Monday 10 August 1713, we read the following:

TUESDAY 22ND APRIL 1712.
The Famous Water-Theatre of the late Ingenious Mr Winstanley, there is the greateſt Curioſities in Water-Works, the like was never Perform'd before by any. It is ſhown for the Benefit of his Widow every Evening, between 5 and 6 of the Clock, with ſeveral new Additions made this Spring: As 3 new Stages, Sea-Gods, and Goddeſſes, Nymphs,

Maremaids and Satyrs, all of them playing of Water as fuitable, and a Sea Triumph round the Barrel that plays fo many Liquors: And all is taken away after it hath perform'd its Part, and the Barrel is broke in Pieces before the Spectators. Boxes 2s. 6d. Pit 2s. firft Gallery 1s. 6d. Upper Gallery 6d. It is at the lower End of Pickadilly, and is known by the Wind-Mill on the Top of it.

MONDAY 10TH AUGUST 1713

THE Mathematical Water-Theatre of the late Ingenious Mr Winstanley will continue to be fhewn every Evening between 5 and 6 a Clock, for 6 Days and no longer this Seafon. This Evening the curious Barril will be made a Spring-Garden, entertaining the Boxes and Pit, with Cool Tankards, Spaw-Water, Bilquits, Milk, Ale, Beer, Sullibubs, Cakes and Cheefecakes, and Flowers playing of Water: And a very delightful Part will be added to the 3 Parts that are ufually performed. There is Galuthehs's Flight from Polyheme, and as fhe is carried in State by Neptune attended by many Figures playing of Water, and fome with Fire mingling with it: then will be a great Tempeft of Thunder and Lightning, and burning Flames roling in Great Cafcades of Water, to the Expence of 300 Tun extraordinary. Boxes 3s. Pit 2s. 6d. Firft Gallery 1s. 6d. Upper Gallery 6d. This is at the Lower-End of Piccadilly near Hide Park, and is for the Benefit of his Widow.

A copperplate engraving of Winstanley's lighthouse was sold at the Water Gardens in London and also at his home in Littlebury, where anyone with sixpence could see a model of it.

The engraving was dedicated to Prince George of Denmark, then the Lord High Admiral of England. It read:

To His Royal Highness ye Prince Lord High Admiral of England, &c.
This Draught of the Light House on ye Edystone, is humbly presented, Great Sir.
By your most Obedient Servant,
— HEN WINSTANLEY

Winstanley's lighthouse was a unique building, its interior extremely well furnished for the comfort of the lightkeepers or visitors to the tower; in his description of his construction, Winstanley wrote:

A DESCRIPTION OF YE LIGHT-HOUSE

A The Rock on ye landing side with ye strong iron Rail leading to ye entering Door where is shown ye Bolts and Eyes to ffasten ye door, and round iron steps for entrance.

B An Engine Crane yt parts at joynts to be taken off when not in use, the rest being fasten'd to ye side of ye house to save it in time of storms, and it is to be made use of to help landing on ye Rock, which, without, is very difficult.

C The window of a very fine Bedchamber, with a Chimney and Closet, ye Room being richly Gilded and Painted and ye outside Shutters very strongly Barr'd.

D A Gallery to take in Goods and Provisions from ye Boat to the store Room.

E The State Room being 10 square 19 foot wide and 12 foot high, very well Carv'd and Painted, with a Chimney and 2 Closets, and 2 Sash Windows with strong shutters to Bar and Bolt.

F The Airry or open Gallery where is Conveniency to Crane up Goods and a great Leaden Cestern to hold ye rain Water that falls from ye upper roofs in leaden Pipes and to let ye Sea pass through in time of Storms.

G The Kitchen where is a large Closet and large standing Bed and c.

H A Bedchamber with 2 Cabbin Beds and all Conveniences for a Dining Room with large Lockers to hold a great store of Candles for light.

I The Lanthorn yt holds ye light is 8 square 11 foot Diameter 15 foot high in ye upright Wall: having 8 great Glass windows ...

for squares and conveniency to burn 60 Candles at a time besides a great hanging Lamp.

There is a door to go into ye Gallery, that is all removed to cleanse ye glass of ye Lanthorn which is often dim'd by saltwater yt washes over them.

K Is great wooden Candlesticks or Ornaments but ye irons yt bars them is very useful to stay a ladder to clean ye Glass.

L Is Funnels to let out ye steam yt riseth from ye light.

M Is a Compass Painted on ye under side.

N Is a Gallery to go out to put out ye Ensign to Salute or make a Signal.

O Is a vessel to let float on ye water to take in Small things from a Boat on ye West side of ye Rock, then there is no landing on ye other side.

P Is a large standing Crane to take things at a Distance when no Boats can come near the Rock.

Q Is a small Iron Turning Crane to take things into ye Airry or ye store Room below.

R Is a moving Engine Trough to cast down Stones to defend ye landing Place in case of need.

S Is the View of Maystone and part of Devonshire Land.

T Is Ramehead and part of Cornish Land and towards ye House and behind it lie ye Sound and Town of Plymouth.

LOVETT'S LEGACY

THE NEXT lighthouse erected on the Eddystone reef would be made of English oak and stand on a solid stone and wooden base, clamped in iron. The proposal to build the new structure was a revolutionary architectural concept for lighthouse construction but equal to that used in naval shipbuilding techniques.

The tower would be much taller and stronger than Winstanley's and visually very different. Being gracefully slim, the column, tapering upwards, was to be round throughout its length. It would also have a smooth exterior, being well jointed, giving it a clean appearance. Only a narrow cornice at the lantern gallery protruded from its wall. This lighthouse was to be a functional building, its job quite simple: to provide a sea-mark and beacon to those mariners who came close to the Eddystone Reef.

The man asked to design and build the next lighthouse was John Rudyerd.

Rudyerd's life is difficult to trace, as little is known about him. Some say that he was of local origin and that his childhood was spent in great poverty within a family renowned for their criminal activities. Indeed, they were once described by a clergyman "a worthless set of ragged beggars, whom almost nobody would employ, on account of the badness of their characters".

There is some evidence that the family were employed as labourers, who had moved from Staffordshire to work in Cornwall. However, the facts relating to John Rudyerd have been romanticised over the years. He is portrayed as a boy of good character and it is suggested that he was liked by the village community. The story implies that the youngster was unhappy and felt trapped between a brutish family of thieves and the outside world, which as he grew older, began to look a far more attractive alternative for him to explore.

He bided his time, making plans, waiting for an opportunity to run away and leave behind his sad and unpleasant existence.

Accounts of this period in his life make colourful reading, with a few writers stating that he became a cabin boy. Unfortunately, there is so little information available to the researcher, that the actual facts can sometimes be overlooked, with some authors preferring to accept the story which has been handed down through generations.

Of course, it is possible that John Rudyerd did travel from his Cornish home to the busy port of Plymouth seeking work. The traditional accounts tell of his experiences there, spending many an hour waiting outside the old ale houses in the Barbican area of Plymouth, hoping to persuade a sea captain to offer him work on board a ship.

It is said that after a few days of walking the streets of the busy port, he was eventually spotted by a Plymouth gentleman and offered a position within his household, which although it was not what he had expected, would eventually turn out to be the most important opportunity that he had ever taken.

His new job would be that of a "domestic manservant" to a wealthy couple who had no children of their own.

Within a very short time, it is stated that Rudyerd proved his worth in the house and was soon regarded, not simply as a servant but as part of the family itself, almost as an adopted son. The old gentleman who had employed him also recognised his special quality, because a suitable place of schooling was found and the education, probably his first, proved to be the boy's making, as he did remarkably well in every subject taught to him. Sciences and the English language became important subjects to young Rudyerd and through his enthusiasm, with the help of caring folk, this eager pupil became a very good scholar, especially in mathematics.

Very little is known about the period after his education, but historical accounts refer to him becoming a silk merchant in London.

From my own research on John Rudyerd, I can confirm the following:

The name Rudyerd appears relating to "sojourners" in the village of Landrake, Cornwall, which indicates that the original story of him living there is perhaps correct, in as much as the family were considered to be "travellers", although no evidence indicates that John Rudyerd was born there.

He is mentioned in the Skinners Company Register of Apprentice Bindings and Freedom Admissions, 1603–94. It refers to "John Ruddyerd sonne of Anthonye Ruddyerd, late of Deulecres in the countye of Stafford".

The account may support reports that the family came from Staffordshire; it is also suggested that Anthonye Rudyerd was a miner who arrived at Landrake during the early 1600s with his wife and six children, which included sons John, Thomas and Raphe. If correct, this would give some further credibility to the stories of Rudyerd's early life.

Unfortunately, I have been unsuccessful in acquiring any relevant local information about the family, either on where they worked or indeed any evidence at all connecting Rudyerd with his employer in Plymouth.

He did certainly move to London, where we find him as a young man of about 20, working as "an apprentice to a Robert Morris, citizen and skinner of London, for 7 years from the 9th of November 1666".

It must be remembered that thousands of people were encouraged to enter London after the Great Fire and to rebuild the city. This date and his whereabouts is thefore consistant with the records found about him.

By the late 17th century, Rudyerd it seems had established himself as a fine mercer, providing many wealthy clients, including Lord and Lady Shirley, with silks, furs and cottons. From his accounts to them we read that on 14 February 1674 he supplied Sir Robert Shirley with an Indian gown and two pairs of slippers, and on 7 December 1675 Lady Shirley bought another boy's Indian gown.

He had completed his apprenticeship with Morris and Thomas Byfield successfully, gaining his indentures on 2 November 1686, although it appears that he had already set up in business by then.

Also in that year it is documented that he leased "a messuage in Great Brickhill, (la) in Common Field, Home Close, Penn Close and Greate Close".

At this time, Rudyerd was married to Sarah Jackman, of St Andrew's Parish in Holbourne, Middlesex, whose father, Thomas, of St Bride's in London had provided land, possibly as a dowry for his daughter's union with Rudyerd. The couple had at least one child: it is known that a daughter, also named Sarah, was born on 18 September 1677 and baptised at St Martin in the Fields, Westminster.

The Jackman family had also been mercers in London for many years and were quite wealthy, which would have undoubtedly helped raise Rudyerd's standing in society.

But in any case, Rudyerd was a "citizen and skinner of London", a respected silk merchant and fur trader who owned premises at the top of Ludgate Hill, close to St. Paul's Cathedral. The established business, which I suspect had been given to Rudyerd by Sarah's father, gained even greater success for the couple. This period proved to be another important chapter in Rudyerd's life, as it was through his association with his clients that he would eventually meet and befriend Colonel John Lovett, a man who was to be instrumental in Rudyerd's next business venture as architect and builder of the new Eddystone Lighthouse.

The Eddystone lease was then owned by a Colonel Lovett, who was a member of the Irish Parliament and who had been an acquaintance of the previous lease owner, William Whitfield. It would appear that an agreement between these two men enabled Lovett to automatically become the new lease owner, in the event of Whitfield withdrawing from the venture through death or other cause. So when Whitfield was no longer involved with the lighthouse, Lovett became principal owner, although Trinity House would later challenge that arrangement.

However, when the legal situation was finally resolved, an amended lease between Trinity House and John Lovett was signed on 12 January 1705, although an Act of Parliament allowing him to proceed with the construction was still required by the Elder Brethren. The Bill for erecting the new Eddystone Lighthouse was promoted by Lovett's father-in-law, Lord Fermanagh, the draft being written by him and his associates. In a letter from Fermanagh to Lovett in 1705, we read:

> The Bill has been well drawn by good lawyers and that every vote in the Commons for the Bill is of importance. I won't have it till it is past all danger, which I hope for Friday next.

The Act was finally passed in the House of Commons on 26 March 1706 and Trinity House again held the Letter Patent for the Eddystone site itself. The deal they offered to Lovett gave him a 99-year lease. He would pay an annual rent of £100 to the authority, but was required to build his lighthouse within seven years, after which he would be authorised to collect light dues from passing ships to offset the construction costs. The source of income also provided the necessary financial stability which allowed them to support his venture.

John Lovett had been associated with a high-standing Buckinghamshire family, the Lovetts of Liscombe, with his father Christopher being the second son of Sir Robert Lovett who had earlier emigrated to Ireland, becoming an Alderman and Mayor of Dublin in 1676. Christopher Lovett also held the office of Auditor and Master of the City Works. Lovett enjoyed his father's determination and good fortune and soon the young man would rise in the ranks of the Bucks Militia to that of Colonel; in 1703, through family connections, he was to accept a parliamentary seat as the member for Phillipstown in the Irish House of Commons. Lovett was a popular figure and known in the highest echelons of Dublin society. Unfortunately, his mother did not enjoy such favour there, due to her background, and was kept very much in the shadows. Before marriage, her maiden name was Frances O'More, the daughter of Prizad O'More, an Irish rebel chief, who had assisted in the thirteen risings against the English some years earlier.

However, her son had proven himself a worthy inhabitant of the city, being successful in business and a much respected individual.

He was first married to Susanna, his cousin, the daughter of Lovett's own uncle, Lawrence of Eythorpe, and between them they had several children, with Robert and Christopher outliving a girl called Fanny and other baby boys. Sadly, Susanna died shortly after the deaths of her children, leaving him a young widower.

Happily, his lonely grief and sadness soon disappeared. On a business trip to London in 1702, Lovett, then 34, fell in love with Mary "Molly" Verney, who was the daughter of Lord Fermanagh. After a frustrating courtship due to her father's unease about Lovett's financial position, they were finally married on 20 July 1703 and a dowry of £5,000 was awarded.

With the financial boost, Lovett was able to set up a new business venture, in the belief that it would benefit his entire family. Unfortunately, this project was to be based in England and so would prevent the happy couple from spending much time together.

Lovett decided to accept a 35-year lease from his friend Lord Meath on an estate in Kilruddery, Ireland, which would be the couple's summer residence, while during the winter months they were to live at Clancarty House, opposite Parliament House in Dublin.

Lovett had many friends in the English Government and Admiralty. He enjoyed a variety of business and financial dealings while other members of the family were involved in the linen trade. But Lovett's commitment was to his new lighthouse project. He had wanted to build and own a lighthouse for many years and, with the loss of Winstanley's, a great opportunity had offered itself to him.

Lovett calculated that the initial investment from his wife's £5,000 would yield at least £700 per year clear profit and that the scheme would be most beneficial to the Lovett family.

He wrote to Mary's father: "I wish your daughter joy of a very good estate."

The first known correspondence between Lovett and Rudyerd is dated in various letters around 1700, and we read that "his friend of long standing was John Rudyerd" and that "Rudyerd's father was a miner in Cornwall, his brothers being described as a worthless set of beggars."

Lovett frequented Rudyerd's shop on Ludgate Hill and went to his home on numerous occasions. In a letter he wrote in 1703 he tells us of his respect for Rudyerd, describing him as his "business advisor, my friend of long acquaintance" and that "to risk

COL JOHN LOVETT BY SIR GODFREY KNELLER
THE AUTHOR'S COLLECTION

a pennyworth, he would neither advise nor suffer me". Lovett also reports that Rudyerd was born in Cornwall and had much experience in the use of mechanics and building materials.

So it is clear that Lovett's friend had the abilities necessary to take up the challenge asked of him, to design and build the next lighthouse to stand on the Eddystone.

The partnership and friendship continued throughout their lifetime and Lovett's venture would take them both into the annals of maritime history, like Winstanley before them.

Rudyerd had accepted the position of "architect and surveyor", along with two talented shipwrights, Smith and Norcutt, who worked at the Woolwich Naval Dockyard.

In their agreement, Rudyerd was asked to contribute financially to the venture only during the initial stages of the work, then after its completion he would be guaranteed an annual income of £250, with the same sum for his wife, paid yearly throughout their lifetimes.

First, the men had to design their lighthouse, but needed an appropriate workyard to set up the project. Luckily, Lovett, through Norcutt and Smith, had obtained agreement from the Admiralty to use a part of the Woolwich yard, and it was there that they discussed structural design and subsequently made models of the previous Eddystone towers before deciding on their own possibilities. The planned beacon was also built as a scale model with everyone agreeing to use normal shipbuilding techniques, which could be adapted quite successfully in creating their solid structure. The men would then work in the same way, as if building a ship, with the only significant difference being that it was to be built on its end, as if standing on its stern.

Their decision to proceed on the same lines as maritime structures, rather than of shore erections, was a revolutionary concept which enabled the ships' carpenters to produce a clean vertical shaft. The sturdy frame was weighted in its lower storeys by heavy stones, to act as ballast. When complete, the building would, as Rudyerd said, "rise like a mast of some high admiral" from the waters.

Rudyerd's lighthouse was to be far less ornate than Winstanley's had been, altogether a much more slender and elegant looking tower, being both tapering and circular, so that the new design would provide the elements with less resistance when the sea crashed against its frame.

Not only in shape did it differ from the previous Eddystone Lighthouse, but also in the construction materials used. Although granite was still a vital component in the base to anchor and secure the lighthouse to the rock's surface, English oak would provide the tower's strength. It was the main material used, enabling Norcutt, Smith and Rudyerd to show their remarkable skills in construction.

When the lighthouse design was finalised it was drawn to scale and offered for approval by Lovett to Trinity House. The Brethren observed that the proposed tower was very plain but functional, free of any projections; even the windows when closed were flush with the outside wall; and only the cornice protruding from the top of the building, around the lantern gallery itself, diverted the eye from the otherwise smooth column. But the cornice was a vital part in the building's design, enabling waves to shoot outwards, thereby shielding the lantern's glass from damage. Rudyerd and his two shipwrights believed they could offer an acceptable proposal to Trinity House which would ensure their support in the new venture.

Like Winstanley before him, Rudyerd found a passion so strong that it was to take him and his employer Lovett on a quest so important that their lives would be changed forever.

> Think not of rest; though dreams be sweet
> Start up and ply your heavenward feet,
> Is not God's oath upon your head
> Ne'er to sink back on a lothful bed,
> Never again your loins untie,
> Nor let your torches waste and die,
> Till, when the shadows thickest fall,
> Ye hear your Master's midnight call?
>
> — KEBLE

So once again the dangerous outcrop had a warrior to fight its menacing evil, someone with fresh ideas and imagination to beat the beast.

Trinity House, although surprised by the material to be used in the building, were nonetheless pleased with what they saw and accepted Lovett's project wholeheartedly; so began the next chapter of the Eddystone's story.

The reef presented the same difficulties in building as Winstanley had found before and nothing much had changed in the development of tools during those few short years. Everything would still have to be undertaken by hand.

On his return to Plymouth, Rudyerd immediately took a boat to the lonely rock mass and viewed for himself the rusty remains of Winstanley's iron braces. He realised at once that a critically accurate base plan would be needed if his team were to have any chance of success. Design of the upright iron anchors to hold the tower's base would have to be even better than his predecessor's effort and would have to be positioned correctly, to a fraction of an inch.

Working again with only pick-axes and heavy chisel-ended drills, the Cornish quarry-men or tinners chipped into the hard stone. Once more the work was incredibly hard and difficult, with rushing sea water constantly covering the workers' boots.

During the first season's work only 36 holes had been drilled into the rock to hold the tailor-made iron branches, becoming the 20-foot circular foundation brace for Rudyerd's structure. The irons were six feet long and weighed up to a quarter of a ton each. The work had been Rudyerd's first task and he knew that it was the most crucial part of the construction process, something that he had to get right.

A new workyard on the Cornish side of the Hamoaze had been acquired to base the small workforce and the tiny harbour at Empacombe allowed Rudyerd to use large barges and open boats, capable of taking all the building materials out to the Eddystone.

Along the stone harbour quayside he built a row of cottages. One was for his family, who had moved from their home in London to be with him. The others were occupied by Smith, Norcutt and senior members of the work party. Its location was ideal with even a conveniently placed inn nearby.

Both on the rock and at the small harbour, progress continued smoothly under the expert supervision of Rudyerd's two shipwrights, where the winter-felled oak was shaped and planed, then numbered before being sent to the Eddystone.

In a letter from the Secretary of Trinity House to Rudyerd dated 11 March 1706, replying to concerns over the safety of his workforce from press gangs and French privateers, we read that the Secretary "thinks that the workmen need not fear being troubled, since the person that molested those formerly employed (Winstanley and his men) was severely punished by the French King, and the men sent back again."

There were again many unforeseen difficulties for Rudyerd to overcome, mostly concerning the uncooperative weather but especially at the rock itself where the sea water was a continual problem and nearly always covered the working area, filling up the all-important holes that were critical in holding the tower's upright iron legs. His solution produced an ingenious method in which hot tallow wax would be heated to boiling point and immediately poured into a dried-out hole, where in a matter of seconds it cooled and hardened, sealing the space within the rock, which prevented further fillings by the sea water.

A coal forge which had been borrowed from the Plymouth naval dockyard was positioned on a tender, moored near the workplace, where it was used continuously during the first stages of building. So by heating the iron rods to a bluish colour, at approximately 550 degrees F, it was easy for the builders to rapidly push the irons into their individual slots, which caused the melting candle wax to spurt out. Each iron was then held firmly when the remaining wax hardened about it. Next, molten lead was poured around the upright and as it hardened off the surrounding area was topped up with pewter, poured into any tiny gap left between rock and stanchion, thereby fusing rock and iron together, which made a sealed plug and a totally watertight fitting.

Having secured the 36 irons to the rock's surface, a strong base was needed to support the building itself. Large oak and stone blocks were bolted together in criss-cross layers within the framework, onto the rock's surface, which itself had been levelled into steps. A solid wooden/granite platform was then built up to 24 feet and became the solid foundation base of the lighthouse. Slowly, the timber and granite stone sandwich rose from the Eddystone's surface, forming a plinth.

Every section was fitted together beforehand at the harbour workshop, numbered and then sent out to the reef, which allowed the builders to swiftly erect their beacon. With each timber and stone bolted and clamped by vertical iron straps to the rock's surface, Rudyerd and his men soon constructed a 36-foot platform for their creation. Over 500 tons of granite were sandwiched between strong timbers in the base, acting as ballast for the whole tower. Eighty tons of iron would be used throughout the building and 35 tons of lead would secure the various joints, with 2,500 screws, trenails and rack bolts anchoring each sinew of the structure together. However, the pharos was to be encased by 71 timber uprights, in lengths of 10 to 20 foot wide at the bottom and tapering to but a few inches at the top. The 71 uprights would be planed by craftsmen, then joined together before the seams themselves were caulked with oakum and coated with pitch to provide a smooth finish on the outer surface.

An iron ladder to the lower entrance door from the rock's surface would allow access into the tower. At its centre a stairwell would take you into a store area. On the next floor was another store room with the living room cum kitchen above. Next came the bedroom and finally the lantern above that floor, its cupola made from ironwork and lead. The base was completed on 22 June 1707. It was 42 feet high.

On 7 September 1707, the end of the second season's work, Lovett wrote a letter saying:

> Such of the work as can be done on shore is finished and that he has carried up the lighthouse as high as he has gone on the rock, to the great satisfaction of all the sea commanders and others,

that has seen it, or has been with him, and having a guard-ship which has been very serviceable all the summer.

In a letter Rudyerd wrote to Lovett, he told him:

> My Lord Dunley, Sir George Byng and Sir John Innary, have dined with me and they are to be with me this week, They are very pleased.

The Cornish moorstone used in the tower's base had been bought locally from Peter Trevelan and his son Walter of Lanlivery quarry and taken to Par Sands by horse and cart in one-ton pieces.

It was loaded onto vessels which had been beached near the shoreline. Next, at high tide, the heavy cargo was transported along the Cornish coast and brought to the Empacombe harbour workyard.

The importance of the Eddystone lighthouse being erected quickly was such a priority for the Admiralty that they felt it necessary to protect Rudyerd's workforce from the dangers of the press gangs.

An order was passed to station the Navy's finest warships, including the *Roebuck* with its 42 guns, the *Charles Galley* with 36 guns, the *Swallows Prize* with 32 guns and the *Albrow* with 24 guns, near the reef during the entire period of the building work.

At the beginning of the third working season, Lovett reported to Lord Fermanagh with news of his progress. In his letter of 25 March 1708 we read the following:

> Mr Rudyerd has been on ye rock and found everything has been left them and all the winter has not done him a penny damage, and that his man of warr is ready at his command and that he has received his orders to have what men and stores out of her majesty's yard at Plymouth he likes, so that he wants nothing but good weather.

Rudyerd had proven his abilities and efficiency by building a lighthouse, using a method of keying and securing all the materials together within his construction – a skill associated with excellent engineering techniques – and so the tower was seen as a brilliant achievement by most engineers of the day. Rudyerd's description of his achievement contained the following details (see picture on page 36):

A Shews the rock.

B The landing place.

aa The steps or flats to which the rock was reduced.

bb The branches.

c Floors.

cc Floors of wood laid lengthwise of the steps.

dd The floors laid crossways of the same.

ee Courses of compass timber.

D Five courses of moor stone which with two courses of compass timber marked E completed the entire solid, to the top of which led

F The Iron Ladder to

G The Entry Door and through GH The entry or passage into

HI The Well hole for the stair case

KL The Mast

M Five courses of moor stone, the height of which composed the entry or passage.

N Two beds of compass timber making good the passage to the stairs.

O Fours beds of moor stone capped with two beds of compass timber after which succeeded courses of timber alternately cross and cross with compass courses interposed as shewn in the section.

PQ Shew the upright timbers as they appear externally being 71 in number.

Pa The same in the upright section.

I The store room and R The door of the store room: which was so much further to the North than the entry that when casks and stores were drawn up perpendicularly by a tackle, suspended from above, they would clear the iron ladder.

S The state room.

T The bedchamber.

V The kitchen.

W The balcony.

X The lantern.

Y The lantern door into the balcony and to the cupola and ball.

H Four curved pipes for venting the smoke from the candles in the lantern.

g The top of the copper funnel which passed through the lantern from the kitchen fireplace which was brick.

h The upper bevil, or projection by way of

cornice for throwing off the sea, to prevent it from breaking the lantern windows in time of storms which was necessary, though the panes were of ground glass on account of strength.

i Knees to strengthen the junction of the uprights with the balcony floor, and also part to support the weight of the lantern.

kkk The original kirbs of compass timbers to form the uprights to a circle and support the weight of the floors.

mmm Kirbs applied of late years for strengthening the frame of the building.

nn The kant at the foot of the uprights and oo One of the stanchions by which the kants were fastened down.

In a letter from Lovett to Lord Fermanagh, written on May Day 1708, he wrote:

I have been so bissey at Trinity House with Setteling the Methods and way of Instruction and Deputations with the advice of Sir Edward Northey, that I have not finished with the African Company. Thank God all things goes well at Eddystone, and if Mr Rudyerd has eight or ten more days good weather, you will see the light in the Gazett'.

[This was a reference to a notice he would advertise to all mariners, to be published in the *London Gazette* on completion of the lighthouse]. Tell Deare Bess her Pearle Necklas is come, and I will send or bring it with me, I intend to give the Commissioners of The Revenue a Dish of Meate because I am to have from them A Letter to all the Collectors which will be of servis.

On completion of the lighthouse Lovett made a journey to every major port and harbour around the British south coast. He also arranged for respected and trusted individuals to be employed as Eddystone Agents. It was their responsibility to collect light dues from ship owners whose vessels had passed the lighthouse, so guiding their way.

In a letter sent from London, he suggested that a further gentleman be sent to the ports in the north and wrote:

I'll send another gentleman the coast way, from this, to Scotland and between him and I, We shall settle the business over this Kingdom.

RUDYERD'S LIGHTHOUSE
THE AUTHOR'S COLLECTION

Unfortunately for Lovett, light dues could not be collected at any Irish port and the situation was to have severe ramifications on his cash-flow in servicing the venture, which would eventually lead to a crisis and the introduction of further investment from new business associates.

Lovett wrote to Lord Fermanagh again on 22 June 1708:

> By Mr Rudyerd's last Letter he has finished all the Sollid part, which is now 42 foote high, which is 36 above High Water Marck... I have finished all matters with the Trinity House, as to the Methods of the Deputation and Instructions, Receipts, etc.; I have Sir Ed Northey's opinion and I hope to have Mr Cooper's to Back it, and hope in the beginning of next month to goe on my Western Jorney.

On 30 June he wrote once more to his father-in-law:

> I expect to hear from Mr Rudyerd that he has fixed his Lights, for I have sent them down what other things he wanted from hence... We think it not so well to surprise the world with a Light, as that in Tomorrow's Gazette we prepare them to Expect it.

The entry in the *London Gazette* edition of Monday 2 August to Thursday 5 August 1708 states:

NOTICE TO MARINERS

The Master, Wardens and Assistants of Trinity House of Deptford Strond, do give Notice to all Masters of Ships passing thro' the Channel, that they have received Advice from Mr John Rudyerd The Builder of The Eddystone Light-house; That after many hazards and Difficulties, and of very great expense, On Wednesday night, being The 28th July last, a light was plac'd in the Light-house, rebuilt on the Edistone Rock off Plimouth pursuant to an Act of Parliament made in The Fourth and five years of her present Majesty's Reign, for rebuilding The same: And The Duties granted by The Said Act of Parliament for new Erecting, and constantly keeping and maintaining The Said Light-house, being to be paid from and after The Kindling or placing a Light Therein: All Masters of Ships, Hoys and Barks, passing by the same are accordingly asked to take Notice, That The Said Duties commence, and are payable from The 28th Day of July last past as a foresaid.

Further correspondence continued in haste, as the excitement of the forthcoming event neared.

On 1 July he sent a message to Lord Fermanagh:

> All Affaires goes on well and hope next Saturday seven night to have the Light up and good habitation to live there... Mr Rudyerd writes to me, my Lord Dursley, Sir George Byng, and Sir John Jennings, hee dines with. They are to be with him this week, and well pleased, and when it's up it will be a great Sattisfaction to your Lordship's Obedient Son and Servant.
>
> — JOHN LOVETT

Lovett continued his business with various ship owners in London before returning to Plymouth and was arranging the final details of light due payment; success was near and he was happy to find the time to buy gifts for his family. He wrote to his father-in-law on 29 July:

> I thank God the Lantorne is sett and all provision, Bedding, Candles etcetera, went off to the Person who was to live in it... bad weather forced them back, but by Mr Rudyerd's letter yesterday after the storme, all things was very well, and only staid for 8 houres good weather to Lodge the men and everything they should want for six months. One Mr Wilkesson goes to the Northward to Scotland and Liverpool with all things proper for the Collecrs., and the Commrs. of the Revenue, to put the Act in due force... Corporations has promised me to do all that I ask of them... I have been so bissey I have not waited on my friends, but they must pardon me, I came to do bisness, and not complyments. I long to finish my Circuit in order to goe home. I have been a Long time but it can't be avoyded without Loss, and it's the only time of my Life I will ever be parted from your Daughter, who I will vallew and Love to the last Moment of my Life.

THE COMPLETED LIGHTHOUSE OF JOHN RUDYERD AND JOHN LOVETT 1708, PAINTED BY JOHN INNS

PICTURE BY KIND PERMISSION OF EDMUND VERNEY; PRIVATE LETTERS COURTESY OF SIR RALPH VERNEY AND THE CLAYDON TRUST

Fermanagh's reply to his son-in-law read:

AUG 1ST 1708.
I heartily rejoyce that you have brought your 'grate worke' so near to finishing, and I hope with God's protection it will redound to your proffitt as well as your Honour, in soe short a time goeing and thro' soe difficult a business. Noebody can wish you more success than myself, and all other friends here doe... You are putting foot in stirrup; we all wish you a good journey in your Tour d'Angleterre.

It was a time of great satisfaction for the whole team, who were toasting their success in Plymouth. They had achieved so much and their work was being rewarded. The lighting ceremony itself proved a great success and the evening was a wonderful experience for Lovett, Rudyerd and his family, along with the rest of the gathering. During the following day and on reflection, John Rudyerd put pen to paper and wrote the following letter to a man who, although absent from the event, was the one person most responsible for steering the original proposal through Parliament which allowed Lovett and Rudyerd to build their lighthouse. To Lord Fermanagh he wrote:

It is with great sattisfaction I send your Lordship the good news that the Light was put up this sennight, being the 28th of last month, and will be in tomorrow's Gazette in due Forme. I have sent your Lordship a picture of the lighthouse by John Inns, which I beg your acceptance of. One more I give to The Prince, as Lord High Admirall, one to the Corporation of Trinity House and one goes for Ireland. [John Lovett's home was in Dublin].

Talking about the painting, he explained:

In it is four men of warr that Attended on the worck, The Roebuck, The Charles Gally, The Albrough and The Swallow. The rest is shipps of all Nations.

There was a postscript to the correspondence which explains the delay in posting. It read:

When I sent to the painter, it [the picture] was not don, soe it will be next week before it will be your Lordship's.

Lord Fermanagh replied on receipt of his picture from John Lovett, his letter dated 19 August 1708, saying:

I recd. your letter and the Picture, a singular favour which we all heare much admire. We are going to Church, this being the Thanksgiving Day, where we shall sing a Laudamus for the Light-house with hearty wishes for its prosperity to you and yours.

In another rare published print attributed to Rudyerd, produced some time after the completion of his lighthouse and entitled *A Prospect and Section of the Lighthouse On The Edystone Rock off Plymouth*, we find it was dedicated to Thomas, Earl of Pembroke, Lord High Admiral of Great Britain and Ireland, with the motto *Furit natura coercet ars*, illustrated by B Lens and engraved by I Sturt.

John Lovett had been away from his young wife for many months overseeing the venture, staying in Plymouth and London. She found their separation hard to bear, but soon her husband was coming home and Mary hoped they could continue to live their lives together again as a family.

Lovett's final business was to discharge the workmen at Plymouth and settle his accounts there. He had also to make the long journey by horse around the British coast to recruit further agents. The work had made him very tired and he was an exhausted man eager to get back to his home in Ireland, but the remaining appointments were important to the financial success of the project and would only take him a further five weeks. In vague correspondence relating to his last task, we find that in August 1708 he was pleased to be able to stay with his cousin in Corfe near Tawstock in North Devon for a break, before undertaking the hard slog around the rest of the country. Everybody he met on his journey congratulated him on his achievement, which pleasantly surprised him. He wrote:

I have been used with all the respect possible; last Thursday I was on the Rock, and in the House of the Commr. of the Dock, and I went in his 10 Ores Boate, and had a Yacht and a Smack to attend upon us. He as well as I was plesed with everything, and those that Lives in it is very easy and happy, and the late Stormes did them no damage nor anyway made them uneasy. There went off severall boates, and in them women. The whole Country is very kind and civill to me, and gives mee a great many thankes for what is don.... Tell my Deare Little Bess I will bring her something from the Bath.

Before leaving the South-West, he met up with the Rudyerds in Exeter. They had already left their temporary home at Empacombe and were returning to their London address in Southwark, via Blandford in Dorset. He wrote:

Everything is completed and the whole Rudyerd family are going to start for Town within the fortnight.

Lovett travelled first to Bristol, then on to Bath, before reaching London, where he stayed with Lord Pembroke for several months.
On 10 November he wrote:

I was in great hopes to have finished all my Bisness before this, but the gentleman from Scotland had a great Trouble to settle with those obstinate people, but he now has the whole Kingdom to my sattisfaction... As to news, my Lord Prembroke is made Lord Admirall, Lord Wharton Lord Lt of Irland, Lord Somers Ld. President of the Council; my brother Pearse raising his Regiment... my service to dear Bess.

John Lovett had been obliged to remain in London much longer than he had hoped, but the time was well spent and he often visited the offices of Trinity House and also enjoyed his celebrity status with the London elite.

By Christmas Day, he finally arrived back at the family home in Ireland, where his long-suffering wife Mary had waited so patiently for his return.

In a letter to her father Lord Fermanagh, addressed to his home at Claydon and dated Christmas Day 1708 she wrote:

Christmas Day, 10 at night, I can, I thank God, with great joy send you the welcome news of Mr Lovett's being safe at home, after a very bad journey by Land, and a dangerous passage by Sea. I cannot express my joy to see him, and I believe he is very well pleased to be at home. I hope we shall part no more till Death. Your letters were A great Cordiall to me, when I was in a very malloncolly way, but now I hope I shall rub off all that, and with great reason return God thankes for the mercy I have received.

Lovett's health had been adversely affected by the pressure placed on him, especially over the last few of years involving financial worries relating to the lighthouse venture. But now at last he was able to rest in quiet surroundings and enjoy the company of his family, and most of all be with his loving wife who had herself suffered by his absence.
On 12 February 1709, Lovett wrote from his home in Dublin to Lord Fermanagh:

I was so weary and tired after a very sadd Jorny by Land and bad passage by Sea, that the night I landed I desir'd my wife to give your Lordship my duty. I thank God I found all my famhly very well and in good order... We are very barren of news, only that we have had the hardest weather this winter that ever was known in this Kingdom. My Cousin Tighe was married, and are now at Kilrudery, which we have lent them... Our blessing to dear little Bess, and we are very proud of her.

After a short rest, Lovett regained enough strength to continue the management of the Eddystone business; the lighthouse itself was still to be finished and although a light did shine from its lantern, many other matters took up Lovett's time and once again he was hard at work and away from home. In July he wrote:

The whole is intirely fixt and completed. It has been very chargeable, but I almost know the end of it, and hope that the Incomb will fully Answer my trouble, Hazard and Expence. I hope Mr Rudyerd will be in London next month and we hope with my Sister to leave Dublin for Chester with the first convenience.

On 8 August he wrote to Lord Fermanagh, after arriving in Chester:

I thank God after being eighteen hours at sea, we came safe to Park-Gate, and last night to this place; we leave this afternoon for Nantwich. We call on Mrs Rudyerd, who is near Litchfield, and hope to be at Sir Thomas Cave's on Thursday or Friday.

By the autumn, the Eddystone would once again plague Lovett with problems and he was often found in London dealing with them. On 24 November 1709 he was still there, overseeing the payment of light dues, and in a letter to Lord Fermanagh he apologised for not visiting him at Claydon:

I did intend to have paid my duty to your Lordp. at Claydon, but most of the Admeralls coming to town while my friend Sir John Lake was there, I chose rather to do the needfull with them and some of my Collrs.; and now the fleets are coming hom, to see that they pay a third full Tunnage... and prefer'd my family's welfare before my own pleasure... I have a very handsome Certificate of Trinity House signed by Sir John Lake, Sir George Bing, Sir John Jennings, Sir Thomas Hardy, and all the Captns. and Commandrs. in town which I hope will be of great Servis to me and little Verney.

In December Lovett joined his wife and family at Lord Fermanagh's Claydon home where they enjoyed a wonderful Christmas together. Lovett's wife was expecting another child and gave birth to a daughter on 18 January.

Unfortunately the child did not survive and in deep sadness the family decided to stay with John's brother-in-law, Brigadier Ed Pearce in Epsom, so that they could come to terms with the loss in the company of relatives.

It was also a convenient location for Lovett, as his Eddystone difficulties continued to mount up.

A major dispute had arisen concerning his contract with Trinity House and ownership of the lighthouse lease, which legally belonged to Lovett. For various reasons his enemies tried to oust him from the Eddystone business and a fight was necessary to protect his interests.

Immediately he sought the services of his father-in-law to help him and travelled with his wife to central London, where he would bitterly fight the case.

Lord Fermanagh brought the unjust situation to the attention of Parliament and on 21 March 1710 wrote:

My bill was read a 2nd. time and went through the Commitee., so now it Lyes only for the last reading which I hope for tomorrow and then it only waits the Queen's Act.

Unfortunately, there was much opposition to the proposed Bill and the Lords disagreed with the amendment. Lovett's letter continued:

I hope it will be a satisfaction to your Lordship. haveing the House of Commons on my side and most of the house of Lords. I have disobliged a great many of my Country, but it makes no disturbance in my mind.

The ownership battle of the lease was not yet won and during the week of 22 March Lovett's health became much worse, which concerned Mary.

His livelihood and standing depended solely on him winning the Bill and as the tension increased, so too did it begin to drain the family of their strength.

In a letter to her mother, Mary wrote:

I think we stand much as when I writ last, and if Mr Lovett's business will permit, we desine next week to try Epsom Air, which I pray God may doe him Good. His Act of Parlt. is not yet determined but we fear the enemy is too powerful, but this week will put us out of all doubt and then he will write to my Father.

A very tense couple of days followed as the debate continued and the Lovetts waited for the House to vote on the Bill; they were totally exhausted from their difficulties.

In a letter dated 1 April 1710, Colonel John Lovett wrote to his father-in-law, saying:

> After many days waiting on proper persons and doeing the needful in all places, I have carried my poynt against the great Lord Wharton, for after an hour's debate in the House, and many speeches, and some very hard ones, on a devission I carried it by 2, viz. 17 against 15, so that I am safe. We shall only stay in town for the Royal Assent, and then for Epsom and a little quiet and Country Aire which with this good success I hope will make me quite well.

Lovett had narrowly secured his position by just two votes.

On 6 April, Mary wrote to her father with the news:

> Yesterday the Queen went to the house of Lords, where with severall more she passed Mr Lovett's Bill, which Agreeable sight I and my neeces went to see. I hope now Mr Lovett will begin to take some care of himself and get out of town A Satterday, for he indeed very much wants it; but I shall stay in town tell next Thursday, being desired by my Aunt Dunck to be at the Grand Entertainment and represent her, which I promised to doe.

In his final letter dated 6 April, addressed to his father-in-law, who had been so instrumental in the Eddystone venture, the ailing Lovett wrote, enclosing a copy of his successful Bill:

> My Lord, I hope the Enclosed will be a satisfaction to your Lordp. as its to me. I have got it printed that this night it may goe to Dublin and the proper places, and now God willing I will goe to Epsom for a few days to be Easy and have a little quiet, butt my wife is next week to be a great Lady at my Ld. Mayor's... I have so many Letters to write... I will trouble your Lordship with no more than that I am and will ever be, my Ld., Your Lordship's dutyfull and obedient Son and Servant,
>
> — JOHN LOVETT

During the next few days he became gravely ill and those with him saw a massive decline in his health; on 22 April Brigadier Pearce anxiously wrote to Lord Fermanagh:

> My Lord, I find The aire of this place is not so beneficiall to my brother Lovett as we hop'd for, by the advice of Mr Rudyerd, Mr Jess and my own, we carry him to London tomorrow. Your Lordship has a greater influence over him than wee, and if it suits with your convienience, the sooner you could be in Towne, the better.

Mary, who was with her husband in Epsom, also wrote on the back of the same letter:

> I am in soe much trouble I know not what to write, onely I joyn with my Brother Pearce and Mr Rudyerd in beging to see you as soon as possible, for I find a great Change in my Dear and never to be forgotten Mr Lovett. I fear his affaires are not soe well settled as they might be, soe wish I had your advise what to doe, for I fear I am your Unfortunate, though Obedient Daughter till death,
>
> — M LOVETT

Unfortunately John Loverr's health deteriorated still further and then suddenly on 24 April 1710 he died. He was buried at Soulbury Church in the family vault; Mary, st the age of 28, became a widow.

Throughout her marriage to John Lovett, Mary was often left to cope alone in bringing up their children. Two boys, Verney and John, had remained with her at the family home in Ireland while a daughter, Elizabeth, was cared for at the home of Lord and Lady Fermanagh in England. The other child, a baby called Mary, had died soon after birth.

It had not been an easy life for Mrs Lovett, but she had loved her husband dearly and continued to support him until the end.

Her marriage had lasted seven years, and through most of it her husband lavished most of his attention on his business dealings, namely the Eddystone lighthouse venture, leaving her to cope alone.

The project had woven its own magical spell on him, one which Mary had been unable to break, having resigned herself to

RUDYERD'S LIGHTHOUSE
THE AUTHOR'S COLLECTION

sharing her husband with his other great love.

Throughout her marriage the "enchanted Eddystone" had been no friend, because it was taking Lovett from her; in time it would prove to be her worst enemy.

His will instructed that his son Verney should be charged with continuing the ownership of the Eddystone lease, when of age, but until that time his wife should oversee the running of the business.

In the event, Verney would receive a payment of £8,000 from the sale of the lease.

The Eddystone Lighthouse was continuing to serve the mariner well and became a symbol of Lovett's determination, standing proud as the years passed by.

The following information is taken from a bill for painting work carried out at the Eddystone Lighthouse by a Mr Brooking of Plymouth, from 1710 to 1713. It read:

1710/11.
THE EDDYSTONE LIGHT HOUSE TO CHA: BROOKING IS DR. FEB 28.

To the wrighting of 85 letters on a board in gold att 21/2d per letter by Mr Rudyerd' order –
14/-: 81/2d.
To the doing the ground of the board blue –
5/-: 5d.
To the joyner paied him for the board –
1/-: 6d.

1713. JULY 21.
To plaine colors once painted on the outside of 424 yards att 31/2d per yard –
£6: 3/- : 8d.
To Sash Squares in the Lanthorn twice painted numbering 162: att 2d each –
£1: 7/-.
For 24 lb of Putty att 5d per pound –
10/-.
For 20 dayes worke att 1/-: 8d per daye. –
£1: 13/-: 4d
For what I am to have over & above these prices in consideration of its being so much weather beaten & its having so many caulked seames about it which lying deep takes up a considerable quantity of colors more than usuall –
£1.
Total charge to Mr Rudyerd –
£11: 15/-: 2 1/2d.

In 1711 a Mr Partinton had become one of the Irish agents for the deceased Lovett. His duties included the collection of Eddystone light dues, and in his account dated May and June of 1711 we read the following:

Acct of what has been recd by Mr Partinton on Acct of ye Eddistone Light house.

May 15 1711. Recd from Warham Jernett Esq, the ballance of his acct of money recd of ye light house at Cork. = £24: 9/-: 9d.

June 6. Recd from Henry Arkwright on ditto account at Galway. = £2: 16/-: 2d.

June 25. Recd from John Kapper – at Limerick on ditto Acct. = £7: 2/-: 3d.

————————

Total = £34: 8/-: 4d.

The construction materials consisted of the following items: 500 tons of rough-cut stone; 1,200 tons of winter-felled English oak; 80 tons of iron; 35 tons of lead; 2,500 trenails; 2,500 screws; and 2,500 rack bolts.

In our sails all soft and sweetly,
Yet with bold, resistless force,
Breathe the winds of heaven, and fleetly,
Wing us on our watery course;
Swift and swifter furrowing deep,
Through the mighty waves that keep,
Not a trace where we have been:
On we speed to lands unseen.
Be our voyage, brethren, such,
That if direst peril come,
Wreck and ruin could not touch,
Aught but this our weary frame;
That may gladly sleep the while,
Still and blest the soul shall smile,
In the eternal peace of heaven,
That our God hath surely given

— FOUQUE

The Eddystone lease was the property of Mary Lovett, until such time as her son Verney was of age to manage the business. The arrangement seems to have upset the other members of the syndicate and from then on problems and conflict between the individuals produced ill-feeling and a division of loyalty.

However a more pressing situation required Mary's attention as Lovett's business had left many outstanding unpaid bills, all linked to the lighthouse venture. At first she was not unduly worried by the financial difficulties, believing that her late husband had made the necessary provision for his family. But on reading his will it became clear that there were complicated financial problems to sort out.

Lovett's nephew, Richard Tighe, a "true friend", and Mary were co-executors of the will and they were both charged to deal with mounting financial difficulties as the many creditors and legal people fought for a share of the lighthouse estate. Even Rudyerd himself, Lovett's long-time friend, appeared to have shown indifference to Mary's troubles.

In a letter to her father on 9 May, just before the will was read, she wrote:

Hond. Sir, – Your unfortunate daughter begs leave to express her Duty as well as sence of all kindnesse showed to me in my great necessity, for I hope God will preserve you to be a Father to the poor Fatherless and Husband to the Widdow indeed, which I hope will always be a Widdow indeed, and stand by the remains of that Dear Man, whose Memorye shall ever be graven in my heart.

Two days later, on 11 May, she sent copies of letters from Mr Tighe to a Mr Jess and Rudyerd (the latter asking for more money) stating that Mr Tighe was very apprehensive that the affairs of the lighthouse would prove extremely intricate, "but I am resolved to doe the best I can to serve the family of the man that I had soe perfect an esteem and value for." Mary entreated her father to direct her what to do. The letter was written after 11pm and she obviously felt very lonely.

I have not one friend now in this world whose advice I would give A Pin for but yours; and this is a thing of soe great moment that I hope you will think my poor family worth a little of your care, tomorrow or next day at furthest we expect the will.

On 6 July 1710, Mary wrote once more to her father:

Mr Tighe and I have taken out Letters of Administration, and I hope in God in time we shall make the family easy. Mr Tighe has stood tightly to it, otherwise the Plate and everything else had been gone... I find I should have been tore all in peaces if Mr Tighe had not stood with me but he is a true friend and a man of much honour...The was resolved not to administer till I gave my consent to sell or Sett the Lighthouse. He is averse to Mr. Rudyerd's having anything to do with the Lighthouse, or anything, he fearing that he has got too much already, for they all believe here that a much less sum of money would have built it if well managed. We cannot get any money here from the ships, till we have an exemplificitation of the Act Of Parliament from England under the Broad Seal, which we have sent for; it is only their Duty cunning to put us to what charge they can. I thank God my Dear Mr Lovett's memory bears a great Carrecter here, even amongst his very Enimyes, which indeed occasion much kindness and Civility and Respect to be shown to me from everybody, and doubt not but God will bring me through all my troubles save the loss of that just and good man which is never to be forgotten. Mr Rudyerd has writ to us for more money and power to call the Collrs. to an account which Mr Tighe will not give... first I think it best to pay every one what is due to them but I have found he [Rudyerd] is for gratifying all his people never considering what we have to pay. Tomorrow, we all desine for Kilrudery to see my poor children and how matters stand there.

In her father's reply, relating to John Rudyerd, he said:

Tis too soon yet to discover my thoughts of him, but its my opinion that he has gott more by Col. Lovett then he gott in 30 years tradeing, yet I see the meaness of his Spiritt extends still to getting if it be but trifles in comparison of what he hath gott from that Good man. And tho' he might, I believe, yet be made use of, I would put as little power into his hands as possible, especially of money concerns, the Lighthouse affaires excepted, and I doubt he is not capacited to Inspect other men's Accounts. But these matters I knowe Mr. Tighe's more mature Judgement will well consider and act for the best. I am very glad the Creditors seem so easy, and I dare say there will be such a just performance of the Trust, by honest Mr Lovett's Exrs. that they will be fully satisfied with Mr. Tighe and your Integrity. As to the Lighthouse... I much doubt whether it will at long run answer the End by keeping, God onely knows, yet with Peace and his blessing that may happen; but for my part I wish your husband had never undertaken it... and whether Sell, Sett or Kept, God direct you both for the best... I wish Ld. Wharton liked Kilrudery so well that he'd buy it, but it seems you have small hopes of selling it [the lease] to advantage... this is a frightful long letter, therefore Ile conclude praying for you and your small frye [children].

The settlement of her dead husband's estate could not adequately be dealt with and soon her financial difficulties became enormous.

Richard Tighe helped all he could, but the mounting legal pressures proved very complex, so much so that Mary was even forced to consider selling her own home.

In a letter to her father dated 6 September 1710, she wrote:

My thoughts of being in England by this time made me defer giving you thanks for the favour of yours long before now, but I find its very tedious to undertake anything when one depends on other people. Mr Rudyerd has finished all and left Plimouth... I fear we shall find Malloncolly accounts there as well as here for all people brings in their debts... I have had all the goods of both houses and plate valued by sworn Appraisers, and their value of them comes to above £600.

During the next couple of months, Mary continued to ponder her situation. She decided to visit her father at Claydon to discuss the financial implications and in November made the journey from Ireland to England.

After an uncomfortable voyage across the Irish Sea, Mary, accompanied by her eldest son Verney, was involved in an accident; their coach turned over and they and six other passengers were lucky to survive, but on arriving in London an even greater worry overshadowed Mary's pressing lighthouse business, when the young boy fell ill with fever.

The family lawyers were eager to take up Mary's case, although the situation as it stood would undoubtedly take a very long time to conclude, as the complicated legal proceedings involved Trinity House and the Court of Chancery as well as the House of Commons.

Sadly in 1711 Mary had no alternative but to sell her home in Ireland, which at least raised most of the money needed to settle the outstanding debts from a variety of creditors, who were constantly petitioning her. The lighthouse became a millstone around Mary's neck as the legal battles continued.

Although with no home of her own, she was able to find temporary accommodation with relations in London.

It was the mark and courage of the woman to persevere in her efforts in trying to settle all outstanding business transactions relating to her late husband's lighthouse. Most notably, however, Rudyerd and his associates proved very tiresome with persistent demands and they opposed her efforts continuously.

Mary fought hard to keep the Eddystone lease in spite of her own financial worries, believing it to be an act of honour to her dead husband. Finally she gained a legal agreement covering lease ownership which allowed Verney, the eldest son, to take possession, in the event of her death, thereby keeping the lease in the Lovett name. However, Mary's monetary difficulties continued and all thoughts of retaining the lighthouse looked very remote. By 1713, Mary was exhausted and had reluctantly decided to sell the Eddystone. Her children at least would benefit from the sale, but it would also end the constant wretched legal arguments which had overwhelmed her. The lighthouse structure itself was still providing immense help to every mariner on the English Channel, but to Mrs Lovett it had brought nothing but heartache into her life. There were going to be even more complications in selling her lease and once again it would take time and money to finalise all the legal documentation.

On 28 May 1713, she wrote to her father:

> The copy of what Mr [Robert] Weston writ to me, the bill in Chancery for sale of the Lighthouse must be brought in the names of some of the mortgagees against the executors of Coll. Lovett and his son Verney, and if my trustees haveing the first mortgage wou'd be plantives with the other mortgagees it wou'd be more easie and less expensive then to be defendants, and save them the trouble of putting in answers.

The legal wheeling and dealing continued, although some money was being sent to Mary from the light due payments. But much of it was to be used for lawyers' fees or paid to the others associated with the lighthouse venture.

In 1714, the entire Eddystone syndicate were greatly worried about the possibility of two new lighthouses being erected at Land's End, which they knew would decrease the value of their own lighthouse. In the event, however, Trinity House objected to the proposals. The decision strengthened the division in the Lovett partnership and resulted in Mary's opponents mounting a takeover bid to purchase the lease outright and obtain ownership through its planned sale. Rudyerd, Weston and others offered her £24,000 for the lease and between them a deal was struck.

In Mary's correspondence to her family we read:

> The creditors press for the sale of the lighthouse, which for my part, I should be glad were done, for I believe that nothing but rogues and knaves belong to it.

By the end of 1714 a decree was passed allowing the sale of the lighthouse to proceed, and although it took the form of a public auction the syndicate who bought it were, as expected, Lovett's old business associates. Indeed, their leader, Robert Weston, had been involved with the previous venture since its very beginning, having been instrumental in partially funding Lovett's original work.

At the end of March 1715, Mary was in London with her solicitors, finalising the sale. On 16 July 1715, she wrote to her father about the forthcoming business:

I hope to have told you something of my fate with the Corporation [Trinity House] but they keep me still depending. Mr Noyes [a member of the syndicate about to buy the lease] gives me all the assurance in the world it will be done at the next Court but for my part I see so many tricks and turnes in the world that I only depend upon what I see done and now not what people say. When I told him he should have the present Mr Bernard intimated to him, it put A chearfull readyness in his countenance to serve me, I was allmost provoked by him but I conquered myselfe and thanked him for what I must really pay him. I should rejoice to leave sweet hot London and see my young fri but till Mr Bernard gives me leave I dare not stirr, for he's the only man I depend on.

By 16 July 1716, the lease had been sold to her enemies and neither Mary nor her son Verney would have any further involvement with the Eddystone lighthouse business.

The eight-man syndicate was headed by Robert Weston of Norfolk Street, Inner Temple, London, with his associates, Richard Noyes of Grays Inn and a Dublin alderman called Mr Cheetham, all known to John Lovett before his death. Even John Rudyerd's name is noted as being a shareholder in the new Eddystone venture, but whether it was that of Rudyerd or his son is unclear.

Lovett's widow received payment from the sale on Lady Day 1716. Mary announced that she was glad to be rid of it, although she thought the purchasers had a great bargain.

In letters referring to the period we read of her indignation and disgust at the small price received for the lease, just £24,000.

During the next 14 years little happened to discourage the proprietors in their new business: indeed it appears to have been a very profitable period for them. The ownership of the Eddystone was with Robert Weston, who was named its leaseholder. His family would be the chief owners of the lease for the next 80 years, in which time another lighthouse would have been built on the Eddystone.

Rudyerd's design proved to be a masterpiece in architectural achievement, completely silencing all of his critics. As the years unfolded, the people of Plymouth became ever more confident in their fine lighthouse.

Although minor repairs were continuously required to the tower's wall, there were few major difficulties regarding its maintenance. However, it did prove necessary to seal up all of the lower windows in the store room as the sea water always penetrated the compartment in times of bad weather and rough seas.

The two Plymouth dockyard shipwrights John Holland and his assistant Josiah Jessop, who was in charge of the building, soon developed unique skills and special knowledge of lighthouse construction complexities and became vital to the operation, which had moved its base from Empacombe to a bigger site at Millbay.

Life in the tower was sedate and the gentle existence only changed during inclement weather, or if the relief boat was delayed, when the keepers became excitable and anxious.

Just as it had been for Winstanley's men, most days were a routine of cleaning lamps, cooking, more cleaning and preparing for the evening. Those were the lightkeepers' daily chores and, for most, it was a comfortable existence they enjoyed.

A continuous source of home comfort was the kitchen's coal stove, lit throughout the day and night, where light broth was always available.

Fresh fish was caught from the rocks during calm periods, or from the lantern gallery by kite, and it was usual to find dead seabirds around the lantern housing after they had accidentally flown into the glass, encouraged by the candle's light. Their misfortune provided fresh meat which became especially plentiful during stormier times.

Most of the keepers would have had some experience of sea life, either in the navy or as fishermen. But in any case, to be a lightkeeper was regarded as a very responsible position, although the isolated way of life endeared itself to a unique breed and many land people thought it a strange and lonely kind of employment to be involved in.

Originally, in Rudyerd's lighthouse, only two keepers worked together at any one time, being employed on a rota basis and each working a 12-hour shift, while another man remained on shore for relief duties. It was very important therefore for the pair in the tower to have a good working relationship, for the smooth running of the lighthouse and especially when both men were to be confined inside the small beacon, sometimes for months at a time.

Unfortunately, through the years there have been many accounts of keepers fighting, or not communicating with one another, the latter being the most common problem to overcome. But even greater difficulties arose in their eating habits and some were even known to steal from their colleague's rations, or simply not eat what had been cooked for them, when adopting more communal working practices. However, a solution to the problem was endorsed in the entire service and eventually every man would accept responsibility for his own requirements, having to purchase, cook and eat his own individual stores.

Trinity House was a well-respected lighthouse authority even in Europe, but especially in France whose own naval and commercial shipping used the Eddystone light during voyages up and down the English Channel. When one considers that their lighthouse, the Tour de Cordouan, was regarded as a masterpiece of lighthouse design by the English engineers, it is quite remarkable to learn that the French maritime authorities were so impressed by the new Eddystone tower that they wrote to "Messieurs les Officiers de l'Amirauté de Londres a Londres" for technical advice.

From a letter written in Bordeaux on 28 September 1724, we read:

Gentleman,
It is the intention of the Court to raise the top of the Cordouan Tower, at the entrance to the [Gironde] river, to the height it used to be, namely 22 feet more than at present. Several plans have been offered for the construction of the fire-pan, or cresset [reschaut], in which the fire is kept that is lit every night to indicate to navigators the entrance to the river. I have been told that the kind used in England is better and handier and keeps the fire in better; I am also informed that

coal is better than wood, that it keeps alight much longer and does not get put out by rain. I should be much obliged if you would send me a sketch of the cressets used in the towers in which lights are lit on your coasts, and also inform me what sort of coal you use to keep the fires going for a longer time, and prevent them getting extinguished.

I take the pleasant opportunity of assuring you that nobody has the honour, Gentlemen, of being more completely your most humble and most obedient servant,

— BOUCHER

It was also true to say that many French officials believed that their own lighthouse system, operated by La Commission des Phares, was unquestionably superior, being better equipped and managed than the English authority, especially in harbour lighting and other less important subsidiary lights. What can't be denied is that England and France were quickly developing their own lighthouse bodies and both countries realised the immense importance of sea beacons.

RUDYERD'S LANTERN AND GALLERY
THE AUTHOR'S COLLECTION

On both sides of the Channel, brave men had chosen to live their lives in solitude, cocooned in tiny light towers away from the majority of their fellow beings. It was not surprising therefore that their employment differed little from those in other lands and so a common bond and respect was acknowledged throughout the centuries.

Meanwhile, back at the Eddystone, the daily routines were being carried out by the keepers. During the day, cleaning, cooking and lookout was their main activity, then, when evening fell, it brought a different pattern of work. Within the lantern, suspended on a metal chandelier, was its reason for being: 24 tallow candles hung in readiness to brighten the dark night sky. When lit, each one had to be snuffed every half an hour, continuously checked and maintained in good order. Although it was a hot and smelly job, it was nonetheless the most important job of all. Nineteen small candles sat in the outer circle, producing tiny flames, while five larger torches weighing two pounds each were placed at the centre of the array of light.

Outside the wooden tower the mighty waves bashed at its sturdy frame, especially in stormy weather, where they would rush up the column and climb over the entire structure.

The creaking of the lighthouse sounded like that of a ship in heavy seas and in such weather a continuous shudder would be experienced by those inside, with the keeper's trenchers being thrown from the shelves of the kitchen.

However, Rudyerd's lighthouse was regarded as a comfortable place to work, even though the sleeping quarters were occasionally damp from the sea's constant spray on the structure, although the design was such that any heat produced by the kitchen fires allowed for some warmth to penetrate the bed chamber.

The keepers felt able to trust in its strong construction, finding the tower secure and safe. To many it felt like their second home and most found the place had a decent quality which offered them a special and satisfying lifestyle.

Financial accounts of the lighthouse for the year of 1721 show us that its overall expenditure amounted to just £511, while the revenue of light dues collected by the Eddystone agents had been £1520 – a profitable return of £1009.

Unfortunately, as time progressed so too did the repairs, causing costs to rise. John Holland was in charge of maintenance but had recently been promoted to the role of assistant builder at the Woolwich naval yard in London, so it was decided that the daily responsibility should be given to the local man, Jessop.

He quickly established himself by confidently undertaking every new problem set before him. However, in 1729 a crisis arose which threatened to render the lighthouse useless, a situation even Jessop was unable to solve.

The purser responsible for the provisioning of the keepers was Pentecost Barker and in his diary of 8 December 1729 he wrote:

> A day of great trouble and perplexity – under great concern about the people at Eddystone who have no candles and as this is in some measure under my care, I so teaz'd and fretted myself that I had near brought on my fits.

Provisioning of the lighthouse was an important task for the purser in charge and the crew's skill in shipping the vital cargo was legendary. The food taken to the lighthouse included winter potatoes, cabbage, turnips and other vegetables throughout the year, while tea, sugar and beer were in constant demand. Chicken, mutton, ham were regularly eaten by the keepers. Coal and candles would also dominate any order to the lighthouse, along with the news and letters from home.

In an incident which is also attributed to the Smalls lighthouse near the Pembrokeshire coastline, a sad story focused the minds of the public on the keepers' precarious existence and lifestyle at the Eddystone.

Soon after completion of the lighthouse a tragedy occurred, the gravity of which forced changes to the working practices of the entire lighthouse service.

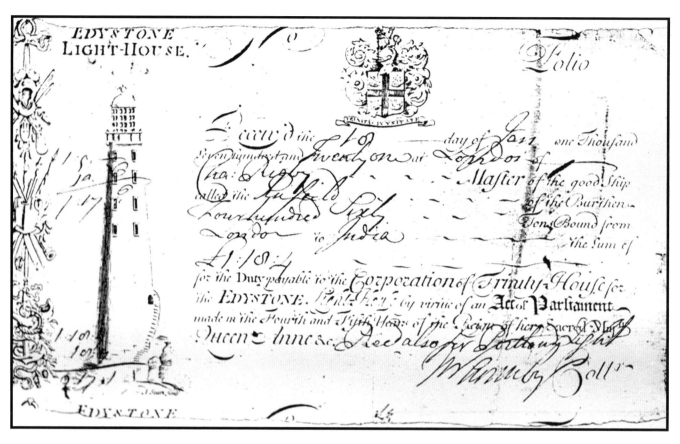

AN EDDYSTONE LIGHT DUE RECEIPT DATED 1721 – PAID TO THE CORPORATION OF TRINITY HOUSE
BY KIND PERMISSION OF THE CORPORATION OF TRINITY HOUSE

During continued bad weather, which had lasted several weeks, growing concern for the keepers' wellbeing filled the minds of those on land, as no relief boat had been able to reach the Eddystone with their vital supplies.

Because of the inclement weather, a lookout had been posted to watch for a signal from the keepers in the tower. His base was the tiny chapel on Rame Head, which was once a light beacon and home to a hermit years before.

Signalling from the lighthouse to shore was still in its infancy. Although the lookout had a large mounted telescope at his disposal, it was known that on innumerable occasions he could not even see the structure, let alone any flags flying from its lantern gallery, due to the poor visibility and the ocean climbing over the entire tower.

Due to the seriousness of the situation a reward of half a guinea was offered to any person who contacted the workyard with news from the stricken lighthouse, or sent word to the agent and collector of light dues, based at the Custom House on the Barbican,

Plymouth. The incentive ensured that many people kept their eyes peeled, both from the Hoe and on the clifftops near Rame.

The long period of stormy weather continued preventing the relief boats from reaching the isolated tower. Anxiously, the townspeople waited for a signal, but most feared the worst.

Then, in the early hours of a bright but still windy morning, a flag was seen flying from the lantern rails of the lighthouse. However, no-one knew what it meant and only speculation was possible. Perhaps the keepers' food had run out or there had been a terrible accident? No-one could say. There was no let-up in the storm and the mountainous seas continued to pound against the lonely tower, while the wind blew stronger and everyone waited for a break in the tempest.

The wives of the keepers were very anxious, especially with regard to the mysterious flag signal, and they too desperately kept watch until in the end the women could bear it no longer and pleaded with local boatmen to sail once more to the Eddystone.

At the Millbay workshops and in the harbour taverns, people talked about the awful predicament and fate of those out on the rock. No-one could tell just what was wrong at the lighthouse and people were confused by the sight of the lantern's candles which would shine every evening, when darkness fell. The workmen at Millbay agreed that the lighthouse was a most durable structure and should stand firm in the prolonged storms, but what was being signalled by the keepers was a question no-one could answer.

Persistent pleas by the women encouraged the Eddystone boatmen to risk their lives and make the earliest possible attempt in trying to reach "the stone". So eventually, when a chance finally did offer itself, a brave crew made the difficult journey to the stranded lightkeepers, not knowing what they would find waiting for them.

The foaming sea was high and remained rough as the boat left Millbay yard during the early hours of the morning. Through heavy waves the men rowed slowly beyond the relative safety of Plymouth Sound and on into the dangerous swirling Channel. The passage was slow and it took many hours of hard effort before they reached the reef. No signs of life appeared from the tower as the party moved carefully between the threatening rocks. They were able to moor next to the base of the "house rock" beneath the wooden lighthouse and secured the boat by throwing hooked lines onto the rock.

Climbing the iron stairway, they would soon discover the truth about the problem.

On opening the entrance door they were met by a disgusting stench. Peering inside the damp and gloomy darkened interior, they saw to their horror a decomposing corpse, laid out in a makeshift coffin. The overwhelming smell penetrated the building as they climbed the inner staircase, looking for the other keeper. On the top floor they found the remaining man, trembling with fear, looking thin and pallid and crouched in the corner of the cold, eery, silent room.

The facts about the terrible ordeal were that the lightkeeper's friend and colleague had died, perhaps a month previously, quite suddenly. Due to the fact that only the one keeper remained, he believed it was his duty to keep the light burning at night. On realising that the weather was too bad for the relief boat to reach him, he took it on himself to continue there as long as possible. His original thought was of throwing the body into the sea, but then he became worried about the possibility of being seen as a murderer and so made a coffin for the body. Anxiety and despair then took over his life in the days which passed and the smell slowly crept up to the kitchen and bedroom, making him feel ill.

For more than four weeks he made sure the candles were lit at night, but as the food ran out his will to live also disappeared.

If it were not for the relief boatmen making their courageous effort in reaching the lighthouse, it is certain that two bodies would have been discovered there later.

The sailors reported the scene in the following manner:

> One was already decomposed and the other haggard and livid, it was like a corpse being guarded by a ghost.

After this incident both Trinity House and the lease owners agreed that in future three men, not two, would be needed to work at the lighthouse, and the practice was soon adopted by all in the lighthouse service. Pay was £25 a year with a month's leave for each keeper. Rudyerd's lighthouse had proven its worth for over a decade, but slowly the might of the ocean was beginning to tell on the structure – not so much due to the waves beating on the tower, but rather due to a tiny sea creature, a type of worm, eating its way into the base of the lighthouse itself, boring through into the thick timbers of the foundations; it had become a major concern.

The Navy allowed the old foreman Holland to visit Plymouth and help sort out the problem, but on inspection he soon accepted that little could be done, other than the continual replacement of the timber cladding. By 1723 the problem became more serious and urgent repairs were required. The operation needed carpenters of immense skill,

EVOLUTE OF RUDYERD'S LIGHTHOUSE, DRAWN BY JOHN HOLLAND IN 1734, SHOWING REPAIR WORK

BY KIND PERMISSION OF THE NATIONAL MUSEUMS OF SCOTLAND

as the water-sodden base timbers had to be hacked out and reinforced with new tight-fitting blocks. The laborious work continued until 1734, when after 25 years of service, the tower's solid base started to deteriorate still further. Mr Holland, then King's Builder, was again able to leave his Deptford post and visit the Eddystone site to confer with Jessop on whether any permanent solution could be found. The men finally agreed to undertake a very difficult work programme in an attempt to kill off the ever-present woodworm. The bottom part of the lighthouse would be fully repaired using new timbers; next the tower's cladding would be encased in copper plating, a method then used by the Navy to kill woodworm, a common problem in the fleet. So, with the wooden uprights binding themselves to the copper sheeting on the outer surface and with lead filling the inner, Messrs Holland and Jessop and the local maintenance team waited to see if their battle plan had worked. Unfortunately no progress was made in eradicating the tiny seaworm from the foot of the lighthouse and so, with no alternative available to them, the team resumed the arduous task of continually replacing the lower base timbers.

In John Holland's evolute, or flat plan of the structure, we see the entire outer surface of the lighthouse, a reference to every outer plank. On the right-hand side he wrote cante, timber and stone, and the four floors, a storeroom, chamber, dining room and cookroom. At the base he listed all of the timbers destroyed, shifted, coppered and leaded between 1730 and 1734. It also showed the scarfing and butting of the timber uprights.

A yet more dangerous incident was to occur in 1744, a particularly tough year and one which would prove very difficult for Josiah, his skills being constantly tested to the full.

In a letter sent to Trinity House on 11 August by the local agent, we read that an application "for a protection against imprest for the boatmen employed in attending the service of the Eddystone Lighthouse, where very material repairs are now in hand" was asked for. Not only did Josiah Jessop need

great practical skills to do the repairs out at the rock, but also the patience of a saint and a hope that his men would not be press-ganged while engaged in their duties.

August proved a very uncomfortable time for the keepers at the reef; no boats were able to take stores out to the men due to the heavy sea. As time slipped by, even greater difficulties lay ahead for the Eddystone team.

After the increasingly violent storms, Jessop felt certain that damage to the tower would be immense and so anxiously waited for the wind to die, which would allow him to go out and check.

Then on 26 September greater problems arose. Thirty of the 71 timber uprights were ripped from the battered structure, leaving the tower close to disaster. Jessop and his men then had no choice but to head for the Eddystone immediately.

From October through to 14 December Jessop and his team laboured courageously in deteriorating conditions until they had finished their remarkable work. For it is certain that if those repairs had not been completed, Rudyerd's tower would have succumbed to the power of wind and tide by the end of the year.

It had been a terrible time for the repair workers on the outside of the tower, facing the furious winds, crashing waves, torrential rain and bitter cold, and also for the keepers inside their ailing structure; nonetheless the candles still shone and the building held firm against all the odds.

The servicing of the lighthouse had continued under the supervision of John Holland and Josiah Jessop for 44 years and it was a fact that they had systematised a tradition of lighthouse maintenance which set the pattern for future working techniques.

In 1752 John Holland died, leaving Josiah in full control of the lighthouse. For the next three years everything went according to plan.

But on 2 December 1755 disaster would once more visit the Eddystone.

This time it was not the mighty ocean which was to blame, but a fire which totally destroyed the majestic building.

The first people to notice the fire in the early morning were some Cawsand fishermen who were netting off Penlee Point in their small boats. The weather was wintry, a frosty south-easterly wind wrapping its icy fingers around them. Unfortunately, although they could clearly see the flames raging from the lighthouse, with such small craft at hand they were unable to go to the rescue of any lightkeeper. Instead, their only option was to row back to the villages of Kingsand and Cawsand to raise the alarm.

From the tiny villages snuggling side by side in a gentle valley, it was not possible to view the Eddystone reef and so no-one was aware of the fire in the lighthouse until the fishermen returned.

As soon as the men were back on shore they headed for the local squire, Mr Edwards of Rame, who was most respected for his humanity to others.

It was still not light and the early morning chill bit into the elderly man as he greeted the men at his door, but his only thoughts on hearing the news were for the keepers.

Edwards soon organised a rescue attempt and rode his beloved horse through the bitterly cold wind at great speed to the local cottages of skilled boatmen he believed would be willing to help him.

However, it was no easy task for Edwards to persuade them and many would not even consider the risk, due understandably to their experiences of terrible sea conditions in wintertime; anyway, the reef was nine miles away and would not be reached easily. The severely cold wind had increased, becoming an easterly, and most men knew it would be the worst weather to go out in.

As news of the fire spread among the waking communities, many of the villagers started to gather along the cold bleak clifftop towards Rame Head, where in the distance they could see the light of the burning tower.

Edwards continued in his efforts and eventually persuaded a boat's crew to attempt the rescue. By 10am the good souls were rowing into the chilly wind and on towards the leaping red flames of the burning lighthouse. Through the pounding waves they struggled, knowing they would take at least three hours to reach the Eddystone. Their way

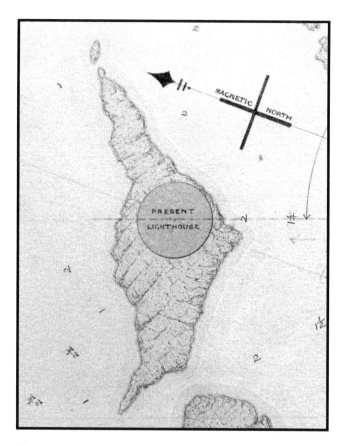

THE HOUSE ROCK HOLDING RUDYERD'S TOWER
THE AUTHOR'S COLLECTION

was lit by the towering flames, and as they rowed closer to the reef their hopes of finding survivors grew fainter.

With the fierce waves showering them with icy spray, they were soon near enough to feel the great heat and to hear the crackle and snap from the incredible inferno before them; the experience for the boatmen was dangerous and terrifying as they searched the black rocks for any survivor.

The situation looked hopeless as the waves crashed over the base of the tower and the fire raged in fury from its top; all seemed in vain.

The crew could not get close enough to climb the rocky outcrops in search of life, so from their boat they looked hard into the rock crevasses, rowing back and forth in the small gullies of the reef, while the fire soared overhead, throwing glowing debris at them.

Then, to their amazement, they saw three tiny figures huddled together in a hollow. With little regard for their own safety the boatmen threw ropes to the stranded men and hauled each one to safety, although all had been badly burnt.

Alderman Tolcher, the Trinity House agent, and his son Joseph were in the second boat to arrive. They had travelled from Plymouth in a private sloop and were devastated by what they saw. Within an hour another vessel arrived with Mr Jessop on board. He had asked Admiral West at the dockyard for assistance and was supplied with a naval fire crew and water pump. However their attempt to put out the fire was useless and nearly resulted in the whole party being drowned when their boat was lifted up by huge waves onto the reef mass itself, smashing the fire engine pipes, then they were dragged back by the swirling tide into a small gully.

The injured lighthouse keepers were nearing the safety of Stonehouse and the local hospital, where a few days later the old squire Mr Edwards was to die from pneumonia, probably brought about by the events of that terrible winter's day.

An extract from a letter sent by Tolcher to C Ambrose, dated 2 December 1755, read:

> This comes to you by express, lest any hasty letters by the post should bring a worse account of the fire on the Eddystone than may be true, and by means create a greater alarm than is needful.
>
> I must now acquaint you, that this morning on looking to The Eddystone, as I generally do from my own house, I discovered through my telescope a smoke more than ordinary from the top of the house, and there upon hasted into the town, and found it was there reported that the Eddystone was on fire.
>
> Upon this I got a reflecting telescope and carried it upon the Hoa, and through this I could easily discern a much greater quantity of smoke than I imagine could come from an ordinary fire.
>
> I then immediately sent my son to Cawsand, and wrote a letter to send off from thence a boat and proper hands, assuring the fishermen to whom I sent it that I would pay the people to their content. And then I went immediately to Admiral West, to pray that he would be pleased to send off one of the men of war's boats, at anchor in the Sound. Upon my coming to the Admiral he said that he had sent out a sloop.

An extract from a letter by Mr Tolcher to Robert Weston dated 4 December 1755, regarding the survivors, read:

> They were found sitting in a stupified manner, one of them had his shoulder bone put out of joint. This poor man is hardly sensible and is very much scalded with the melted lead which ran down upon him from the cupola. The other was also scalded an old sailor, a sensible man, and I am inclined to think behaved very well in endeavouring to extinguish the fire. The third appears not hurt but much stupified.

Richard Hall, who is also referred to as William or Henry in other publications, was aged 84 (94 according to some accounts) and the oldest of the keepers at the Eddystone on that fateful night, the other two being Thomas Strout and Roger Short.

Hall, although of a great age, was a favourite to all who knew him, constantly telling stories of his vast experiences and seafaring life. Even Jessop the foreman enjoyed the company of the old seadog, becoming a close friend.

Hall was a local man who lived in the village of Stonehouse and loved the life of a lightkeeper. He was the first to discover the smoke in the lantern of the lighthouse and had tried in vain to deal with the problem.

However, it soon became clear that a serious situation had arisen and he called out to his two colleagues in the room below for help.

Unfortunately due to the noise from the wind and crashing seas against the lighthouse wall, he could not get an answer from them.

It is also probable that his colleagues were the worse for wear from their consumption of gin, which had arrived that afternoon on the supply boat.

In his exhaustive efforts to extinguish the fire above his head in the roof of the lantern, he threw a pitiful amount of water into the flaming cupola. On looking up, he swallowed molten lead which was falling from the roof covering. Not unnaturally his story was disbelieved by all who were to hear it and although he was noticeably burned about the head and shoulders, it was felt that for a man of such age to have experienced and survived the trauma alone was in itself a miracle, but to have swallowed lead was simply unbelievable.

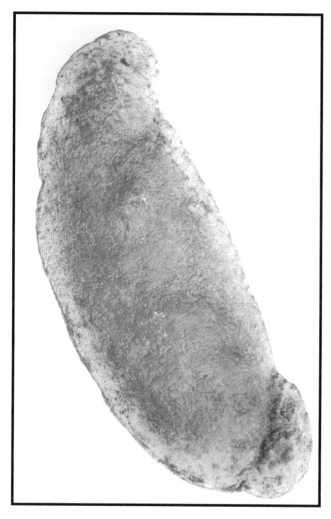

THE LEAD PIECE TAKEN FROM HALL'S STOMACH
BY KIND PERMISSION OF THE NATIONAL MUSEUMS OF SCOTLAND

The three keepers were taken to Stonehouse Quay, where a large group of people had gathered. Hall asked to be taken home, where his daughter and another woman lived. The other keepers were carried to the nearby hospital, badly burnt and in shock.

It soon became obvious that Hall was very ill and Dr Spry, a Plymouth physician attending to him daily, felt his patient would have a chance of recovery if left quietly.

Hall endured his agony for 12 days, always insisting that his story was true. Suddenly he was dead.

Dr Spry decided an autopsy should be performed and asked Hall's friend from the workyard, Josiah Jessop, to witness the proceedings. He declined, but two of Hall's relatives went to the hospital. They also did not want to witness the autopsy being performed, preferring to wait outside the mortuary.

Spry cut open the body of the dead man and found a flat oval piece of lead as big as the palm of a hand inside Hall's stomach.

> The tongues of dying men
> Enforce attention like deep harmony;
> Where words are scarce, they are seldom spent in
>   vain,
> For they breathe truth, that breathe their words in
>   pain.
> He, that no more must say, is listened more
> Than they, whom youth and ease have taught to
>   glose;
> More are men's ends marked than their lives
>   before;
> The setting sun, and music at the close,
> As the last taste of sweets, is sweetest last;
> Writ in remembrance, more than things long past
> — SHAKESPEARE (RICHARD III)

An extract from a letter by Mr Jessop to Robert Weston dated 12 December 1755, read:

> They are all living; Richard Hall and Thomas Strout are in a miserable condition, when, please God, the weather is favourable, I intend to go off and see what condition the rock is in.
> — J JESSOP

A letter transcribed by Captain Chaplin, written by the Superintendent of Plymouth Dockyard on 12 December 1755 after he had interviewed the survivors, read:

> I have received your letter of the 6th and am informed by the Men who were at the Edystone when it took, that on Monday afternoon the 1st Instant they received a supply of Candles and Provisions from the Edystone boat, when Wm Hall one of the three Men attending there desir'd the Master of the boat to acquaint the people ashore he had discovered a defect in the Chimney, just by the Cupola about six weeks before (during which time no boat had been there) that the

Smoak frequently issued out from there and when the Wind blew hard, or there was a great sea the Scarphe Opened. They declared they all attended the Lighting of the Candles at five that evening, and were sober. That Thomas Short who had the first watch snuffed the Candles every Half-Hour as usual and perceived no Smoak or appearance of a Fire. About Nine that Night Wm Hall who was in the Kitchen with the said Short where (they say) was a small Fire, accidentally went up the Lantern and found it so full of Smoak he could not see the Candles, from whence he went to the Gallery to discover the Occasion of it and a flame of the Fire came against him out of the said Scarphe, he returned immediately into the Lanthorn and endeavoured to put out the Fire with Water in two Caske there, a quarter part full, he extinguished the Fire in one of the Pillars, and did all he could to put out the Whole, but for want of more help could not effect it, tho' he frequently call'd the other Two Men to come and assist Him, and Short often answered he was coming, he did not come till Hall had been there nearly three quarters of an Hour and the Cupola was all afire, they were soon after obliged to retire down stairs, and from thence to the Rocks as the Fire was encreasing very fast, the Wind blowing fresh N.E. They remained on the Rocks with the Melted Lead and pieces of Burning Timber frequently falling upon them, till about three the next afternoon, when some men in a Cawsand Boat got them off. Whether this Accident proceeded from their Drinking too much of three Pints of Gin received with the Provisions and Candles that Evening, or having too great a Fire in the Chimney I can not discover, but must observe at the time the Fire was discovered there was but one Bucket in the House and what I think very improper they have never been allowed small Candles for the necessary uses about the House, but have always burnt the Ends of Large ones that were taken from the Lantern and stuck on a piece of Wood between three Nails, for a Candlestick which is certainly attended with great Danger.

The lighthouse was 46 years old and because of that the whole interior of the tower had become extremely dry, especially about the lantern room, where soot from the burning candles had gathered over the years, making the entire structure particularly vulnerable to fire. The tragic event resulted in greater safety measures being incorporated into the working practices of the lighthouse service, but it would also leave a frightening legacy for future generations of lightkeepers in that their workplace substituted as an excellent chimney for any fire. Since that terrible day, keepers everywhere fear a fire in their isolated towers.

An extract from a letter by the foreman Josiah Jessop to Robert Weston dated December 1755 read:

Roger Short having the first watch went up to the lantern at 8 thirty to snuff the candles and then returned to Richard Hall in the cook room, Thomas Strout was in bed.

Richard Hall at 9 pm went up into the lanthorn and to his great surprise found it full of smoak; but saw no fire until he had opened the lanthorn door and went outside the lanthorn where he found the upright of the lanthorn next to the copper funnel all afire.

He called to Short and Strout to bring him water and come to his assistance for the lanthorn was on fire.

They brought him water to the foot of the lanthorn stairs in a bucket but would not go up into the lanthorn to his assistance.

He made use of the water in the lanthorn which was about half a hogshead.

The fire increased to that degree that it melted the lead on the top of the cupola and burnt his face and hands so that he was forced to go down into the cook room.

They had not continued long there, but they were forced to go from room to room and at last to the coal pit where they continued until day break and ultimately were obliged to go to the rock.

A piece of upright fell down upon Richard Hall and bruised him very much so that they thought him dead for sometime.

Another fell down upon Thomas Strout and put his shoulder bone out and bruised him very much. Roger Short received no damage.

At one thirty pm, a fishing boat took them off the rock by throwing a line to them.

There were 70 stairs to the top of the lighthouse and so it would have been a very difficult for Short and Strout to supply Hall with enough water to put out the inferno.

The fire was so intense that it lasted for five days, leaving just a few twisted irons on the rock. Little could have been done to save the building when the rescuers arrived, but the incident served as a warning to all in the lighthouse service.

A macabre story was to follow the tragic events of Richard Hall's death in that Dr Spry, although annoyed at himself for not believing his patient, decided to undertake experiments involving burns investigations and present his findings to the Royal Society in London.

Being an ambitious man, he wanted to make a name for himself, and after his experience with Hall he went about his pursuit in the name of "medical science", carrying out many awful experiments with living creatures and recording how much molten lead would be needed to kill dogs, cats and other animals.

His reports showed that the poor creatures could take large quantities of boiling liquid being poured down their throats. One cockerel, after taking three ounces of lead, "tackled its grain more heartily after the event than it had before".

An account by Spry dated 19 December 1755 and addressed to members of the Royal Society read:

FROM TRANSACTIONS OF THE ROYAL SOCIETY 1756.

On Thursday the fourth of December, 1755 at three in the afternoon, Henry Hall, of East Stone House, near Plymouth, aged 84 years (94 according to some accounts), of a good constitution, and extremely active for one of that age, being one of the three unfortunate men, who suffered by the fire of the light-house at Eddystone, nine miles from Plymouth, having been greatly hurt by the accident, with much difficulty returned to his own house.

I being sent for to his assistance found him in his bed, complaining of extreme pains all over his body; especially to his left side, below the short ribs, in the breast, mouth and throat.

He said likewise, as well as he could, with a hoarse voice, scarce to be heard, that melted lead had run down his throat into his body.

Having taken the proper care of his right leg, which was much bruised and cut on the tibia, I examined his body, and found it all cover'd with livid spots and blisters; and the left side of the head and face, with the eye, extremely burnt; which having washed with linnen dipt in an emollient fomentation, and having applied things used in cases of burning, I then inspected his throat, the root of his tongue, and the parts contiguous, as the uvula, tonsils, etc, which were greatly scorched by the melted lead.

Upon this I ordered him to drink frequently of water-gruel or some such draught; and returning to my own house, sent him the oily mixture of which he took often two or three spoonfuls.

The next day he was much worse, all the symptoms of his case being heightened, with a weak pulse; and he could now scarce swallow at all.

The day following there was no change, except that, on account of his too great costiveness, he took six drachmas of manna dissolved in an ounce and half of infusion of senna, which had no effect till the day following, when just as a clyster was going to be administered, he had a very fetid discharge by stool.

That day he was better till night, when he grew feverish.

The next day, having slept well the preceding night, and thrown up by coughing a little matter, he was much better.

He began now to speak with less difficulty, and for three or four days to recover gradually; but then suddenly grew worse daily from the first, now reddened a little and swelled; to which I applied the emplaster of gums.

But all methods proved ineffectual, for the next day being seiz'd with cold sweats and spasms in the tendons, he soon expired.

Examining the body, and making an incision thro' the left abdomen, I found the diaphragmatic upper mouth of the stomach greatly inflamed and ulcerated, and the tunica in the lower part of the stomach burnt; and from the great cavity of it took out a great piece of lead the shape and weight here described.

It will perhaps be thought difficult to explain the manner by which the lead entered the stomach: But the account, which the deceased gave me and others, was, that as he was endeavouring to extinguish the flames, which were at a considerable height above his head, the lead of the lanthorn being melted dropped down, before he was aware of it, with great force into his mouth then lifted up and open, and in such a quantity, as to cover not only his face, but all his clothes.

The piece of lead weighed exactly seven ounces, five drachms, and eighteen grains.

Richard (Henry) Hall was buried at St George's Church in the old fishing village of Stonehouse on 16 December 1755.

The account of the incident by Edmund Spry was not believed by all in the profession and it so incensed him that he wrote many more letters to the Royal Society in order to prove his credibility.

In a letter to the body's President, the Earl of Macclesfield, dated Plymouth, 30 January 1756 and read to the Society on 5 February, he wrote:

My Lord,
As the late case I took the liberty of troubling your lordship with, was so very singular, as to make it by some gentlemen greatly doubted, on account of their imagining, that the degree of heat in melted lead was too great to be borne in the stomach, without immediate death, or at least much more sudden than happened in this case; I herein can not only convince your lordship of its fact, by my own and (if requisite) the oaths of others, but also by the following experiments, which from similarity of circumstances must not only render that probable, but (in the most convincing manner) the absolute possibility of my assertion.

I extracted three pieces, from the stomach of a small dog, six drachms, one scruple of lead, which I had poured down his throat the day before.

NB: The mucus lining of the oesophagus seemed very viscid, and the stomach much corrugated, tho' its internal coat was no-ways excoriated.

The dog had nothing to eat or drink after, nor for twenty-fours hours before the experiment, when, being very brisk, I killed him.

I also took from the stomach of a large dog (in several pieces) six ounces and two drachms of lead, three days after thrown in.

The pharynx and cardiac orifice of the stomach

were a little inflamed and excoriated; but the oesophagus and stomach seemed in no manner affected.

I gave this dog a half a pint of milk just before I poured down the lead; very soon after which also he ate thereof freely, as if nothing ailed him, which he daily continued to do, being very lively at the time I killed him.

From the crop of a full grown fowl, I (in company with Dr Huxham F.R.S.) extracted of lead, one solid piece weighing two ounces and a half, together with nine other small portions, weighing half an ounce, which lead was thrown down the fowl's throat, twenty-five hours before.

The fowl was kept without meat for twenty-four hours, before and after the experiment, eating (being very lively just before we killed him) dry barley, as fast, and with nigh, if not quite, the same ease as before.

The mucus on the larynx and oesophagus was somewhat hardened.

The external coat of the crop appeared in a very small degree livid; and the internal, somewhat corrugated.

The barley was partly in the oesophagus, tho' mostly in the craw, which was almost full with the lead.

I took two ounces one scruple from the crop of another fowl, three days after the experiment, which fowl was very brisk to the last.

Allowing for a further satisfaction, that the experiment be tried, it is requisite in making thereof, that the melted lead be poured into a funnel, whose spout being as large as the throat of the animal (whose neck must be kept firmly erect) will conveniently admit of, must be forced down the oesophagus, somewhat below the larynx, lest any of the lead might fall therein; and according to the quantity, either by totally, or partly obstructing the aspera arteria, causing immediate, or a lingering death; which accidents happening, in my first experiments on two dogs, directed me to proceed in the above manner.

At present I have a dog with lead in his stomach, which I intend to keep, to prove how long he may live.

My lord, your lordship may depend on it, that so far from my asserting anything in the least degree uncertain, that, I always have, I always shall act with so much circumspection and integrity (especially in these tender points, where my character is at stake) as to be able easily to prove what I may assert, as in the present case, so very extraordinary, that scarce any of the faculty (unless particularly acquainted with me) would give credit to, till I demonstrated it by the above experiments; which I doubt not in the least, will be sufficiently satisfactory to your lordship, and to the honourable Society; to serve which venerable body, as much as lies in my power, will at all times, give the greatest pleasure to, My Lord,

Your Lordship's most obedient and most humble servant,

EDMUND SPRY

To further his credibility and application to join the Royal Society, Edmund Spry asked John Huxham MD FRS to support his case findings.

In a letter he wrote to Mr William Watson FRS on 31 January 1756 we read:

Dear Sir,

I think there are few things remarkable, in art or nature, in this part of the country, that do not, sooner or later, come to my knowledge.

Our worthy commissioner, Fred Rogers Esq, sent me the lead you mention, three days after it was said to be taken out of the man (Hall), who was said to have swallowed it.

I immediately sent for Mr Edmund Spry, an ingenious young surgeon, of this town, who attended this Hall during his illness and extracted the lead from his stomach (as was reported) when dead.

Mr Spry solemnly assured me that he did actually take the lead, that was sent me, out of the man's stomach and offered to make oath of it.

This Hall lived twelve days after the accident happened and swallowed several things solid and liquid, during that time; and he spoke tolerably plain, tho' his voice was very hoarse and he constantly affirmed, that he had swallowed melted lead.

However, as the story seemed very extraordinary and not a little improbable, I did not choose to transmit any account of it to the Royal Society, as I could have wished for more unexceptionable evidence; for Mr Spry had no one with him when he did extract the lead, but one woman (Phillips) the daughter of Hall and another woman, who

were also in the house, not being able, as said, to see the operation, but immediately called in after it, and Mr Spry showed them the lead.

I sent a very sensible gentleman to enquire into this affair and he had this account from them: "This Mr Spry is, to the best of my knowledge a person of veracity and I think would not utter an untruth.

But, what is more, last Wednesday he brought me a live young cock, into the crop or craw of which, he had the day before poured somewhat more than three ounces of melted lead.

The cock indeed seemed dull, but very readily pecked and swallowed several barley-corns, that were thrown to him.

I had the cock killed and opened in my view and in the crop we found a lump of lead weighing three ounces, less twenty grains and some other little bits of lead.

I make no doubt the cock would have lived several days longer, if had not been then killed.

There seemed a slight escher in the cock's mouth, occasioned by the melted lead and the crop seemed as if parboiled.

This experiment is very easily made, and seems to confirm the probability of Mr Spry's account. I never dispute a matter of fact, when I am fully convinced, that it is so; but I think it my duty to enquire narrowly into the circumstances of it before I admit as such.

With respect to the present case, you now know as much of it as I.

Dear Sir, Your most faithful and obedient servant,

J HUXHAM MD FRS

We know very little of Spry's subsequent activities and career, except that he was censured by the Society for the ill treatment of animals.

The Eddystone Rocks were unlit and the hazard worried mariners. The Eddystone had succeeded once more in removing any trace of Man's attempt to build there. People wondered if it would spell the end of attempts to establish a beacon on the reef.

The lease of The Eddystone was still under the executive control of Robert Weston. He seemed a good man and acted swiftly in trying to find another engineer to undertake the formidable task of building another lighthouse on the Eddystone Reef. He advertised in the London Gazette and other newspapers telling ship owners that all light dues would cease until a further lighthouse had been erected.

His search led him to the Royal Society and the Earl of Macclesfield. The two men agreed there was only one engineer capable of undertaking what had proven so far to be an impossibility.

In February 1756, Weston met the man who would build the next lighthouse to stand on the Eddystone – a challenger called John Smeaton. But would he succeed?

The December storms of 1755 were exceptionally fierce and without a lighthouse on the Eddystone it wasn't long before the danger was experienced by unlucky ships.

From a letter dated 23 December 1755, written in Lyme Regis, for a local newspaper, came the following:

On Thursday last was wonderfully saved in this harbour 'The Beauty of Whitehaven' a four master, bound from Whitehaven for Morlaix and Virginia. She was in sight of Morlaix when the storm began and lost her way by missing the Eddistone lighthouse; it being burnt: which brought her into this bay.

Observing her to be in distress as the storm was very terrible, signals were made in this harbour, and on advanced work of the same, by hoisting ensigns at the masthead, which were soon seen by the distressed, and guided them safely in with the assistance of a boat which advanced a considerable way out to direct them. This is the only place of safety between the river Exe and the road of Portland, from whose Bill it lays north west about seven leagues.

On Saturday last a boat with four men and one woman was drove out of Axmouth Haven and were all lost; two of the men have been since found, and buried.

NB: There is now on the beach near Abbotsbury a french vessel which was conducting to Portsmouth, laden with indigo, coffee and logwood, which might have been saved had the people known of this harbour.

Trinity House had become a more professional lighthouse service and was eagerly buying up lighthouse leases owned by private individuals, who were making large sums of money in their collection of light dues.

Since 1716 the Eddystone lease had been owned by Robert Harcourt Weston, who had a majority share in the surviving syndicate. After he died, his son, Robert Weston, became the lease owner. However, in 1764 there was litigation between Weston and Trinity House. Things would never again be quite the same between the two parties and a change in lighthouse ownership was about to take place.

From 1790 to 1805 William Pitt had been the head of Trinity House, serving as its Master. His role and relationship with the Government enabled him to make many changes to the authority, ensuring its smooth transformation and rapid development as a respected body. The corporation was to establish itself as the leading authority in the world of lighthouse services and would be globally recognised for its ability in lighthouse management.

The number of lighthouses built around the 2,350 miles of the English and Welsh coastline, prior to Pitt's involvement in 1790, was just a handful, but as private landowners realised the probability of the large financial gains being made by their construction, the number rose to 25 during 1780. Trinity House then took sole charge of the lighthouse service and bought out the privately owned stations, many of which were poorly run and of little use to any seafarer. Trinity House was of course guaranteed to benefit enormously from its monopoly.

It is of interest to read the membership duties and structure of Trinity House. In a letter to prospective candidates we are given an insight to the role of this authority:

1st Charter of Incorporation granted them by Henry VIII, on the 20th May 1515. Wherein were confirm'd to them not only All the ancient Rights and Privileges of The Shipmen and Mariners of England, Their Predecessors, but also There several Poffeffions at Deptford: which, together with divers Grants of Queen Elizabeth and King

Charles 2nd, were confirm'd by Letters Patent of the first of James 2nd on the 8th July 1685, by The Name of The Master, Wardens and Assistants of the Guild or Fraternity of The Most Glorious and Undivided Trinity, and of St Clement, in the Parish of Deptford Strond in The County of Kent. This Corporation is governed by a Master, Four Wardens, Eight Assistants and 18 Elder Brethren: The Inferior Members of the Fraternity, denominated Younger Brethren, are of an unlimited Number (for every Master or Mate, expert in Navigation, may be admitted as such) and serve as a continual Nurfery to Supply The Vacancies among The Elder Brethren, when removed by Death or otherwise.

The Master, Wardens, Assistants and Elder Brethren of The Fraternity are by Charter Invested with The following Powers:

1. The examining of The Mathematical Children of Christ's Hospital.

2. The Examination of The Masters of his Majesty's Ships, The appointing of Pilots to conduct Ships in and out of The River Thames, and The amercing all such as shall prefume to act as Master of a Ship of War, or Pilot, without The'ir Approbation, in a pecuniary Mulet of Twenty Pounds.

3. The fettling The several Rates of Pilotage, and erecting Light-houses and other sea Marks upon several Coasts of The Kingdom, for The Security of Navigation.

4. The preventing of Aliens from serving on Board English Ships, without their Licence, upon Penalty of Five Pounds for each Offence.

5. The punishing of Seamen, for Desertion or Mutiny, in The Merchant Service.

6. The Hearing and Determinating The Complaints of Officers and Seamen in The Merchant Service; but subject to an Appeal to The Lord High Admiral, or judge of The Court of Admiralty.

7. The granting of Licences to Poor Seamen (Non Freemen) to row on The River Thames for Their support in the Intervals of Sea Service.

To the Company belongs The Ballast Office, for clearing and deepening The River Thames, by taking from Thence a Sufficient Quantity of Ballast for The Supply of All Ships that fail out of

THE RUDYERD TOWER BEFORE THE FIRE IN AN EARLY 18th - CENTURY WOODCUT DRAWING
THE AUTHOR'S COLLECTION

THE EDDYSTONE ROCKS WERE NOW BARE
THE AUTHOR'S COLLECTION

the said River: in which Service Sixty Barges of The Burden of 30 Tons and Two men each, are continually employed. And in consideration of the great Increase by Their Charter impower'd to purchase In Mortmain, Lands, Tenements and to The Amount of Five Hundred Pounds per Annum: and also to receive charitable Benefactions of well-dispos'd Persons, to The like Amount of Five Hundred Pounds per Annum Clear of Reprizes.

The charitable Benefactions belonging to The Corporation are so very numerous, to advoid Prolixity, it shall suffice to acquaint The Reader, That by The Profits arising Therefrom, together with those of The Ballast Office, Light-houses, Buoys, Beacons and etc. The Company annually relieve about Three Thousand Pounds to Poor Seamen, their Widows and Poor Orphans at The Expense of about Six Thousand Pounds.

On 1 August 1786 the Northern Lighthouse Trustees were established to oversee lighthouse activity in Scotland, while in Ireland the Commissioners of Irish Lights had also evolved, creating the prospect of safe passage for every seafarer sailing in British waters.

When Robert Harcourt Weston applied to renew his lease of the Eddystone in 1807, it was turned down and the acrimonious partnership between Trinity House and the proprietors abruptly ended, with Weston accepting a £300 annuity which he denounced as an "abject and mean supplication coupled with falsehood".

SMEATON'S SENSATION

ON 27 MARCH 1756, John Smeaton, aged 31, arrived in Plymouth after a five-day coach journey from London. Local dignitaries had gathered to greet him and remarked on his impressive appearance. He was a smart man wearing a silk shirt, a three-cornered hat and a long overcoat.

Smeaton expected to complete construction of his new lighthouse in just four seasons, but on the question of expense he said that "in the progress of the work we should lie so widely open to accident that I could not undertake to make any calculation of this part, which might not possibly be exceeded ten-fold."

The young man, already acknowledged as a gifted civil engineer, would show his abilities to the people of Plymouth.

Smeaton was born at Austhorpe Lodge near Leeds on 8 June 1724, his father being a respected attorney. The family also had an historical association with the area and were very wealthy in their own right.

For much of his childhood, Smeaton was educated at home, before moving on to a grammar school. John's young life had been enviable and enjoyable and his exploits are well recorded; he was also a very likeable boy. His parents encouraged him to experience life to the full and indulge himself with hobbies and interests. One of Smeaton's favourite pursuits was in the new science of mechanical and mathematical study, at which he excelled.

His happiest hours were spent constructing working objects such as small windmills or water pumps, and indeed his daily interests lay solely in the field of engineering. Even the masons and carpenters employed at his family home had become aware of Master Smeaton's activities, as on many occasions their tools and materials would go missing, only to be found later in the hands of the eager youngster. Smeaton would constantly ask the workmen questions and learned all he could about building techniques through simply watching them at work. His father soon began to worry about the boy's obsession and decided that something ought be done to offer his son more challenges to satisfy his inquisitive and fertile mind. Soon a decision was made to send the child to grammar school in Leeds, until he reached 16. Smeaton gained further instruction in geometry, arithmetic and English, which excited him greatly. His progress was rapid, but only in the subjects

PORTRAIT OF JOHN SMEATON
BY KIND PERMISSION OF THE CORPORATION OF TRINITY HOUSE

relating to his love of everything mechanical, and so it seemed inevitable the boy's future lay in that area, especially due to his exceptional dexterity and ingenuity in using tools.

John Smeaton Sr remained unhappy about his son's direction and tried to persuade the lad to look at other options. His concern intensified after the boy had pumped dry one of his father's favourite garden ponds by using a home-made pumping device put together from bits and pieces taken from the house.

By the age of 15, Smeaton had already constructed his own turning lathe and other small devices. He could also forge iron and steel and melt metals and had gathered every sort of tool for working in wood, ivory and metal. His father had almost resigned himself to the fact that nothing could change the boy's mind and so reluctantly accepted his son's determination to pursue a career in engineering. He generously purchased all the materials and tools required for his son's experiments and building projects. However, he still believed his son should at least experience life in the "real world" and arranged for him to work in the offices of the family business, where he would be encouraged to copy legal papers and learn details of law. It appears it was a last-ditch attempt to convince him to accept the opportunity on offer and follow in his father's footsteps.

The young Smeaton found that period of his life very difficult and unhappy, although he did make an effort for his father's sake, but alas any enthusiasm was clearly lacking, even when in 1742 he was posted to London on instruction from his parents, who hoped that in a new city environment their boy might just focus his attention more closely on the job at hand and begin to enjoy the work. But the plan failed and he made his views very clear in the correspondence he sent home. On realising that his son would never become an attorney, Smeaton Sr finally agreed to the teenager's wishes and provided him with the escape he had always dreamed of.

Through his father's contacts, Smeaton entered into the service of a philosophical instrument maker and quickly set up a small business, where he confirmed his prowess immediately. During that brief period, he made many mathematical instruments which were to be used in astronomy and navigation. His greatest achievement was in improving the Mariner's Compass, and the work established the young man's reputation. Soon he was attending meetings at the Royal Society and researching into "the Natural Powers of Water and Wind to Turn Mills and other Machines, depending on a Circular Motion"; for that endeavour he was

honoured with the Society's Gold Medal. His progress continued and most considered him vastly superior to others specialising in the new field of science. His work took him to Europe and in 1754 he visited the canals of Holland and Belgium, where he studied water management constructions. Smeaton returned to England the following winter, excited by what he had seen, and was soon eager to get back to work.

1756 was to offer him his greatest challenge; it would be a year he'd remember for the rest of his life.

The Eddystone Rocks beckoned. After Rudyerd's Tower had been burnt to the ground, Robert Weston, the principal lease owner, decided to ask the Royal Society to recommend a civil engineer capable of constructing another lighthouse. Smeaton's name shone out like the beacon he would soon build and the society's President, Lord Macclesfield, had no hesitation in suggesting him.

In Plymouth there was much to be done to prepare for the project, and finding a local workforce was crucial; also an acceptable shore base would be fundamental to Smeaton's plans. However, his first action was to seek out Josiah Jessop, who had so marvellously taken charge of the previous lighthouse. Smeaton knew that Jessop understood far more about the practicalities of lighthouse building than he did, even though his own skills were not in question. Nonetheless, he felt it was important to learn from this highly respected man and to offer him a position in the new Eddystone venture.

Unfortunately, Jessop and Smeaton were awkward in each other's company, perhaps because one was a young gifted engineer from Yorkshire while the other was an old rugged Cornish man with traditional values. Obvious difficulties lay ahead in their new relationship and inevitably the uneasy alliance finally erupted when Smeaton announced that the new tower would be built in stone. Jessop dismissed the idea as youthful naivety and raised considerable objections to Smeaton's proposal; he genuinely believed that, as in the previous structure, wood was the only

PLYMOUTH IN 1736, LOOKING TOWARDS THE BARBICAN AND SOUND
FROM AN OLD ENGRAVING, THE AUTHOR'S COLLECTION

material which could be used and he did not understand why Smeaton wanted to build with such heavy material.

For the first few days, the pair continued in their hostility to one another, but slowly the arguments abated and the two minds became more focused together. Jessop was then offered the job as the builder's assistant.

Smeaton's other priority had been to visit the Eddystone, but prolonged bad weather ensured his confinement to shore, which greatly frustrated the engineer; finally, the weather improved and another opportunity to reach the rocks offered itself and so the men got ready for the journey.

Smeaton's first visit to the reef took more than four hours' sailing and was a disappointing experience, due to the fact that the boat could not get close to the rock on which he intended to build the lighthouse. A further delay, then on 2 April, during his seventh day in Plymouth, they again boarded an old 10-ton wooden vessel known as the *Eddystone Boat,* which had serviced the lighthouse years before. But once more Smeaton could not land and another three days would pass before he could eventually climb onto the rocky outcrop and survey the site, staying for just two and a quarter hours.

The wind always annoyed Smeaton, as it seemed to increase whenever the boat became close to the reef mass. The passage to the Eddystone was unpleasant and difficult, as time and time again the visits would end in failure due to the changing sea state which prevented landing.

The relationship between Smeaton and Jessop grew stronger, their individual working skills and acknowledged abilities encouraging them to work as one – and without realising it, they had gained immense respect for one another's strengths. Genuine exchanges of ideas were also being put forward and slowly the odd couple had become anchored together by their shared desire, for they both had one thing in common: their new Eddystone Lighthouse.

Smeaton soon announced his revolutionary plans to the townspeople of Plymouth, but not surprisingly had an indifferent reception to the proposal. Nobody agreed with his reasoning for using stone in the construction and few felt the idea even worthy of discussion. However, Smeaton had been chosen on merit to build the next lighthouse and those around him were supportive.

Further meetings followed, where he explained his plans in more detail. Stone represented the fundamental ingredient for the building and, in any case, his whole argument had concerned the weight and strength of the lighthouse. Stone was therefore the ideal material to use. It was a natural and plentiful substance found locally and would undoubtedly be essential during the tower's construction.

Rudyerd's wooden beacon had impressed Smeaton, but his own effort would be better, both in design and in strength.

He compared the plans of his proposed lighthouse to that of a branch on a tree, assuming that if the sides of the tower curved inwards from the base like a tree trunk, instead of converging conically in straight lines towards the summit, it would give the structure an ability to withstand anything the sea could throw at it.

Further research and analysis continued to explore every possibility, looking at alternative suggestions and ideas from Jessop. But there was never any doubt in Smeaton's mind and he would always return to the tree-trunk theory. His argument lay in the scientifically proven fact that by lowering the centre of gravity and concentrating more of the tower's weight on a broader base, and at the same time narrowing the upper portion of the structure, it was obvious it would lessen wind and wave resistance still further, allowing less impact on the structure's wall.

Smeaton's plans had finally taken shape and he made many detailed models to convince the sceptics of his intention. He grew in confidence as did everyone around him, feeling that a genuine breakthrough had been achieved – and so everyone agreed that his lighthouse could after all be built of stone.

During his first visit to Plymouth, Smeaton used the time well, establishing many local contacts. He introduced himself to the Commissioner of the King's Dockyard at Stonehouse, asking for support for the venture, and met with many officials of the town, gaining their confidence and the approval he needed to ensure his success.

With the initial visit lasting just two months, his efforts had paid dividends. But he was disappointed that he had only managed to visit the Eddystone Rocks ten times. Smeaton, uncharacteristically, often became very annoyed and frustrated by that, but it did make him realise and appreciate the fundamental difficulty of simply reaching his workplace. Nonetheless, all things considered, he was pleased with his initial progress and happy with a new workyard being made ready for him at Millbay. Things were finally beginning to take shape – and with Jessop at his side, Smeaton knew the lighthouse would soon be built.

His travels had taken him to the local granite quarries outside Plymouth, where to his delight he had found the right type of stone for the construction of the tower.

On his journey back to London at the beginning of June, he pondered his options but genuinely believed he would eventually succeed. The meetings with Robert Weston and the other lease owners were always positive affairs and his new ideas welcomed by the proprietors. Even when talking about his workforce, Smeaton convinced the officials of their individual importance and value to the project.

The welfare of his men and their working conditions would be a vital ingredient to any successful construction, each member of the team holding a unique responsibility. Smeaton realised he needed a detailed management contract for his labourers, but there were no such things as workers' rights and all employees were at the mercy of their bosses, which often meant low pay and long hours, usually in a very poor environment.

Smeaton would become one of the first people to offer an "employment contract" to his workforce and the practice was soon adopted by other fair-minded visionaries.

The following details represented a contract of employment for his men known as "Management of the workmen":

1/ That the Eddystone service should by all reasonable inducements be rendered preferable to any other common employment.

2/ That therefore (as a punishment) any one failing his duty should be immediately discharged.

3/ That workmen should be divided into two companies; one company to be out at the rock, the other to be employed in the workyard on shore.

4/ That every Saturday, the weather permitting, these two companies to change places; but the out-company not to return home till the in-company is carried out to relieve them.

5/ Every man to have certain fixed wages weekly; and the same whether out or in.

6/ Every man to receive something per hour over and above the fixed wages, for every hour he works upon the rock.

7/ Every out-man to take all opportunities of landing upon the rock to work, when the weather serves, whether night or day, Sunday or work days.

8/ The in-company not to work either nights or on Sundays, except in case of necessity, and then

9/ All extra work on shore to be paid for in proportion to double the fixed wages for the like time.

10/ The seamen to be also at constant weekly wages, with an addition of a fee certain and proportionable every tide's work upon the rock.

11/ Each company to have a foreman constantly with them while working upon the rock; to be paid more than the common workmen, and in the same proportion.

12/ The engineer and his deputy to go off alternately week for week; and each week go off as often, and stay as long as weather will permit, or service required.

13/ In case of sickness, or necessary absence of either the engineer or deputy, the whole (if possible) to be taken care of by the other.

14/ All persons to victual themselves, but a bowl of punch to be allowed each company on their return ashore.

15/ The foremen, workmen and seamen, to be paid every time the respective companies return on shore.

16/ All work tools to be provided and repaired at a charge of the proprietors, and to have a mark put upon each of them peculiar to the Eddystone.

17/ Every person hurt or maimed in the out-service to receive his common wages while under the surgeon. This to be allowed on the certificate of the engineer, deputy or agent.

18/ Any person desirous of quitting the service, to give a week's notice to the engineer or deputy.

19/ The foreman on shore to take account of everything received into or sent out of the workyard; as also of the day's works of the company with him; under the check of the engineer or his deputy when on shore.

20/ All smith's and plumber's work to be seen weighed by the foreman, engineer or deputy on shore; and all timber or wood work to be measured and other materials taken account of by the same on receiving them.

21/ The foreman afloat to take account of time and landings upon the rock, to be checked by the engineer or his deputy when afloat.

22/ An account of all matters done on shore to be given in weekly to the agent or accountant; and of all things done afloat by the proper foreman at the time of landing.

So the scene was set, Smeaton's work was about to commence, and everyone was happy with his proposal. The design had been commended by Trinity House and the proprietors had every confidence in their builder. The local pieces of the jigsaw were being put together in Plymouth. As with the previous lighthouse constructions, finding the right men to fill the positions was difficult, but plenty of individuals came forward. Smeaton's confidence rose, knowing it was just a matter of time before the Eddystone would once again have a lighthouse on it.

A century later Alan Stevenson, the Scottish lighthouse engineer, pointed out:

It is obvious, indeed, that Smeaton has unconsciously contrived to obscure his own clear conceptions in his attempt to connect them with a fancied natural analogy between a tree which is shaken by the wind acting on its bushy top, and which resists its enemy by the strength of its fibrous texture and wide-spreading ligamentous roots, and a tower of masonry, whose weight and friction alone enable it to meet the assault of the waves which wash around its base...

One is tempted to conclude that Smeaton had, in the first place, reasoned quite soundly, and arrived, by a perfectly legitimate process, at his true conclusion; and that it was only in the vain attempt to justify these conclusions to others, and convey to them conceptions which a large class of minds can never receive, that he has misrepresented his own mode of reasoning.

The fact remained, however, that Smeaton had not only solved his own immediate problem but had stumbled upon what was later to be accepted throughout the world as the definitive design for stone-built wave-swept towers.

Smeaton's initial visit to Plymouth continued and on 3 August 1756 he sailed once more to the Eddystone. Due to good weather he was able to climb onto the rock's surface, mark out the area of his intended tower and fix the centre point of the foundations.

His target for the first season's work was to cut the rock into flat steps to hold his dovetailed blocks.

Back in London, Smeaton worked on producing scale models of the designs in order to make clear his plans and modifications to the work. Final drawings of his proposals were soon completed and approved by Robert Weston, the Lords of the Admiralty and the Trinity House Brethren.

Many meetings continued with the lease owners and Trinity House who were all delighted by his efforts and in the presentations he gave, allowing them to express their own thoughts. They were excited by his ideas, but especially so when they were able to understand the technical aspects and theory of dovetailing the stone blocks together for reinforcement of the tower. The meetings continued throughout the construction period, normally held at 21 Ludgate Hill in London, with Mr Platt, a legal representative, Robert Weston and the other lease owners. The talks often lasted three hours before the proprietors left under no illusion as to the importance of the task which lay before them.

The journey between London and Plymouth would often take five days, and the poor roads made each trip by horse-drawn coach

A PLAN AND PERSPECTIVE ELEVATION OF THE EDDYSTONE ROCKS, FEATURING THE FOUNDATION STEPS
THE AUTHOR'S COLLECTION

an uncomfortable experience for Smeaton, who believed it a tedious routine to undertake. However, to improve the situation, he had his own carriage built, thus easing the monotonous journeys. Sadly, no drawings exist of the magnificent coach but it was reputed to have been most luxurious and comfortable.

In Plymouth, Jessop had been promoted and William Tyrrel became the yard foreman, with Mr J Harrison being made Clerk of the works.

The Millbay company employed two identical working groups of twelve men, each under the direction of one foreman.

Six masons provided the muscle power to cut the large stones and build the lighthouse, while six tinners were engaged to fit windows, construct the lantern gallery and other tasks. That meant there would always be one team able to work at the Eddystone while the other was busy in the workyard; additional workers were also drafted onto the payroll at a later date.

In a letter written by Smeaton to Robert Weston, dated Plymouth, 18 January 1757, we read a passage which endorses the respect and friendship which had developed between Smeaton and Mr Jessop:

> I hope it is counterbalanced by Mr Jessop's calmness, whom I think Providence has put along with me to keep me out of dangers that I might sometimes run into...

On Sunday 12 June 1757 the first stone was laid, weighing two tons. The following day another three were locked together and by Tuesday the 14th, nine more were in place. However, a storm on the 15th washed away five of the stones, which resulted in the masons working day and night to catch up the time lost. They cut the duplicate blocks in two days and their effort enabled Smeaton to complete his second course of the building by the evening of 30 June 1757.

In order to speed the construction of his tower, Smeaton realised that the journey to and from the Eddystone reef prevented continuous working schedules. It could take anything up to five hours' sailing time in one

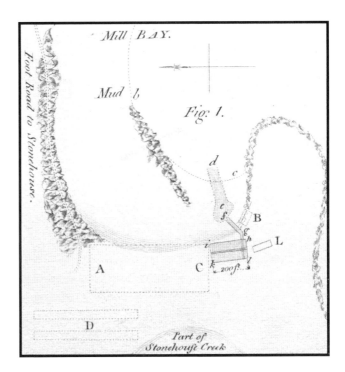

THE MILLBAY WORKYARD
THE AUTHOR'S COLLECTION

direction to reach either the Eddystone or his Plymouth shore base and meant that the men would have very little opportunity of completing long working periods on the rock face. His solution lay in a request to the proprietors to allow him an extra vessel, one which was capable of remaining anchored at the Eddystone Reef in gale conditions. It would be utilised as a multi-purpose extension to the Millbay yard, with the advantage of being constantly stationed at the work site, allowing the possibility of long-term working on the rock itself and of course ending the long daily journeys to and from the Eddystone for his workforce.

Smeaton's request was granted in the autumn of 1757 and an 80-ton herring fishing vessel was eventually found for his use. It was brought to Stonehouse Creek to be fettled out and made ready.

The harbour was next to the Millbay workyard and convenient for the likes of Smeaton and Jessop to oversee the conversion. The boat, renamed the *Neptune Buss*, was ready for her first journey to the Eddystone on 24 November 1757. At 4am, Smeaton, Jessop, William Hill the foreman, the 12 workers and four seamen climbed aboard the large craft. It was decided that they would be towed out to their intended destination by Thomas Richardson, the foreman of the second team, with his crew of the smaller *Eddystone Boat*.

As they sailed slowly into Plymouth Sound and beyond Penlee Point, the dark morning broke into a bright clear day. Both parties eventually arrived at the Eddystone just after noon and anchored their vessels near one another. It was to be a day of preparation for all, as a large cork buoy was to be brought from Plymouth on the following day's high tide, to be secured by heavy chains, where the *Neptune Buss* would be moored at her permanent station.

Unfortunately during the afternoon the wind started to increase and continued in its easterly direction. Richardson and his crew were finding the conditions becoming very difficult as their vessel was much smaller than Smeaton's. It soon became apparent that should the weather continue to worsen during the night, Richardson might be in trouble and the *Eddystone Boat* might not be able to stay roped together with the larger vessel for safety.

Smeaton signalled to Richardson and his men to make homeward for Plymouth, already realising that the situation was becoming very dangerous. Within a few minutes Richardson's men acknowledged the signal and raised their boat's sails for the journey to shore, leaving behind the tossing but anchored *Neptune Buss*.

With encroaching darkness falling about the lonely vessel, the strong winds increased still further, giving little option to Smeaton and his men but to up anchor and head for Plymouth.

The early evening brought great activity to the crew of the large vessel. She was big and bulky to handle and her sails had been modified to the extent that they were really only for emergency use. Steering her homeward proved difficult in the angry waters and after travelling only a short way from the reef the wind changed its direction and began to come right at them over the bow of the boat. The crew could do little to persuade their vessel to continue forward and the decision was made to head west along the coast, perhaps 20 miles or so to the relative safety of Fowey.

With the gale-force winds persisting, Smeaton and Jessop retired below deck and spent the next few hours resting in their cabin.

It was not a pleasant journey for anyone on board but they knew that Fowey would offer a safe haven and suitable refreshment. However, Smeaton awoke in his cabin three hours later when he heard a great commotion up on deck.

Without properly dressing and with immense difficulty from the rolling motion of the boat, he climbed the ladder to the cold outdoors. The scene before him was incredibly dramatic and he was terrified by what he saw. Within the biting, wet blackness that surrounded him, his eyes peered at the distant danger that awaited the struggling vessel. In front of him beckoned a white phosphorus curtain of tide smashing on an unfamiliar reef, the crew darting about, frantically trying to evade imminent disaster. All hands were tearing at ropes and battling with the boat's wheel. James Bowden, a seaman, yelled at Smeaton: "For God's sake heave hard at this rope if you mean to save our lives." They were desperate and Smeaton was only too willing to help his fellow men.

The frightening, icy wind screamed at the luckless sailors while the heavy rain combining with the freezing seas soaked everyone on board. The men knew their lives were in peril and thoughts of reaching Fowey's port were now a distant memory. They continued to fight the elements that bore against them, pulling on ropes and trying to steer another course away from certain death. The 18 men hauled and heaved, while several of the seamen struggled at the helm. Then, with immense effort from all concerned, they managed slowly to turn the *Buss* around and sail her away, preventing a tragedy.

The boat strained as it ploughed through the mountainous seas as their nightmare continued, when, with a loud crack, the jib broke and large amounts of water crashed over the entire vessel. Their fight for life lasted almost an hour before eventually they were making slow headway southward, into deeper water.

Although the ocean's fury tested the crew's experience and nerve, they pressed on, but not far away lay the rocks of the Deadman Point and Trewardreth Bay, which had to be avoided at all costs.

Steering their large boat into the Channel and away from the mainland, another challenge beset them. Suddenly the foresail split, leaving only the mainsail intact. By daybreak the weary crew looked about the threatening waters, the storm persisted and there was poor visibility, but no sight of land.

A tiny yawl boat that had been tied behind the *Buss* for ancillary uses was beginning to sink through damage sustained during the evening's terrible ordeal. It was also causing extra problems for the helmsman in steering

WORK IN PROGRESS
THE AUTHOR'S COLLECTION

the wooden 80-ton vessel and so they cut her loose to enable better control and a speedier passage. However, they estimated that their course was taking them into the Bay of Biscay and it was not at all certain whether the damaged boat would be able to make the coast of Spain or France, and more importantly only a week's supply of provisions was available on board the *Buss*.

At noon on Saturday 25th, with the sea still carrying them along, land was sighted in the distance. To make the landfall was out of the question and it was assumed to be that of the Lizard Peninsula, being many miles to their weatherside. This caused further anxiety to the men, as now their only other option was to try to make for Mount's Bay.

When the cold, black evening fell, they decided that because of the poor weather and the gloom that hung over them, they might

easily miss their last chance of reaching land. The captain advised Smeaton of the dire situation, explaining the possible outcome should they be unable to find Mount's Bay. They decided to lower the anchor where they were, in deep water, and wait till morning. Riding the gale would not be pleasant but in daylight their chances of reaching landfall would be so much better.

Throughout that evening their boat lunged and rolled in the tempest about them. The men huddled together below in sombre silence, all hoping for a break in the weather. They were tired and rested as best they could during the long and uncomfortable hours that followed. When daylight appeared the next morning, they could see Land's End in the distance, which brought even greater despair. They had missed their opportunity of reaching the relative safety of Mount's Bay and were still drifting further out into an open sea.

Should they try for the distant shores of France or Spain, or should they attempt to steer a course to the shores of the Scilly Isles, with the dangerous reefs and rocky outcrops that surrounded it?

The dilemma caused much more uncertainty among the men and so a decision was postponed until noon, just in case the weather turned in their favour.

The captain deliberated on his options but decided to make for the Scilly Isles.

Uncertain of a route to avoid the rocky coast of the islands, he considered his plan further then proceeded in the early afternoon. He would try to anchor off the islands until the following morning, allowing him to approach the Scillies in daylight. Smeaton and the crew agreed on the strategy and prepared for the journey ahead. But no sooner had they lifted up the anchor, than the lookout spotted a ship on the horizon. The captain immediately ordered the raising of a distress flag signal and everyone prayed that help was finally at hand.

A large vessel called the *White Hart of Poole*, heading for Guinea, eventually pulled close to the *Buss*, but couldn't tie alongside as the winds were still strong.

Both crews shouted across at one another in great excitement and after many minutes of exchanges, the *Buss's* captain established the correct direction to take for a safe passage to the Scillies.

With hearts lightened the crew were in determined mood; Smeaton and Jessop also felt confident of surviving the ordeal and, as daylight started to fade, the men were happy to remain at anchor until the following morning. The evening's atmosphere below deck was so very different to that of the previous day, when, anxious and fearful, the men could only guess at their fate. But now in the confines of the galley, a good meal was prepared and heartily enjoyed by the whole crew, who retired content to their bunks.

At four in the morning of Sunday 27 November, the *Neptune Buss* lifted her anchor and headed for land. Steadily she pitched and rolled her bows. Unfortunately the weather would again play its games and in a short time the wind abated and changed direction. An hour or so later, the sea's motion had subsided, so that by early evening it had become quite calm. It was extremely frustrating for the men, as with little wind to help them, their prospects of finally reaching the Isles of Scilly grew slim. Their only option was to lie at anchor another night and wait for the morning's outcome. The sea and weather had again conspired against them, leaving the bitterly disappointed crew to contemplate their next action, for they knew that their journey was far from over and could still be an adventure, but at least in that type of weather they were in no real danger.

At 2am the next day the crewmen once more lifted the anchor, but during the laborious task, the wind changed its direction again and freshened to a cold north, north-westerly.

With great joy, they abandoned all thoughts of landing on the Scillies and headed straight back to Plymouth.

Early in the morning on Monday 28 November, five days after leaving Millbay, the men could see the moonlit outline of Rame Head; they had made good time, having passed Fowey an hour or so earlier. At 5am they rounded the cliffs and on into the safe waters of Plymouth Sound.

The workyard of Millbay awaited them and in the approaching daylight they arrived back at the quayside. News of Smeaton's survival spread quickly around the town; it was a great surprise to everyone that he was back, as most had assumed that he and his crew were drowned. But by the time Smeaton's men had moored their vessel to the quay wall, a tremendous welcome from their wives and colleagues awaited them and it was with much relief and humble thanks that each of the men finally stepped ashore.

After a few days of recovery, Smeaton and his company tried again to secure the mooring chains and cork buoy into position near the Eddystone. The *Neptune Buss* was once more towed from Stonehouse Creek and delivered to her station, where she remained.

Smeaton and Jessop's target for the first season's work was to complete the cutting of the rock into flat steps which would provide the platform to the building's foundations. The work was achieved and unquestionably helped by the successful mooring of the *Neptune Buss* and another vessel, a sloop, which provided berths for the whole company.

The *Buss* proved to be a vital staging post for operations and became home for the workmen when off duty at the rock. It was also providing exceptional service as a repair facility and general maintenance craft.

Slowly, the tons of stone began to arrive at the Millbay yard from the harbours of Portland and Par, where craftsmen cut out every block to precise specifications.

Portland stone had been preferred to local granite because it was easier to work on, but would only be used inside the tower itself while the harder local granite moorstone from Lanlivery Quarry near Fowey would give the building its mighty strength in the foundations and outer walls.

Smeaton had made many trips to quarries during his initial visit to the West Country and inspected sites at Hingstone Downs near Calstock, Constantine, Beare, Purbeck and Swanage, before he finally accepted the quality of stone from Lanlivery and Portland.

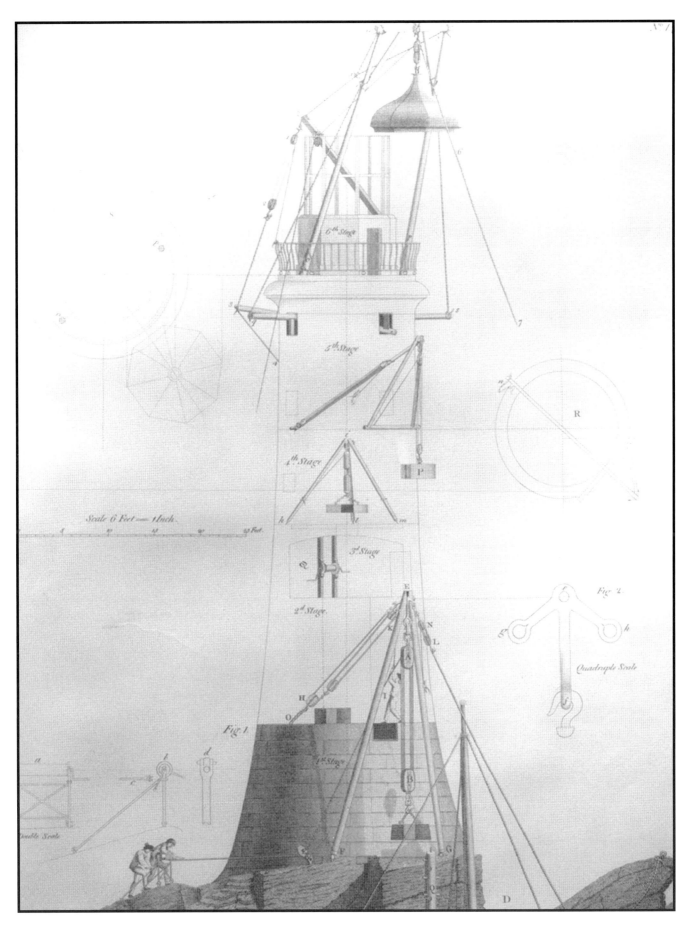

THE PLAN OF THE EDDYSTONE BUILDING PROCESS
THE AUTHOR'S COLLECTION

Smeaton was unquestionably a very hard and physically strong individual; his manual skills, mathematical prowess and use of pulleys, blocks and tackle enabled him to believe in himself. His management abilities had allowed him the satisfaction of knowing he was also a highly regarded and much respected boss.

However, there was one concern which continually troubled Smeaton, that of his men's safety out on the Eddystone. It was not the difficulty of their work which bothered him, although that was bad; it was something that had worried the earlier lighthouse builders, Winstanley and Rudyerd: the presence of indiscriminate press gangs.

They had already become a nuisance to Smeaton and had boarded his Portland ships when carrying the stone blocks along the Channel from Dorset.

So a way to deter the opportunists was necessary to secure the stone deliveries. Immediate action was needed and so Smeaton devised a method of immunity for the men in his care. Each man who was employed on the Eddystone payroll was to be given a small silver medallion, to be carried at all times.

Smeaton's idea was just another safeguard for his men working at the Eddystone. Besides that he also insisted that a large painted figure of the lighthouse be shown on all the mainsails of his cargo ships, so that from a distance, everyone would immediately recognise their special purpose. Smeaton wrote:

> I considered, that if I had a stamp which could not readily be counterfeited, with which one might at pleasure stamp a piece of silver, each man employed by us might thus be furnished with an evident token in his pocket of service to which he belonged. This idea having been communicated to Mr Weston, he soon got a sufficient number of silver medals made for the purpose, and after the distribution of these, and the painting of the sails, we never had any further interruption.

Between 8 January and 22 March 1757, Smeaton and Weston concentrated on the one

THE EDDYSTONE COIN 1757
THE AUTHOR'S COLLECTION

item. Through their correspondence we read a detailed account of the process:

> From Robert Weston dated 8 January 1757:

> I shall apply this day for Admiralty protections, which I will transmit to you as soon as I receive them; and would recommend an Eddystone ensign for their colours.

Again from Weston to Smeaton, 15 January:

> The Secretary of State, to whom I must apply, has a mind full of more momentous matters at present, but I hope to find a proper time soon to lay it before him.

On 11 January Smeaton wrote to Weston:

> I got a couple of Edystone ensigns you advised made up when I first came down, which have served ever since, and though the press boats have very frequently boarded us, none of our men were taken, the service being considered as a protection. I think it would be very useful if you could get a stamp with something of a device representing the lighthouse, capable of stamping a bit of silver to be given to each of the men as a

token of their belonging to the service if separately attacked.

On 29 January Weston replied:

What number of medals shall I send you? The die is in hand, and I expect it in ten days or a fortnight, when I will get as many struck as shall be necessary, on a piece of silver of about three shillings value, of the bigness of a crown. The device is the Edystone, the legend In salutem omnium and on the exergue Edystone Resurgit. 1757.

Smeaton wrote to Weston on 1 February, saying:

Of the medals please send me two or three dozen, and if you please, half a dozen of about the weight of a crown. I do not know whether some may not think the term Resurgit at the bottom of the exergue rather premature, or as the proverb hints, "reckoning our chickens before they are hatched".

Weston continued four days later:

The medals I expect will be done next week. I will not enter into criticism with you now, but I think RESURGIT not unapt, even at this time.

On 19 March Robert Weston again contacted Smeaton by letter, with reference to the coins. The silver tokens had been brought from London to Plymouth in the previous week by one of Weston's associates, but Smeaton did not seem very happy about the design during his initial observation and Weston's letter suggested:

As you think the medals too elegant to be distributed in common, suppose you were to give one to the Commissioner at Plymouth, another to the Admiral, and in short any person we have been, or may be obliged to, and keep the rest to be worn by the workmen in the out service, who on return should resign them to the company that succeeds them, and so while the work is carrying on, to give the workmen the use, but not the property, till all is finished.

By 22 March Smeaton wrote:

I am glad the contents of my last letter gave satisfaction. The medals I will endeavour to dispose of as you propose.

It is to be presumed that this plan was adopted and that the men in the outgoing party received the medals. There were two companies working, each of twelve men, six of whom were masons and six tinners. The Eddystone medals given to each man provided the workers with the reassurance that they needed to complete their task. The silver pieces certainly eased the builders' constant worry of being pressed into service by the navy. However in one incident on 4 January 1758, a press gang from HMS *Duke* landed at the lighthouse site to check the identity of the party and after inspection of the whole workforce, took a J Krugger away, as he could not find his medal, stating to the foreman that Krugger had lost his protection and so they were within their rights to take him.

Back at the Eddystone Rocks, work was well under way. From the lighthouse on 8 September 1757, Smeaton wrote:

We landed at daybreak, and the Eddystone boat having been unloaded, we proceeded to set in position her cargo. Mr Weston not only had the satisfaction of setting in place the centre stone of the Seventh Course, but was also entertained by the appearance of a fleet of more than a hundred ships – Merchantmen from the West Indies and the Mediterranean to whose future safety we could suppose ourselves to be contributing. After setting the centre stone Mr Weston returned to Plymouth. The fineness of the weather now helped to speed our efforts, so that the Eighth Course, which was begun on the 8th, was completed in five days, being finished on the 13th at the same hour.

From Smeaton's diary we read:

Eddystone Lighthouse, 20th September, 1757. And after that the work continued smoothly until 20th September so that in return for the previous interruption of fifteen days, due to bad weather, we had had an uninterrupted working period of eighteen days, by which time the Ninth Course was considerably advanced. But now, although the wind had only been blowing moderately from the East for the past week, there began to roll in so heavy a ground swell from the South-West that all efforts to get the Eddystone boat into the gut and so continue work, had failed. During that fine spell our greatest difficulties arose from the unusual lowness of the tides, which made our vessels, when loaded with stone, liable to be caught by the keel when leaving the jetty in Mill Bay, Plymouth.

To overcome this, Mr Jessop borrowed a Punt [a square, flat-bottomed vessel], which was loaded at the jetty and then hauled out into deep water where her cargo could be transferred into the vessels at any state of the tide. Something occurred, in our use of this punt, that can only be said to demonstrate the extreme degree of malevolence that sometimes possesses the heart of man.

She was loaded in the evening of Monday the 12th and hauled into deep water as usual.

The next morning, on hauling up her moorings, we found that she had been swinging by a single thread, the rest of the rope having been cut with a knife at a point beneath the surface of the water.

No doubt the intention had been that the sabotage should not have been discovered until the punt had been driven upon the rocks, and there sunk with her cargo, with consequent delay to our work. The act, since it benefited nobody, illustrated a degree of tiny-mindedness that one would not have thought existed in human beings.

By then Jessop had engaged his son William, 14, to help him in the final stages of the work. It appears that the young lad possessed all of his father's great skill and talent, because in a very short time, Smeaton responded to William's notable contribution.

Encouraged by Jessop, his son was subsequently offered a clerkship with Smeaton, based at the master builder's own home near Leeds.

Jessop would finally retire in October of 1759 after the completion of the great work. He had served his two masters (Rudyerd and Smeaton) with total devotion and was rightly recognised throughout the land for his

CROSS-SECTION OF SMEATON'S TOWER
THE AUTHOR'S COLLECTION

achievement and experience in lighthouse building.

From the diary of Smeaton we read a letter from him to one of the lease owners, a J

Noyes Jr, dated in Plymouth on 27 June 1758. It gave an idea of the other difficulties the builders had to address and continued:

> Two or three weeks since, some villains in the night broke all the windows of Stonehouse Chapel to pieces; and much about the same time, our dog that laid in the yard at nights was poisoned. I have therefore employed our porter, instead of attending by day, to watch the yard from six at night to six in the morning, with a loaded musket.

All the meticulous preparations for the coming winter season were put into action and the many weeks of experimenting with different types of cement were put to the test.

Smeaton's work had progressed well, but was always dependent on the kindness of the weather; when the sun shone and the air was still the men would labour their hardest and when it was not possible to get to the Eddystone the entire workforce would be found at the Millbay yard.

Every man was fully involved in completing the task set before them, each company trying to outdo the other. Jessop would have successes with his efforts, then Richardson's men would be satisfied in their toil. All, however, would suffer from setbacks, with the weather nearly always playing the role of villain.

Smeaton and his hardy men forged ahead in their laborious task, but even as the tower grew, the construction work remained a dangerous occupation. It continued to be heavy and slow work at the best of times, the tools and stone being awkward to deal with. However, the workers were well-organised and disciplined individuals who were also able to find pleasure and laughter on those extra-special days which stood out from the rest of their routine.

The hardened granite-like men shared a strange sense of humour and would mock their colleagues' misfortunes or minor accidents.

Smeaton found himself on the receiving end when he slipped on a joggle hole, stumbled hopelessly for support, and went crashing from the tower's platform onto the rocks below.

No bones were broken but he did suffer a dislocated thumb which was pulled back on site by the foreman. However, his swollen hand remained useless during the next four weeks.

On another occasion, just before the completion of the lighthouse, he was overcome by fumes and found unconscious in the tower.

Once, during the late evening of 8 July 1757 when the men were on board their *Buss*, the lookout spotted a boat heading towards the reef and in minutes heard her grind on the jagged rocks. They rushed to the rescue and found that the 130-ton brig *Charming Sally*, returning to Dartmouth from Bideford, had foundered on the reef. She had mistaken the black rocks peering out of the sea for small fishing boats and thought her direction a safe one. Luckily the seven men on board were all saved. A lightship had been forced on Smeaton at the insistence of Trinity House and had been stationed two miles from the Eddystone in the previous year, providing its light from 14 August 1756 to prevent such groundings. However, many people said the vessel was useless and incidents like that seemed to prove their point. Critics questioned from the outset whether the light would be strong or high enough to help mariners navigate about the unlit Eddystone reef, and a letter had already been sent by a Mr Connel to the Collector of His Majesty's Customs in Plymouth, dated 19 August 1756, suggesting, like many others, that the new lightship provided little benefit to mariners. It read:

> Gentlemen, There is a boat come this morning into the river with four men and two boys who say they were cast away last night at 10 o clock upon the Edystone rocks, out of their brig the Pelican, 70 tons from Topsham.
> Thomas Butcher master, from Ferrol, in ballast.
> They say they saw a light which they thought was the stone, but it was on board a ship a considerable distance from it, so that they were forced to take to their boat and they afterwards saw the brig sink.

The floating light's effectiveness continued to be criticised, but there was little that could be done until the new lighthouse was finished.

Finding people to man the vessel had been difficult for the authorities because its crew would have to ride out the mountainous seas anchored near the reef. So when the seafarers of Cawsand refused to undertake the duty, the decision by Trinity House to station the lightship at the Eddystone seemed irrelevant. The vessel required experienced men, hardened to life at sea and able to survive a lonely life bobbing up and down on the ocean, day and night; the employment would not suit many.

It was a fortunate coincidence, therefore, that during February 1756, six months before the lightship arrived off Plymouth, a James Hill of Yame wrote to the Eddystone lease owners offering his services. In a letter from Robert Weston to the Master of Trinity House, he wrote:

> James Hill of Yame, a fishing town four miles distance from Plymouth would undertake with three hands more, such as he should get, to look after and manage a floating light.
>
> He says they are all fishermen and well acquainted with the Edystone, that the best place for mooring the vessel would be N or N.E. part of the rock, about 150 fathoms distant from the main rock.

It would appear that the local man got his wish and had already joined the workforce.

In a letter dated 10 August 1756 from Smeaton to Weston, we read:

> James Hill originally engaged by Mr Smart to serve on board your destined light and who, since I came down in the Spring, has been employed in going off to the Edystone, and upon your fixing with Mr Lugger, engaged himself in the Edystone service; him they sent for, to go on board their light; but he told them he was engaged to me and did not choose to quit the service.
>
> Since I came they have also sent for Mr Smart to engage him to carry off stores for the light, as he used to do to the house; but he told them he could not make any such engagement, as he was employed by me.

Besides these matters, Smeaton's concern focused on the quality of the equipment and tools being used in the building work.

It was vital that everything sent out to the Eddystone worked, but unfortunately that was not always the case, as we find in a letter, dated 12 September 1758 and addressed to J Noyes Jr. Smeaton wrote:

> The lamp which was sent with the Buss's lantorn, I fancy was made by some Plymouth man; for upon trial I find it has only one fault, that is, it will not burn at all: So that I shall be obliged to get a new one made, as also something for holding candles; for in some kinds of weather, I believe there will be difficulties in the use of any kind of lamps.
>
> The lanthorn has also a material fault, that is, it will not turn when wet.

In Smeaton's diary of 10 October 1758, we read the following entry:

> Today, I again went up to the Hoe, and though the wind had remained fresh at Nor'-West now for more than twenty-four hours, and so should have done something to reduce the Sou'-Westerly swell, the sea was still breaking over the house, rising up in the form of a white pillar, considerably higher than the building, and of such a size as occasionally to hide every part of it from view But with the air now more clear, in the intervals of the sea's retreat I could distinctly see the triangle standing upon the lighthouse and the stone suspended from it. However, to my great concern I found that the Buss had really gone from her moorings and was nowhere to be seen. Indeed, this proved to be a day of unrelieved disappointment, for besides the uncertainty of the fate of the Neptune Buss I received the decision of a General Court of the Corporation of Trinity House on my proposal of the 28th September regarding the exhibition of a temporary light upon the Eddystone. And it was a decision which much more effectually put a stop to further progress this year than the parting of the Buss from her moorings. Their answer was to the effect that having given careful consideration to my proposals. "On reading the acts of parliament, the application from the merchants and owners of ships, the patent for the floating

Light, and the enclosed Account of the first lighthouse erected there (Mr Winstanley's), they are of the opinion that a light cannot be exhibited on the Eddystone rock until the lighthouse is rebuilt".

This set-back, I must confess, disappointed me greatly, not only that I should apparently fall short of the speed which my predecessors Mr Winstanley and Mr Rudyerd had shown in providing a temporary light in the course of the third working season, but that my considerable efforts in this direction were thus frustrated.

This evening at ten o'clock Mr Jessop returned to Plymouth, and to my no small joy and satisfaction brought news that the Buss was safe at anchor in Dartmouth Harbour.

He told me that on Sunday, about two hours after I left them, it began to blow a stern from the Sou'-Sou'-West and he ordered the decks to be cleared and everything put in order. He did not hoist the mainsail because by holding wind, it might cause them to break loose from their moorings. Towards nightfall, however, the storm increased, and the sea frequently hid from them all sight of the building, as the broken column of water rose considerably higher than the top of the triangle. With the coming of night the storm continued to increase, and at about eleven o'clock the cable parted at the bows. Upon this they hoisted their foresail and mizzen and tried to make for land, but the sea proved so tempestuous that with the small amount of sail they had they could not keep a proper steerage, and it being excessively rainy and dark they were afraid of running on shore before they could see it. They therefore decided to lay her to, with her head to the South East, so that they might have daylight before they made for the land~ At about two o'clock that morning the wind went West, and at daybreak they found themselves about three leagues from, and abreast of, Start Point~ They then bent their mainsail, hoisted their jib, and stood in for the land~ But the Neptune was so slow a sailer that it was four in the afternoon before they got off at Dartmouth: they then by the help of a pilot, came to an anchor in the Road, the next morning warped themselves into the harbour~ Having seen the vessel safely moored, Mr Jessop and most of the workmen returned to Plymouth.

From Smeaton's diary we find an account of his thoughts dating from the Spring to the Autumn 1759:

During my stay in London in the early part of this year I received regular reports of the work in progress at Mill Bay, Plymouth, which was being carried on with all the speed I could wish, while I myself was busy designing the iron rails for the balcony, and the cast ironwork, the wrought ironwork, and the copperwork for the lantern; all of which, together with the plate glasswork, was made in London.

The first report I had of the condition of the works at the Eddystone itself was contained in a letter from Mr Jessop dated 27th March, in which he told me that on the 21st, he seized the first opportunity after the violent storm on the 9th (which had done great damage to ships, houses and buildings at Plymouth) to visit the Eddystone. While still some distance off they had seen the triangle, with the stone still hanging as we had left it last season, and it was therefore with considerable surprise that on arriving they found the Transport buoy had gone ! Where upon they dropped anchor, went into the Gut in small boats, and landed.

They found only two respects in which the sea had altered the arrangements on the rock as we had left them at the end of last year's work: one was that one of the two wooden fenders that prevent the boats chafing on the rock when they are tied up in the Gut unloading their cargo of stone, had gone; the other, that from the top of the wall one of the loose stones that I had drawn within the circumference of the work had been washed away.

Finding that otherwise everything was firm, they lowered the stone from the triangle and stowed the triangle itself in the well-hole of the stairs (the stairs themselves were not yet in position).

A further search revealed no trace of the mooring buoy, and Mr Jessop informed me that he had put in hand the preparation of a new one, and also a new fender.

At the same time he had given the necessary orders for fitting out The Buss to sweep for the moorings. He added that the forty-fifth course was being worked upon in the stone-yard.

SMEATON'S LIGHTHOUSE AS IT APPEARED AFTER COMPLETION IN 1759
THE AUTHOR'S COLLECTION

After this the seamen frequently went out to sweep for the moorings, but without success; they had been promised £10 if they recovered one set and £20 if they recovered both.

Presently it became apparent that the recovery of the moorings was a doubtful prospect and I decided it was time to set about the preparation of a new set. Therefore on the 29th May I ordered forty fathoms of new chain to be made at Blackwall, intending to send it down to Plymouth overland. This together with some chain which we already had in Plymouth, we thought would meet our needs for this year, in case we did not recover any of the others; and Mr Jessop was directed to look out for a couple of suitable anchors. The casting of the corner pillars of the lantern being attended with some difficulty which placed the work beyond our capabilities of the ordinary workmen in the cast iron foundry, I had them executed by the intelligent and ingenious Mr Prickett, of Farthing Fields, Wapping.

The copper window frames were successfully cast, each in one piece, by Mr Kinman of Shoe Lane, a work he did with credit.

The fitting together of the whole work of the lantern with wrought iron framing, as also the balcony rails, I saw well advanced, and left in the hands of Mr Broadbent, an engine-maker in Piccadilly; of which work he acquitted himself to my full satisfaction.

During my stay in London I appeared more than once before the Board of Trinity House.

On the second occasion, which was on the 2nd June, they wanted my opinion of a proposal that had been made to them by an optician in London, who suggested that all the panes of glass in the lantern should be ground to the shape of circular segments, so that the whole lantern should form a glass sphere of fifteen feet diameter.

My answer was to the effect that this was a way of making an easy thing difficult and expensive, without the gaining of any corresponding advantage.

For the proposer seemed to imagine it was necessary that the rays of light should shine out in every direction, upwards as well as sideways, whereas it was the horizontal or sideways rays alone that were seen from the surface of the sea by distant observers; all the rest either going over their heads into the air, or falling down into the sea before they reached them.

For my explanation, which fully convinced the Board of the impracticality of the scheme, I received the thanks of the Deputy Master on behalf of them all.

Smeaton's entries in his diary of August show the work progressing and from 17–18 August 1759 we read:

This day the last pieces of the forty-six course were set, thus completing the main column.

I now let fall a plumb-line from the centre of the man-hole in the balcony floor down to the centre of the bottom of the well-hole, a height of forty-nine and a half feet, and found the building to be leaning one eighth of an inch to the east.

I then measured the heights of the several parts of the building and found them as follows:

The six foundation courses to the top of the rock = 8ft 4 3/4 inches.

The eight courses to the entry door = 12ft 1/2 inch

The ten courses of the well-hole to the storeroom door = 15ft 2 1/4 inches.

The height of the four rooms to the balcony floor 34ft 4 1/2 inches.

Height of the main column, containing forty-six courses = 70 feet.

We proceeded to set up and lead in position the balcony rails, and completed them; and then made the holes by means of which the window frames, when they arrived, would be secured to the stonework. Furthermore, in order to permit Mr Richardson's company to lodge in the lighthouse, I fixed a temporary cover to the hole in the balcony floor (through which, when it was completed, access would be had to the lantern) which made it water tight. Presently the Eddystone boat arrived with the first of the six courses of stone for the lantern, and was unloaded this evening.

From the Eddystone lighthouse on 18 August 1759, Smeaton wrote:

This day we all landed at four in the morning and proceeded to set the first course of the lantern.

While this was being done and having left instructions with Mr Richardson for the completion of the rest of the stone-work, including the stone stairs in the well-hole, I returned to Plymouth to speed the work of completing the lantern, and arrived there at noon. Among the many annoyances and disappointments met with in the course of the building of this lighthouse, not only from the uncertainties of wind and weather, but from the negligence and carelessness of others, it was not one of the least that the carrier employed to bring the lantern-work by land from London, by land, for express purpose of avoiding delay!, had, for his Own Convenience, left most of it at Exeter a week before. I now found it was still not arrived, which prevented our finishing the last course of stone in the work-yard; the course into which was to fit the iron rim of the lantern.

The groove for it was indeed roughly cut into the stone, but not trimmed up; and as I had never trusted to anything fitting at the Eddystone that had not first had its parts assembled at Mill Bay, I did not think it wise to dispense with this rule; unless absolutely necessary.

It is never possible to estimate how much time will be needed to make parts fit together; particular difficulties may arise and what had seemed a simple task may become quite complicated.

However, this evening the lantern-work did arrive, which greatly relieved my annoyance.

September soon arrived and with the work nearing completion Smeaton wrote in his diary on the 28th the following details of his efforts:

Since the 23rd the leading and glazing work had been going on very well, the weather in general having been moderate and dry. Today the wood workers finished their work, which consisted of the following items:- Three cabin bunks to hold one man each, with three drawers and two lockers underneath each to hold his personal property; these were in the upper room, or bedroom. In the kitchen, besides the fireplace and sink, were two locker-seats, a dresser with drawers, two cupboards and one crockery cupboard, In the lantern, a seat was fixed all round, except at the balcony doorway, serving equally to sit upon, or stand to snuff the candles; and to enable a person to look through the lowest tier of glass panes at distant objects, without needing to go outside the lantern on to the balcony.

In addition, the joiners had fixed ten window frames: that is, two in the upper store-room, facing north and south, and four in each of the two rooms above. These were bedded in putty, but were otherwise held only with two wooden pins above and two below, driven into the holes bored in the stone. They were thus easily removable, should necessity arise.

I would note here that whenever it was necessary to fasten anything to the wall, the fixing-hole was always drilled in the solid stone, and not in the joints between them, which would thereby have been weakened.

It will be noticed that in the present tower I have fixed the beds in the uppermost room, and the kitchen, with its fireplace beneath it.

The reverse was the case in the previous lighthouse with the result, I understand, that in moist weather the beds and bedding generally were in a very damp and disagreeable state.

In the present arrangement the warmth from the chimney passing through the bedroom, and the warmth rising from the kitchen generally, would promote a genial temperature in both living rooms; not that the rooms below suffered in any way from damp. Nor is this surprising, when it is remembered that the walls were wholly moorstone, which will never admit dampness and that there was no plaster at all in the building, each stone, being worked smooth within, making the inner surface of the rooms.

This afternoon the Eddystone boat came out and brought out two chests of candles for the lights, and other stores. She also brought out sixteen cross bars for the windows, with a couple of smiths to fix them; but as by mistake they had only made half the number I ordered – that is, sixteen pairs. I found it necessary to send them home again to forge and prepare the rest, while I proceeded, with such help as was available, to fix those we had.

The boat was expected to bring out a painter, but on hearing of so many being taken ill at the Eddystone, he refused to come. I therefore set one of the masons to work painting the outside of the roof of the cupola.

The copper-smith and mason who had been taken ill yesterday continuing unfit for work, they, with the three joiners and two smiths, returned to Plymouth this evening in the Eddystone boat.

After the boat was gone and it became so dark that we could no longer see to work, I ordered a charcoal fire to be made in the upper store-room, in one of the iron pots we used for melting lead.

The intention was to soften the ends of the iron cross-bars for the windows so that they could be drilled.

Most of the workmen were sitting round the fire, and to make ourselves comfortable we had closed the windows. I remember watching the fire closely, to see that the iron was made hot enough, and not over-heated, and I remember feeling slightly giddy...The next thing I remember was finding myself on the floor of the room below, half drowned with water!

It seems that, almost without warning, the gases given off by the charcoal completely overcame me, so that I fell down upon the floor in a faint.

Had not my companions lowered me into the room below, and doused me liberally with cold water, I should certainly have expired on the spot.

The building was almost finished and one of Smeaton's last tasks was to fix a lightning conductor to the outside of the tower, from top to bottom. It had just been invented by Benjamin Franklin and had never before been used on a lighthouse.

In correspondence from Smeaton to Mr Shuttlewood, written at the Eddystone Lighthouse on 4 October 1759, we learn:

Sir, Pursuant to the directions of the Honourable Corporation of Trinity House, by you transmitted to me, I beg leave to inform them that the Edystone lighthouse is by God's favour, ready for the exhibition of a light therein, in the same manner as formerly having made trial thereof in the daytime and found everything to answer, and that the persons agreed with to keep the light are now in the house. I therefore, accordingly to their worships order, hereby give notice, that on Tuesday the 16th of this present October, in the evening, a light can be exhibited in this house, and, by God's permission, continued therein without interruption: and in further obedience to their worships' order, at this time I dispatched an express to Mr Symonds, Master of the Floating light vessel, to acquaint him with the day of lighting as above, and in consequence that he will not need to show a light on board his vessel after the night between Monday 15th and Tuesday

16th inst and I am, with the greatest respect to the gentlemen of the Corporation, P.S. The lanthorn was glazed and everything ready on the 29th ult but till this day no boats have been able to land. All hands have lived here since the 12th ult.

Feverishly, the work continued, and, a week before the lighthouse was due to be ready, two of the newly appointed lightkeepers went to the Eddystone to learn more about their role.

It was their first visit to the reef and the men were said to have been quite nervous about the task which lay ahead. As the boat neared the rocks, both of them seemed uneasy

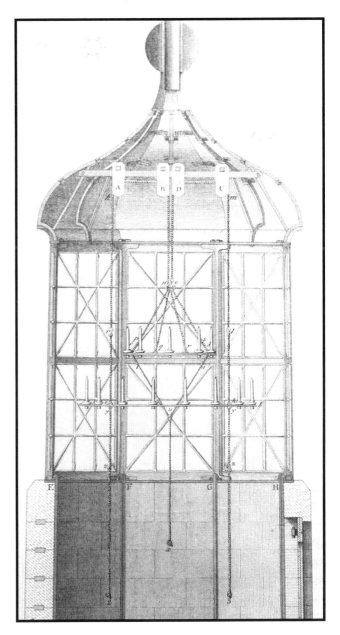

The tower's lantern and housing
The author's collection

and showed no enthusiasm for what they were about to undertake. With a heavy swell rolling over the stony outcrop, the new keepers prepared to jump from the boat. Unfortunately, as the first man leaped towards the rock's surface, he fell badly and dislocated his arm. In great pain he lay there, hoping that his colleague would soon join him from the craft. However the second keeper refused to leave the safety of the vessel and insisted that he would have no more to do with the lighthouse and demanded to be returned home. Other men already at the tower were waiting for their replacements to climb up the iron rungs to the entrance room. However they saw what had happened and ran to help the injured man back into the boat, only to see it cast off from the mooring rope and head back towards Plymouth. Angry, their concern was not for the keeper who fell, but because that they remained stranded at the tower.

It appeared that the impending lighting ceremony would be a disaster, with no keeper able to light the tower's candles. On hearing of the unexpected predicament, Jessop searched for the necessary employees and on 8 October 1759 three more lightkeepers were installed at the lighthouse to play their part in maritime history. Smeaton knew his final hours of hard work were almost over and was excited about the forthcoming historic event.

But a twist of fate intervened. Smeaton would be foiled by bad weather and not be able to light his 24 six-pound tallow candles at the Eddystone. Instead he would acknowledge his triumph as a spectator, along with hundreds of other people who stared out to sea from Plymouth Hoe during the night of Tuesday 16 October 1759.

The light vessel which had remained at her moorings at the insistence of Trinity House was no longer needed and so ordered to leave her position at the end of that week, just so long as there were no problems with the lighting of the tower. Nothing untoward happened and three days later, on Friday 19 October 1759, she pulled up her anchor and sailed away from the new lighthouse, giving three cheers to the keepers waving from the tower's lantern gallery. Smeaton wrote soon after:

In the stormy weather that happened during this interval at Plymouth, I took several opportunities of viewing the lighthouse with my telescope from the Hoa and also from the Garrison, both of which places are sufficiently elevated to see the base of the building, and the whole rock at low water, in clear weather; and though I had many occasions of viewing the unfinished building when buried in the waves in a storm at south west, yet never before having had a view of it under this circumstance in its finished state, I was astonished to find that the account given by Mr Winstanley did not appear to be at all exaggerated; at intervals of a minute, and sometimes two or three, I suppose when a combination happened to produce one overgrown wave, it would strike the rock and the building conjointly, and fly up in a white column, enwrapping it like a sheet, rising at least to double the height of the house, and totally intercepting it from sight; and this appearance being momentary, both as to its rising and falling, one was enabled to judge of the comparative height very nearly by the comparative spaces alternately occupied by the house, and by the column of water in the field of the telescope.

Of this column I made an eye sketch at the time; and must further observe that, while I was in the lighthouse during the last interval of finishing, in which time we had more than one hard gale that obliged us to shut the windward ports of the uppermost rooms, I particularly noticed the manner in which the waves began to gather as soon as they came so near the house as to be sensible of the sloping rocks underneath them; those waves by degrees towering higher as they came nearer, formed a deep hollow sea at the foot of the building; and then falling into it, struck it with all imaginable fury.

Smeaton was not able to reach his lighthouse until 19 October, but during his brief stay he spoke animatedly with the triumphant keepers, thoroughly enjoying the enthusiastic welcome he received.

He returned to Plymouth a few hours later and in the Eddystone Journal, dated 20 October 1759, a crewman wrote:

All hands, except the lightkeepers, went on board the boats at noon, but the wind being Northerly, we did not arrive at Plymouth till Sunday morning.

During this passage, the air being clear, Mr Smeaton observed the light very distinctly; at the first lighting we were about seven or eight miles distant, and the light appeared very strong and bright, till the lanthorn was sunk below the apparent horizon which happened near the island of St Nicholas, after we had passed the men of war riding in the sound...

On the granite cornice running round the second store room are the following words, which have never been used more appropriately:

Except the Lord build the house, they labour in vain that build it.

On the last stone of the edifice, above the door of the lantern, the joyous and grateful architect inscribed "Laus Deo".

It was a wonderful achievement for the modest Yorkshireman and in his diary he wrote:

I generally visited The Hoa every clear evening, being curious to observe what appearance the light made from thence.

It was a fact universally agreed in, that the light in the old lighthouse had never been discerned from thence; whatever appearance, therefore, it now made, was so much gained by the different fabric of the lanthorn; the candles themselves, their disposition and number, being the same as before.

I found it required the air to be clear to see it at all, and then it appeared like a star of the fourth magnitude: but when the air was very clear, it appeared as a star of the third magnitude, and doubtless could have been seen several miles further.

The year 1759 concluded with a series of very stormy weather and it was not until the month of January succeeding, that there was any prospect of boats going off.

I have a letter from Mr Jessop, dated 13th of January 1760, in which he mentions, that upon the 8th instant, the Eddystone boat went off, wind at east and moderate, but a great swell.

They got thither at four o'clock in the afternoon, but could not land.

However, going to the west side of the house, they conveyed some small stores into it by means of the keg; and by it received a letter from Henry Edwards directed to Mr Jessop.

The purpose of it was to acquaint him that they had had such very bad weather that the sea frequently ran over the house, so that for twelve days together they could not open the door of the lanthorn, nor any other.

He further mentioned that upon the 5th December, at night, they had a very great storm; the wind being at east, so that the ladder which was lashed below the entry door loosed, and was washed away.

Also upon the 13th, there was so violent a storm of wind that he thought the house would overset; and at midnight the sea broke one pane of glass S.E. side of the lanthorn.

That they had had a very melancholy time of it, having had besides a great deal of thunder and lightning.

Mr Jessop further informed me that upon the 10th the boat went out again but the wind at east blew too fresh for her to be got into the gut; that with some difficulty they landed some fresh provisions by means of the small boat; the candles, water, and beer they could not land; but as there were several chests of candles remaining, and a sufficient quantity of water, there could be no real want for some time.

Soon after this, a violent storm happened at SW and I was informed that Admiral Boscawen had mentioned to the Admiralty that it was the greatest storm that had been known by the oldest person on board his ship; I therefore excepted a still more formidable account from Mr Jessop of its effects upon the lighthouse.

But no account being received in course of the post, I wrote to him on the 21st February, desiring that, as soon as possible, inquiry might be made into the state of the house; as likewise whether it has more motion with the wind at E or at S.W., and whether they were sensible of the seas striking the cornice.

To this I received an answer, March 2nd, that Smart and Bowden had been off the 29th February to land stores; that they stayed at the house two hours and viewed it all over carefully, inside and out; but could not discover any of the mortar started, nor the joints anyways cracked; and that all the damage sustained by the last storm was that the electrical strap, which went from the sink pipe down to the rock, was washed away; the glass of the lanthorn was all sound, the pane excepted that was before mentioned.

Apart from Smeaton's own pride in his work, the elderly Jessop had something to remember in the remaining years of his life, for he had been a remarkably skilled and hard-working ally to both Rudyerd and Smeaton. His achievements were also honoured as he was acknowledged as one of the most devoted shipwright/quartermen the Plymouth Dockyard had ever seen; He died in 1761.

The youngest man employed at the lighthouse in 1759 was a John Hatherley, and in a letter written by him after a violent storm we read:

> The house did shake as if a man had been up in a great tree.
> The old men were frightened almost out of their lives, wishing they had never seen the place, and cursing those that first persuaded them to go there.
> The fear seized them in the back, but rubbing them with oil and turpentine gave them relief.

Smeaton often thought about "his" lightkeepers while at home in Yorkshire, but especially during periods of bad weather.

Although he was involved with less adventurous work, he did keep in touch with his "family" in Plymouth.

On a visit in 1761 for Jessop's funeral, he took a boat out to his tower and found it clean and in good order but with its lower half covered with marine vegetation and limpets which gave the appearance that the lighthouse was just a natural growth on the rock itself. Smeaton wrote:

> The year 1762 was ushered in with stormy weather and indeed produced a tempest of the first magnitude, the rage of which was so great that one of those who had been used to predict its downfall, was heard to say, "If the Eddystone lighthouse is now standing, it will stand till the day of judgement!" and in reality, from this time its existence has been so entirely laid out of men's minds, that in the greatest storms, no inquiry has been made concerning it.

Witness the storm in which the Halsewell, Indiaman, was lost! And though the public papers were full of immense damages done by it at Plymouth and in the Sound (in particular a ship in the harbour, that broke loose and beat down a house, will be very well remembered), yet not a single word was said about the Eddystone Lighthouse.

Mr Richardson, though a very sound hardy mason, was not a man conversant in literary descriptions; the pen was therefore taken up on this occasion by my very valuable friend, Dr John Mudge, who gave me two letters upon the subject of this storm; and which coming warm from the heart, so much exceed any thing I can compose, that I cannot do better than insert them.

PLYMOUTH, FRIDAY 15TH JAN 1762.

Dear Sir, Accept my most sincere congratulations on the safety of the Eddystone; as well from the danger that has threatened it, as that I think the dreadful storm it has withstood will for ever remove any anxiety about its being injured in future, by the united force of the wind and sea.

It blew very hard the beginning of last Monday night, but increased with incredible fury towards Tuesday morning; when, about six, partly from long southerly winds, but principally by its concurring with the spring tides, it afforded the most horrible scene of devastation.

This tide rose full two feet higher than when the Victory was lost, and when the fish-house was carried away; or than was ever known in the memory of the oldest man living.

The seas came in bodily over the Barbican wall; but one wave with such irresistible violence, that it swept away the parapet below its foundation; and in its return carried off five people then upon it, all of whom were drowned.

The new Lammy Pier was swept clean away.

Prodigious losses have been sustained by the shopkeepers on the quays; as in some of the shops near the Barbican, the water was as high as their counters: and the quays themselves are in so ruinous a condition and so much of them carried away, that had the gale continued until the next tide, it is highly probable some of them would have been wholly swept away, and the houses with them.

In the midst of this confusion there were no less than six large merchant ships wrecked in the very harbour, some of which were bent to pieces, but all lost, and this in the short space of three hundred yards, betwixt Treat's Hill and Bear Head.

There were nine men-of-war in the Sound, several of which were constantly firing signal guns of distress.

Some cut away one, others two, another three and one lost all her masts and bowsprit.

Three of them only escaped with all their masts standing; one of which to avoid immediate destruction on the south side of Mount Batten, was, by the great dexterity of the pilot, brought in within the Fisher's Nose, and run ashore under the Lammy; but this was when the ebb had made considerably; so that she was safely got off the next tide.

But it exhibited a very uncommon appearance; as I believe it was the first time ever a man-of-war was seen in that place.

In the Hamoaze the men-of-war were all this while firing signals of distress and some ran foul of each other.

The sea came over the dock gates into the dock where the Magnanime was; but as there did not come in enough to float her, it did no considerable damage.

The new dock was likewise filled.

I will only mention one circumstance more to give you some idea of the extreme agitation of the sea, the froth of it flew clean over the walls of the Garrison, and in such quantity, that in one place a sentinel was obliged to quit his post.

In the midst of all this horror and confusion, my friend may be assured that I was not insensible to his honour and credit; yet in spite of the high opinion and confidence I had of his judgement and abilities, I could not but feel the utmost anxiety for the fate of the Eddystone; and I believe poor Richardson was not a little uneasy.

Several times a day I swept with my telescope, from the Garrison, as near as I could imagine the line of the horizon; but it was so extremely black, fretful, and hazy, that nothing could be seen; and I was obliged to go to bed that night with a mortifying uncertainty: but the next morning early I had great joy to see that the gilded ball had triumphed over the fury of the storm and such a one as before I had not conception of.

I saw the whole so distinctly from the bottom to the top, that I could be very sure the lanthorn had suffered nothing.

It is my most steady belief, as well as everybody's here, that its inhabitants are rather more secure in a storm, under the united force of wind and water, than we are in our houses from the former only.

I received the above letter in Yorkshire where we had had very stormy weather; the account of my friend was therefore equally agreeable and astonishing: yet notwithstanding his letter announced the general safety of the building, and that nothing very bad could have happened, even to the lanthorn, I could not conceive that this expression, the lanthorn had suffered nothing, could be strictly and literally true; I therefore wrote in return desiring he would send me a circumstantial account of the damages, after the house had been visited.

The following is an extract of the second letter sent to Smeaton from Plymouth, dated 24 January 1762:

The boat went off with an intention to land on Friday se'nnight; but there was so great a sea, and the wind being too much to the south, they desisted till the next day, when the wind being a point to the north of the west, and better weather, they got near the house, landed their things, and had a conversation with the people.

Smart tells me that the ladder was carried away; and some small matter of putty, which was cracked by last summer's heat, was washed off from the lanthorn.

This was all that the violence of the sea had effected; that there was not so much as a single pane of glass broken.

That the lanthorn was secured by that perfection of ornament, the cornice; which, when the sea rose to the top of the house, blanched it off like a sheet. They insisted on it that the sea went bodily over the top, for that it came in through the vents of the ball, and filled the sockets of the candlesticks. They were asked whether they had been under any uneasiness; they said, not in the least, as the house had not been affected by it in any other way than they had before experienced.

The storm in the evening of Monday began at the SE and they then felt very sensibly a tremor from every stroke of the sea, so that while it continued there to act upon the natural cavern of the rock, it gave them some uneasiness, which, though they now believed unnecessary, yet they could not help wishing it was filled up.

Now though I look upon this as a proof that no storm will affect the house, as it is a plain smooth surface, and though a less sea has a greater influence on the rock at low water, than a mighty one has upon the house itself; yet I must say that I concur with them in wishing it was done; and that for two reasons.

One is, that I should be glad to see every the least appearance of defect removed; and the other, that I should hope it would give me the chance of seeing my dear friend once more here.

In earnest I wish you would complete the rock too as well as the house; for so many vibratory strokes can do it no service.

You seem to have been greatly affected by the little I have said of the horror of this storm; but, believe me, it cannot give you even a tolerable idea of it.

It has upon a moderate computation done about £80,000 worth of damage in the harbour and Sound, and I cannot help repeating again that you may for ever rid yourself of an uneasy thought of the house, as to its danger from wind and sea.

Visitors to the Eddystone were many, as the structure projected a romantic and wondrous image. They included Sir Joshua Reynolds, Dr Johnson and other celebrities of the day.

Most of the keepers enjoyed their existence at the rock, but for one poor soul it seemed to have taken over his whole life.

In a true story told to Smeaton on a visit in 1777, he learned of one man who liked the lighthouse so much that for two years he spent every day there, not even taking entitled shore leave.

He had already worked at the Eddystone for 14 years and was in no hurry to go anywhere, but his colleagues insisted that he took a break and so reluctantly he went ashore.

However, the experience proved catastrophic for the quiet and sober fellow, as on arrival in Plymouth he went straight into an ale house where he remained, intoxicated with liquor, for the entire month of his leave.

On returning to the lighthouse, he had to be first carried to the boat, still in a drunken stupor (although this was a common event for most returning keepers), then pulled up into the tower. Unfortunately, his colleagues could do little for him, and during the next three days his state of health worsened until he died.

Smeaton visited his lighthouse for the last time in 1787. It had taken the Yorkshireman three-and-a-half years of his life to create and build a lighthouse on the infamous reef. It has been estimated that his payment for the undertaking was a modest two guineas for a full day's work, which amounted to less than £2,000 on completion of the tower, though he was known for his indifference to money matters. His endearing character was tested to the full when at an influential London gathering he turned down a lucrative offer to work for Catherine the Great in Russia, from the Princess Dashkoff who was attending.

Her parting words to John Smeaton were overheard as these:

> Sir, I honour you, You may have your equal in abilities, perhaps; but in character you stand alone. The English minister Sir Robert Walpole was mistaken and my Sovereign has this misfortune to find one man who has NOT his price.

Smeaton's tower when studied in detail gives the impression of a single stone mass rising from the rocky reef, so closely are the dovetailed granite blocks married together.

The internal arrangements greatly resemble those of all lighthouses, being composed of a kitchen, two store rooms, a bedroom and a lantern.

Various words, letters and figures were sunk into the moorstone of the lighthouse with the point of a sharpened pick.

On the first stone of the foundation is inscribed "1757" and over the entry door it says "1758".

Round the upper store room, on the course under the ceiling, is this inscription:

Except the lord build the house they labour in vain that build it.
Psalm cxxvii

Over the fourth window, on the outside of the dwelling room, or kitchen, is inscribed "1759". Upon the outward faces of the octagon basement of the lantern door are marked NE, SE, S, SW, W and NW and on the last stone set, over the door of the lantern on the east side, it says "24th Augt 1759. Laus Deo".

In a letter from Mr Noyes Jr to J Smeaton we can appreciate the modesty the Yorkshireman possessed, as it read:

With regard to your intended inscription on the entry door, Mr Weston thinks that there should be an addition of your name, as "Built with stone 1758, John Smeaton, Architect".

Smeaton felt it unnecessary to add this. Some of the names of the builders who helped Smeaton in his triumph are found in a few of the old publications and letters of the time and include Roger Cornthwaite, mason, John Watt, painter/glazier, and John Dolland, glazier.

The first keepers to serve in Smeaton's tower were Henry Edwards, Henry Carter and John Hatherley who had been brought in as a replacement for John Michell who had refused to set foot on the Eddystone after his acceptance of duty.

Stores for the keepers continued to be a vital requirement and in one shipment of provisions sent to the Eddystone Lighthouse in October 1759 by the proprietors, as winter stock, we find the following items:

Coals, in half hogshead
cask 64 bushels,
Water-No16,
Lamp oil-No 2,
Salted beef 2 cwt,
Salted pork 1 cwt,
Large candles 10 chests,

Small candles 1 chest,
Biscuit 3 cwt,
Boiling pease, 2 bushels,
Oatmeal, 2 bushels,
For six months supply.

Although it may be hard to understand why anyone should endure life as a lighthouse keeper, it must be remembered that so long as each man accepted his colleagues, a relaxed and trusting environment could be achieved.

Time spent in the structure could be offset with a walk around the lantern gallery and in calm fine weather sitting on the rock ledge with a fishing rod in hand. Activities enjoyed by the keepers ranged from reading, playing cards, draughts, bagatelle, fretwork and picture-frame making to building models of ships and lighthouses.

The Eddystone in the late 1700s
The author's collection

So for men who wanted such a livelihood, it was a pleasurable existence.

However, the winter months were always the most difficult as the keepers would often be confined within the grey walls of the tower throughout their tour of duty.

It was during those long dark days that the men needed to keep their sanity and retain their constitution. The ocean throughout the stormy period of winter would continually pound against the structure of the lighthouse hour after hour, while the cold could penetrate the safe interior and comfort of the kitchen. With the screaming wind wrapping itself around the lighthouse walls outside, shaking its very foundation, the men could only sit it out, the noise making conversation impossible. It was also accepted that the terrible winter storms could pose the biggest threat and test the lighthouse structure to the full.

A situation soon arose which caused great fear to the keepers inside the building.

During a night of heavy seas and increasing gales the main doorway was heard to explode as if a demon had entered the building.

The keepers peered down from the stairwell to see the crashing waves climbing up towards them and a clear opening to the boiling ocean outside.

The heavy door had been torn away from its iron bolts and hinges as if a great force had opened it from within the tower itself.

Later the engineers would explain that this had been caused by pneumatic action and sudden back draught created by the alternating pressure from the mountainous wave motion.

Although the keepers lived monotonous lives when on duty, Smeaton mentioned an instance when a cobbler engaged himself as a lamplighter at the Eddystone.

During the passage to the rocks, the coxswain of the boat asked: "How is it, Master Jacob, that you are going to shut yourself up there, when ashore you could earn half-a-crown or three shillings a day, while as a light keeper you will only receive ten shillings a week?" Jacob answered: "Every man to his liking, I was always fond of independence."

The remark is not without truth, though it may appear strange when applied to a life of seclusion.

It was said that to confine a man by force under such conditions would seem almost a legal barbarity; but from the moment the choice was voluntary, and the isolation was a favour instead of a punishment, the gloomy dungeon would be robbed of half its rigour because there was no longer any feeling of captivity.

Smeaton's activities covered a very wide field including the building of water mills, bridges, harbours and one further lighthouse at Spurn Head.

The Eddystone Lighthouse shows us his ingenuity and imagination at work, especially in the complex system of stone dovetailing he employed for fixing the courses of masonry together.

Cramps and joggles had been used by classical and medieval builders of churches and important historical buildings. Smeaton was aware of that and able to use his knowledge to solve the problems he faced during the construction of his stone lighthouse.

In his diary on 17 August 1757 he wrote:

> I should like to say here that one of my main aims has been to construct a tower whose every part should be strong in direct proportion to the stress it was likely to bear.
>
> For it was eternally dinned into my ears that A Building of STONE upon the Eddystone would certainly be swept away.

He was a unique individual and described by a contemporary as such:

> His style and language had a particular and in some degree a provincial way of expressing himself and conveying ideas, both in speaking and in writing; a way which was very exact and expressive, though his diction was far from what might be called classical or elegant.

Smeaton's lighthouse cost £16,000 to build and it was without doubt the finest in the world. It was said that you could see the light with the naked eye from at least five miles away – and for a time that was acceptable.

Smeaton was a satisfied man, his tower had become his greatest achievement and he had also learned so much about a way of life that was alien to him beforehand.

He liked talking to the keepers and enjoyed hearing their stories, spending many days at the lighthouse whenever he could.

Due to his keen interest in their lifestyle, he soon undertook responsibility for improving their conditions, especially with an important administrative innovation which dramatically improved the provisioning of all lighthouses.

It had often been reported that keepers were forced to eat the lantern's candles when their food ran out. Sometimes no relief was possible due to bad weather, so food would become scarce until the next boat arrived. During the winter months it was not uncommon for the delay to last several weeks, causing great hardship for the keepers.

Provisions had traditionally been basic and never generous. Smeaton devised a system where every six months, the owners would stock up the lighthouse with food. Each keeper would then pay for his own requirements, at the wholesale price, so there could be no food shortage as each man spent what he wanted on his daily needs.

The system soon became standard practice throughout the lighthouse service.

During Smeaton's last visit to his lighthouse, on 3 August 1787, he wrote in his report:

> My visit to the house was on the 3rd August 1787 and I then had the satisfaction to find both stone and iron so very nearly in the same state, as I had found and reported it 21 years ago, in the year 1766.

At 63, Smeaton was writing his memoirs. He would die five years later in 1792 at his birthplace, Austhorpe Lodge in Yorkshire. On his tomb, the inscription reads:

> Sacred to the Memory of JOHN SMEATON, F.R.S.
> A man whom God had endowed with the most extraordinary abilities, which he indefatigably

exerted for the benefit of mankind in works of SCIENCE AND PHILOSOPHICAL RESEARCH; More especially as an Engineer and Mechanic. His principal work, the Eddystone Lighthouse, erected on a rock in the open sea (where one had been washed away by the violence of a storm, and another had been consumed by the rage of fire), secure in its own stability, and the wise precautions for its safety, seems not unlikely to convey to distant ages, as it does to every nation of the Globe, the name of its constructor.

Smeaton will be remembered forever. He once said that "the abilities of the individual are a debt due to the common stock of public well-being". During the last years of Smeaton's life, he met fellow engineers at the Queens Head Tavern in Holborn, London, where they discussed bridge-building techniques, canal making and other engineering projects. The Smeaton Society as it was then known discontinued its meetings on the death of their founder, but within a short time the body of men gathered once more, soon to become

SMEATON'S SPURN HEAD LIGHTHOUSE
The author's collection

known as the Institution of Civil Engineers.

Smeaton's good manners and devotion to duty were principles that future engineers would embrace and respect; indeed no better example of that was offered than by the railway engineer Robert Stephenson, who said of him in 1858:

> Smeaton is the greatest philosopher in our profession this country has yet produced. He was indeed a great man, possessing a truly Baconian mind, for he was an incessant experimenter. The principles of mechanics were never so clearly exhibited as in his writings, more especially with regard to resistance, gravity, the power of water and wind to turn mills, and so on.
>
> His mind was as clear as crystal, and his demonstrations are to be found mathematically conclusive.
>
> To this day there are no writings so valuable as his in the highest walks of scientific engineering; and when young men ask me, as they frequently do, what they should read I invariably say "Go to Smeaton's philosophical papers; read them, master them thoroughly, and nothing will be of greater service to you".

Smeaton, like the beacon he erected in the open sea, shines in solitary splendour above the technological sterility of 18th-century Britain, lighting the way to the wonders of the 19th.

It is therefore a fitting tribute that in creating his masterpiece, which so perfectly reflected the ideas of labour, service and beauty, he happened also to build a lasting personal memorial to everything he believed in and loved.

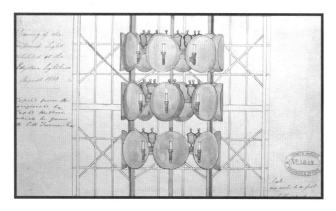

THE LIGHTING SYSTEM IN 1810
BY KIND PERMISSION OF THE CORPORATION OF TRINITY HOUSE

This, you might think, is where our story ends, but no, not just yet, because the Eddystone Reef would once again remind us of the great power of the ocean.

The British Industrial Revolution was about to arrive; in Smeaton's lighthouse, its 24 candles were becoming old-fashioned and inadequate and they would be lit for the very last time in 1807.

Experiments with different lighting systems over the next three years were made and by 10 September 1810, oil lamps were burning at the Eddystone.

Progress was casting its hand over the water, and in France Augustin Jean Fresnel, 22, was to become another great pioneer and inventor of a truly remarkable optical lens.

Fresnel was born in Normandy on 10 May 1788 and was also a prolific experimenter, although his subject was optical science.

He was a modest, quiet individual who was to receive very little recognition during his lifetime. It was not until after his death in 1827 that his work was noticed and although no patent or copyright was ever credited to Fresnel, his invention, a pioneering glass lens, would prove to be of the greatest importance to all seafarers.

Another important figure who advanced lighthouse technology was the Swiss engineer Ami Argand. He, after many years of hard work, perfected a new type of oil lamp and was credited with having created the first circular wick which produced its own air current inside a cylindrical glass funnel.

Furthering that innovation, the French lighthouse engineer Teulère added a parabolic reflector to the system which gathered together the rays of the unprecedentedly bright lamp and projected them forward in a beam for 13 miles.

Lighthouses were to develop greatly during the next 100 years, as more technology became available to the service.

Smeaton's tallow candles burnt at three to four pounds an hour, at a cost of about 1s 6¾d an hour. Financial restraints were becoming important in the lighthouse business and through the development of oil lamps, which consisted of small containers filled with spermaceti (whale) oil or colza oil, with either a fixed or floating wick, a change in lighting sources was under way.

Until the early 1800s, the Eddystone light produced between 20 and 67 candlepower; by 1810 the catoptric reflectors raised it to approximately 1,000 candles. By 1845 the revolving French dioptric lens was producing 3,000 candles, and in 1872 it was 7,000.

Gas was also used at some land lighthouses during the 1900s but had little success. Petroleum or kerosene soon lost out to the incandescent lamps which vapourised the oil by burning it on a mantle, which then produced a very bright white light.

Electricity now provides the power for light almost everywhere but was first used with arc lamps, although they have recently been succeeded by powerful xenon discharge units which produce light infinitely brighter than that of any previous system.

At the Eddystone Lighthouse, then under the sole ownership of Trinity House, the lantern would be supplied with parabolic reflectors of silvered copper, given a dioptric centre in 1845.

Painting the outside of the lighthouse for improved visibility during the day was undertaken many times. Different ideas and colours were considered before the tower was eventually covered in alternate bands of red and white horizontal stripes.

The arrangement had a striking effect many miles from the lighthouse and so was used as a clear ship's mark during daylight.

The Eddystone continued to endure the immense power of the sea and on many occasions would be completely overwhelmed by the mountainous waves heaving against it.

A lightkeeper's log, dated November 1824, reads:

> The sea was tremendous, and broke with such violence on the top and around the building as to demolish in an instant five panes of the lantern glass and sixteen cylinder glasses the former of which is of unusual thickness.
>
> The house shook with so much violence as to occasion considerable motion of the cylinder glasses fixed in the lamps and at times the whole building appeared to jump as if resting on an elastic body.

THE EDDYSTONE LANTERN OF 1810
BY KIND PERMISSION OF THE CORPORATION OF TRINITY HOUSE

> The water came from the top of the building in such quantities that we were overwhelmed and the sea made a breach from the top of the house to the bottom.

The weather continued to affect every aspect of the keepers' working environment and once again just servicing the lighthouse with its provisions was an enormous task for the store boat's crew.

In his report for October and November 1807, the captain of the supply vessel wrote:

> SATURDAY 17TH OCTOBER 1807
> Went out in the morning at Noon, Landed 2 Hampers of greens and Potatoes and Return at Night.

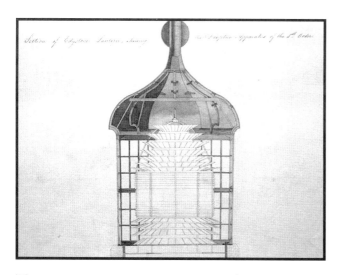

THE DIOPTRIC APPARATUS OF THE 1ST ORDER
BY KIND PERMISSION OF THE CORPORATION OF TRINITY HOUSE

MONDAY 9TH NOVEMBER
Went out 4 AM at one mile without the Ramhead and Returned as Gale came on from the SW, returned 2 Hampers with greens and Potatoes.

FRIDAY 13TH NOVEMBER
Went out 3 AM Light airs to the Northward at 5 AM. Run out a Brest of the Ramhead very squally from the NNE. hauled down the Foresail, hauled up the Jack of the Mainsail. Hove to with her head to the Eastward at 7 AM. Fresh wind Bore up for the Stone Run and at 3 miles to the SW of the Ramhead, Strong wind and a great swell found it impossible to Land at 8 AM. Tacked to Eastward at PM. Returned off The Lamery and Moored – Leaving on board 2 hampers, Greens and Potatoes.

SATURDAY 14TH NOVEMBER
Went out 1/2 Past 5 AM. Light airs from the Northward at 1/2 Past 8 AM Edystone. Bearing SW and W at 5 or 6 Miles. Wind came at SE. Strong Gale and a great sea. We were obliged to Reef our Sails. Found it impossible to Land at 3 PM. Returned to our moorings in the Pool. 2 hampers, with greens and Potatoes on Board.

WEDNESDAY 18TH NOVEMBER
Went out at 7 AM. Light Breeze at NW at PM landed 2 hampers, Greens and Potatoes at the Edystone. Received 3 empty water Casks and 3 empty Candle chests. At 4 PM Returned at the moorings.

MONDAY 30TH NOVEMBER
Went out at 6 AM. Little wind as of NNW and NE. Weather at 11 AM. Landed 2 full Chests of Candles, 1 Bag of Turnips and 1 Bag of Vegetables at the Edystone. Received 1 Empty Water Cask. At 7 PM Little Wind as of NE. Came to Anchor off Cawsand Bay at 3 AM. As of 1st December wayed anchor from Cawsand Bay AT 6 AM Arrived to our Moorings.
Left the People in good Health.

On 10 October 1810, new regulations improved the working conditions of those at the Eddystone Lighthouse. In a letter to the Plymouth agent we read:

The Court have made the following Regulation in Respect to the Tour of Duty, viz -
That Three of the Four Keepers shall be constantly in the Light House, and One onshore, And that each be on shore One month in Rotation.
They have also resolved,
That each Keeper shall be allowed One Quart of good Table Beer daily, And Tea, Sugar and Butter in the following Proportions Viz -
3/4 lb Tea
2 lb Sugar
4 lb Butter
To each Keeper – Per Month.
That the Boat be sent off once every Fortnight instead of Once a Month as heretofore. And it being the Wish of the Board that the Keepers be supplied with fresh Provisions as often as possible. Also, that a supply of Fresh Provisions be sent whenever the Boat goes off to the Rock.

In the following year, further improvements were implemented through the Trinity House Board and the keepers' allowance included 3/4lb of sugar per man per week, 4oz of tea and 1lb of cheese. A keeper's annual salary in 1811 was £30.

Although shipwrecks were a distant memory at the Eddystone, shipping disasters continued.
In the Lloyds Registers for 1854 to 1897, we find that nearly 50,000 vessels had perished.

DRAWING SHOWING THE DAMAGED ROCK
BY KIND PERMISSION OF THE CORPORATION OF TRINITY HOUSE

However, The Eddystone Lighthouse had its own problem, a major crisis which would seal the fate of the old building.

In an 1818 report Scottish engineer Robert Stevenson wrote:

> The house seems to be in a very good state of repair and does not appear to have sustained any injury by the lapse of time. The joints are full of cement and the stones exhibit little appearance of decay... As to the rock on which the tower stood; It is shaken all through, and dips at a considerable angle and being undermined for several feet it has rather an alarming appearance. Were I connected with the charge of this highly important building, I should not feel very easy in my mind for its safety.

Engineers had for some time observed that a crack in the rock beneath the tower's foundations had become bigger, due to the sea's force undermining the stone. In 1877 a decision was taken by Trinity House to build a new structure, so Smeaton's lighthouse would become dark on 3 February 1881.

The old tower remained a solid and secure building, but it did seem inevitable that at some point especially during violent storms, the heavy column of stone might just topple over into the sea. It had been decided purely on safety grounds that another lighthouse would have to be erected as soon as possible to avert a disaster.

Smeaton's great achievement would not be forgotten. It was re-erected on Plymouth Hoe, in the same spot where the old Trinity House Day Mark had been sited, known locally as Drake's Beacon. It was gratifying then that the

THE RED AND WHITE BANDED LIGHTHOUSE
THE AUTHOR'S COLLECTION

wonderful building would still be of use as an unlit day mark to all local boatmen.

And so another chapter closes on the story of the Eddystone. History had shown that each lighthouse built on the rocky outcrop had been better than its predecessor. New times brought different ideas and values; the Victorian era was colourful and exciting, while the industrial revolution provided immense development in the working environment.

Civil engineers were creating magnificent buildings throughout the country, and advanced technology allowed for a quality never before seen in the work produced. The Eddystone reef, too, would also share in the rapidly developing construction industry.

A proposal to erect another lighthouse on the rocks had been accepted by Trinity House. The structure would be the biggest of all the towers which had stood there, although on a different site to its predecessors.

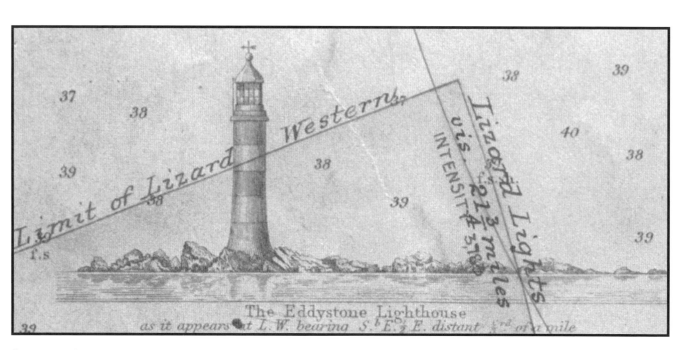

SMEATON'S TOWER WAITING TO BE REMOVED
BY KIND PERMISSION OF THE CORPORATION OF TRINITY HOUSE

SMEATON'S STUMP AT THE EDDYSTONE WITH ITS ORIGINAL ENTRANCE FILLED WITH CONCRETE
PHOTOGRAPH TAKEN BY THE AUTHOR

DOUGLASS'S DESTINY

IT WOULD be left to another respected civil engineer to build the biggest of all the Eddystone lighthouses. James Douglass was born on 16 October 1826 at Bow in Middlesex, although the Douglass family were originally from Northumbria.

His father Nicholas was working for the engineering firm of Hunter & English and was establishing himself as a talented individual.

However, in 1838, Nicholas embarked on a risky business venture with another man, working on the River Thames in a project which combined both his ship-building and engineering skills. Unfortunately, the deal failed sensationally with the sudden withdrawal of his partner and the unforeseen crisis caused him major financial difficulties which resulted in the near ruination of the Douglass family.

James was then just 12 and lived with his aunt in Blaydon-on-Tyne, where he enjoyed a private education. But with the mounting difficulties back at home, it was uncertain whether the privileged schooling could continue and so James returned to London at the end of term.

His mother was never a healthy woman and the unhappy state of affairs caused her even greater anxiety. However, James was a kindhearted boy and cared for her with loving tenderness, and he also looked after the rest of the family as best he could, while his father sought new employment.

The headmaster of James's school graciously waived the boy's fees, which allowed him to continue his studies there.

Luckily the family troubles improved when Nicholas found work with Trinity House, where he became a construction engineer for the corporation in 1839. His new position changed the lives of the Douglass family and an adventurous lifestyle awaited them.

James and his brother William would soon become nomadic and follow their parents around the country's coastal extremities. Lighthouse construction had become Nicholas's role in life and his daily responsibility, which meant a great deal to him. The boys, too, began their own special journey into adolescence and remarkable experiences, something that few of their age could ever have had the opportunity to discover.

Nicholas's employment brought him many accolades as a respected engineer. He enjoyed

PORTRAIT OF SIR JAMES DOUGLASS
BY KIND PERMISSION OF THE CORPORATION OF TRINITY HOUSE

the work and the challenges of the structures he was asked to build. Normally each job would take him a year to complete and the family were constantly moving around, which meant the boys were unable to make close friends. Their temporary homes were in Cardiff, on Flatholm Island, Newton near Bridgend, Tenby and at Land's End, which although unsettling to the teenagers provided James and William with useful experiences.

Even at a young age, they could swim, row and fish with great confidence and their raw education made them aware of the world about them. Normal schooling was sometimes possible but much of it was left up to their parents. Mrs Douglass was considered prudent and capable, being a wise counsellor and loving guide to her sons. However, while living in Newton, Wales, both children became weekly boarders under the tuition of the Rev J E Jones, who was the Unitarian Minister of Bridgend and had a brilliant mathematical mind.

It appears the Rev Jones was an inspiration to James and focused the boy's thoughts to decide on a direction in life and the sort of employment he should consider.

An old friend from these school days, a Mr Price Williams, remembered James:

> I must state that what impressed me most was his splendid temper, his lovable nature, his earnest application to his studies, and the marked ability he showed even then. He was, as I am sure Mr Jones would have testified were he alive, one of his best, if not the very best of his pupils. James often admitted to me that the training he got at Mr Jones' school was of the greatest service to him in his professional career.

When James left school he wanted nothing more than to follow in his father's footsteps and become an engineer. So Nicholas helped his son obtain an engineering apprenticeship at his old firm of Hunter & English.

Immediately it was obvious to everyone that the youngster was naturally gifted. The boy had much enthusiasm for the tasks set before him and besides his engineering abilities he would often be found drawing quality mechanical studies.

His apprenticeship continued successfully and he moved on to another company,

Seaward & Capel, based on the Isle of Dogs, where he remained until 1847.

Brother William had also accepted an engineering apprenticeship at R Stephenson & Company in Newcastle-on-Tyne, but was soon to assist in his father's new appointment on the Isles of Scilly.

Nicholas Douglass had proven to be a remarkable engineer with Trinity House and was building a lighthouse on the Bishop Rock, off the Scilly Isles, at a place where in 1703 many warships of the British Squadron had been lost with 1,800 crew men. Their commander, Sir Cloudesley Shovel, survived the tragedy and was washed ashore alive, only to be murdered by the local wreckers. So the new lighthouse, designed by James Walker at a cost of £12,000, was an important assignment for Nicholas, who with his youngest son William undertook the project with immense pride, beginning in 1847. The lighthouse was an iron screw pile erection which would stand 80 feet tall.

James Douglass worked in London, but he too was encouraged to join his father and brother, being offered the post of Assistant Resident Engineer. Remarkably, the whole Douglass family were once more united in working on the same construction, the Bishop Rock Lighthouse. They were special days for the three men, each bringing to the project individual talents and experiences. The construction workforce acknowledged their unique pedigree and immediately warmed to the Douglass trio.

During rest breaks it was common for all the workers to sit down with their bosses and exchange stories and adventures. James would often play his flute while Nicholas would tell the builders of his sons' early life. In one such story retold to the gathering he reminisced:

> At the age of two years, James was seen running over a plank of wood, laid across at a giddy height, many feet in the air. The workmen were about to shout to the boy to go back, but I ordered them to be silent and so we all watched as the toddler carried on over the plank, where he reached for the safety of my arms, without a care in his eyes.

Life for the Douglasses during the building of the Bishop Rock was a very pleasant one and Nicholas, in his 50s, felt proud of his two boys' obvious skill and abilities.

It was then that James Douglass acquired the nickname of "Cap'n Jim". He was tall and good-looking and embarked on a relationship with a local girl, Mary Tregarthen, who was the second daughter of Captain James Tregarthen, a shipowner in St Mary's (the main port on the Isles of Scilly) and brother of the Trinity House agent there.

The construction work continued, and by the end of 1849 the building was complete, except for its lighting apparatus. However, on 5 February in the following year of 1850, a terrible storm lashed at the new building and destroyed every piece of the structure. Undaunted, the Douglass trio started to rebuild their lighthouse, but this time the designer James Walker would follow Smeaton's example and that of the Eddystone.

As the new work progressed and the foundation stone was laid, James began to feel he had done all he could and looked for a new challenge, away from his close family ties.

Whether he felt trapped or simply stifled by the situation is unclear, but he believed a complete change would benefit him and so during the winter of 1853 he severed his association with Trinity House and moved from Scilly to Newcastle-on-Tyne, where he began work with R J & R Laycocks, a railway carriage works in Stella.

However, his new-found freedom proved unsatisfying as he missed his old life at the Bishop and especially his girlfriend. Inevitably, during the early part of 1854, he returned to the Scillies and on 6 July married his sweetheart, Mary.

He was reinstated by Trinity House and was once again helping his father and brother in the final construction of the Bishop Rock Lighthouse. Within the year, James was offered his first solo appointment, that of Resident Engineer, charged with building the Smalls Lighthouse off the coast of Wales.

Now it would be James's turn to show his skills as an engineer and so, with his new wife beside him, he left the Scilly Isles for Wales.

Douglass enjoyed the new challenge set before him and soon began to gain the respect needed from his workers, so much so that one fellow, a Sam Dimond, who was a stone mason and rhymester, wrote a ballad about his worthy boss. An extract reads:

Our master cheers our spirits up;
he is a gallant man;
The first wherever danger is,
he always leads the van.

The words were justified, as James Douglass proved to be a good leader, someone who, like Smeaton, took an interest in the welfare of his employees.

His building successes continued and, after completion of The Smalls Lighthouse six years later, he was sent back to the West Country to build the Wolf Rock Lighthouse. He would eventually design 20 lighthouses for Trinity House and invent the helically framed lantern.

However, his acknowledged masterpiece came with the construction of the new Eddystone Lighthouse, which he started in 1878. For that single undertaking, he was honoured with a knighthood for his services "to engineering and the humanitarian needs of shipping".

In August 1877 Douglass had already visited Plymouth and met with a section of the British Association. He had told them that their lighthouse, built by Smeaton, was doomed to collapse in the very near future and that as Resident Engineer he would build another lighthouse on the Eddystone. Thomas Edmond would act as his Superintendent in charge of construction, while his son William Tregarthen would be appointed Assistant Engineer. The new building was needed because a portion of the gneiss rock below Smeaton's tower had been undermined, due to the lighthouse being shaken continuously by the heavy seas. Also, it was common knowledge that during stormy weather the mountainous waves rose above the lantern itself and eclipsed the light, rendering it useless or altering its character.

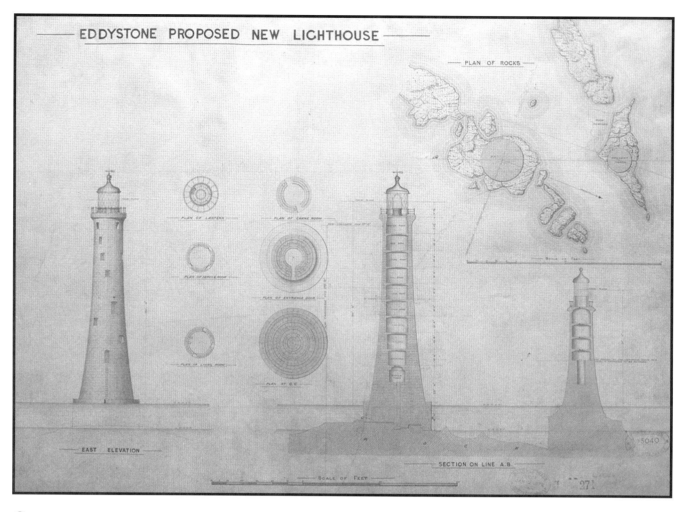

ORIGINAL DRAWING FOR THE PROPOSED NEW LIGHTHOUSE
BY KIND PERMISSION OF THE CORPORATION OF TRINITY HOUSE

In previous years the lighthouse "character" (its individual and distinctive lighting identification signal) seemed of little importance to the designers, due to the small number of coastal lights around the British Isles. However, because more ships were sailing the ocean, a variety of lights at night were always visible to the mariner, being perhaps from other vessels in the Channel or from distant shore lights. So individually recognised lighting identification, especially from lighthouses, was an absolute necessity.

Douglass would build his 120-foot tower away from the site of Smeaton's structure, in the body of the reef mass itself, with the foundations being laid below the level of low-water spring tides. He estimated the cost would be £78,000, which proved a lot less than other tenders submitted. Because of the financial difference, Trinity House asked him to build the lighthouse.

Being nearly twice as tall as Smeaton's tower, the new building would be formidable and again would be built in stone.

The many advances in modern construction practices and design techniques ensured that the Douglass lighthouse would be a massive improvement on its famous predecessor and be even stronger, able to withstand anything the forces of nature could throw at it.

At 52, Cap'n Jim had already lived a full life and was regarded as a practical man and a courageous leader.

John Fulford Owen, an Elder Brother of Trinity House, once spoke of James Douglass as being "not only an engineer, but a blacksmith, a carpenter and a mason, in his own person, as well as a seaman". He was a tall man of immense stature, with a thick black beard and matching side whiskers. His appearance and standing in society seemed to epitomise the eminent Victorian gentleman.

He was seen by outsiders as a strict authoritarian, but in reality preferred to live a quiet and unconventional life, being most comfortable with the working-class people around him and finding value in every experience he had. In leadership on the Eddystone he would shine and once more gain respect from his new team, insisting on working with his men, never leaving their side in times of crisis. His reputation was that of being a man's man, and this contributed still further to the high standing he was held in by those he worked with.

James Douglass was also well aware of his responsibilities to his workforce, doing all he could to ease their burden. If he could find ways of making their job easier, he would introduce new tools and working practices.

On 17 July 1878, James and an executive party landed for the first time on the Eddystone reef, just a few yards away from the tower Smeaton had built 119 years earlier.

The weather was favourable and a large portion of the area was uncovered by low water, so a start was made on the initial work. The preparation of the new site would take nearly a year, as the hard gneiss rock required much work and had to be chiselled and drilled. At the centre of the chosen rock site the workmen began levelling the hard surface in benches and a two-foot well hole was formed for the central crane.

A platform was raised 10 feet above the low-water spring tides which considerably facilitated the progress during the earlier stages of the working schedule, as the men could then land with their tools and materials in readiness to build the foundations. Immediately after the tide had sufficiently ebbed, and with the flood tide also, they were able to continue to work until the last possible moment. Strong sulphuric acid was first used

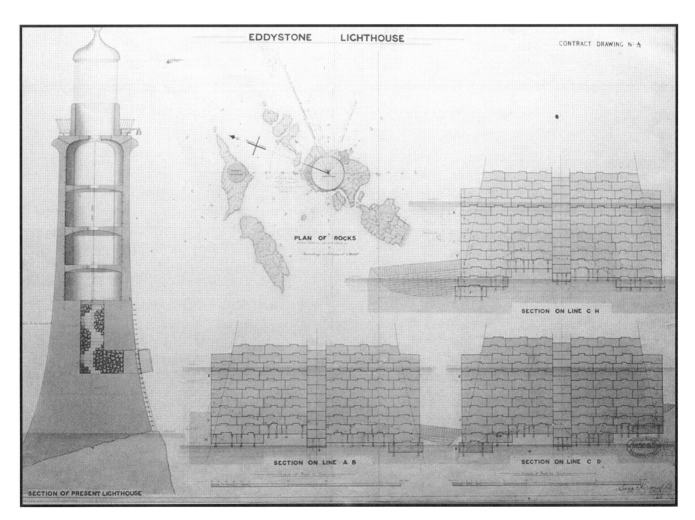

PLANS OF THE NEW DOUGLASS LIGHTHOUSE FOUNDATIONS ALONGSIDE SMEATON'S OLD TOWER
BY KIND PERMISSION OF THE CORPORATION OF TRINITY HOUSE

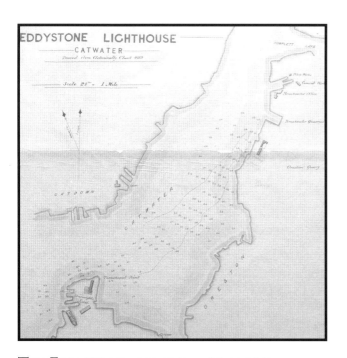

THE EDDYSTONE WORKYARD AT ORESTON
BY KIND PERMISSION OF THE CORPORATION OF TRINITY HOUSE

of well-burnt bricks and fresh-burnt Roman cement was required to stop the Atlantic breakers from engulfing the area. Large pumps were in constant action, clearing away any seawater that penetrated the dam. The noise and bustle of the workmen with their compressed-air drills rattling and pounding on the rock's crust created a grand spectacle for the passengers of pleasure vessels that brought spectators back and forth from Plymouth; the Eddystone had once more become a hive of human activity. Men with "jumpers", cleaving gear and picks hacked into the rock, while the loud Eclipse power drills, specially made by Hathorn & Co, were being used to form a stepped platform on the rock's surface.

The new steam-driven tools dug their way effortlessly into the Eddystone's belly, being powered by the steam ship *Hercules* which lay at anchor just 30 fathoms from the reef. From her decks, two three-inch indiarubber canvas-covered hoses, connected to double-acting pumps of the fore and aft winches on board the vessel, sucked the pools of water from

in smoothing and cleaning the stone's surface so an important coffer dam, seven feet high, could be erected around the site. The barrier

A PHOTOGRAPH TAKEN AT THE EDDYSTONE IN 1879, SHOWING THE WORKMEN AND CRANE
BY KIND PERMISSION OF THE CORPORATION OF TRINITY HOUSE

inside the working area, keeping the men dry.

His team had to work night and day. Douglass pre-empted criticism of Sunday working by insisting that two religious services were held on the Sabbath for his men out at the Eddystone Rock itself. In his usual down-to-earth, honest way, Douglass bonded well with the people he worked alongside. There, as in Wales, he felt able to enjoy the time spent in their company and would often play his flute during rest periods or entertain the company after a hard day's work on board *Hercules*.

O God! Who wert my childhood's love,
My boyhood's pure delight,
A presence felt the livelong day,
A welcome fear at night,
Oh, let me speak to Thee, dear God!
Of those old mercies past,
O'er which new mercies day by day,
Such lengthening shadows cast.

— FABER

It was estimated the construction would be completed in just three years and that the venture would probably cost £60,000. 4,668 tons of stone were to be used in the new lighthouse, 62,133 cubic feet, or 2,171 blocks of heavy granite. In comparison, Smeaton's tower comprised 1,493 blocks, 636 stone joggles, 1,800 oak trenails, 4,570 pairs of oak wedges, eight circular floor chains and 226 iron clamps. Thankfully, modern technical advancement ensured a somewhat easier challenge than that faced by the earlier lighthouse builders.

Nonetheless, it was still going to be an incredibly difficult task for Douglass – and as with Winstanley, Rudyerd and Smeaton before him, the working day would always be determined by the condition of the sea and weather. During initial stages of construction, it was only possible to work on the rock at low water for approximately three or four hours before sea water covered the area.

The majority of stone to be used in the new lighthouse had been supplied by Shearer & Co of Westminster, having been selected from the De Lank quarry in Cornwall; a little more came from Dalbeattie in Scotland. The Cornish quarry was favoured because of the quality of stone and its convenient distance from the Eddystone workyard in Oreston near Plymouth. The site lay on the shores of the Laira River and had been previously used in the construction of the great Plymouth Breakwater. Now it had been placed at the disposal of Trinity House, and wooden jetties, workshops and stores were erected ready for the arrival of the building material. The stone blocks were usually shipped out of Wadebridge, a small harbour on the north coast. They were initially dressed by stonemasons and then taken by boat around Cornwall, passing Land's End and then back up the Channel into Plymouth, where the local workforce prepared the rough-cut stone, shaping it to perfection.

Every block was numbered, painted in red and black lettering on each joint, and packed onto the waiting boats before finally arriving at the Eddystone itself.

In the first year of operations the men at work had to be roped together for their own safety, for it was possible that a rolling wave could crash over the coffer dam, sweeping them out into the ocean. However, to provide as much protection as possible for his workers, Douglass positioned a lookout on top of Smeaton's old lighthouse, which gave the watcher a commanding view of the tide's surface condition.

Soon, the new lighthouse started to rise above the waves and the beacon quickly towered over its quaint neighbour. Smeaton's building had done its job, but had to give way to Victorian progress.

The vertical base would rise eighteen feet nine inches above the low water mark, at which point the curved shaft commenced and had a set-off point or a projection of four feet, so that the lighthouse was seen to be standing on a cylindrical pedestal.

Douglass believed the sea's pounding at that point was heaviest, but it was also the best place for the tower to receive it, besides being the point of least leverage and thus of least destructive effect on the rock below. Douglass said:

A DRAWING OF THE PROPOSED LIGHTHOUSE
BY KIND PERMISSION OF THE CORPORATION OF TRINITY HOUSE

Given great attention to the question of arresting the force of a large ocean wave on a structure of that kind, that a vertical base was the proper form to be adopted.

When completed, the tower's base measured 44 feet in diameter by 22 feet high and the light was 133 feet above high water, with a range of seventeen-and-a-half nautical miles.

Work continued swiftly and Douglass felt confident that everything would be achieved. The designs of his new lighthouse were exciting and on a massive scale. It was an undertaking that he enjoyed, one where he could demonstrate his remarkable building skills.

He was a hands-on boss and happy to work alongside his men. He would often be heard reciting a verse of poetry, a favourite being *Epistle to a Young Friend,* by the bard of Scotia:

> To catch dame Fortune's golden smile
> Assiduous want upon her,
> And gather gear by every wile,
> That's justified by honour;
> Not for to hide it in a hedge,
> Nor for a train attendant,
> But for the glorious privilege
> Of being independent.

The fate of Smeaton's lighthouse was undecided, although several offers to buy the tower had been received by Trinity House, one coming from a Falmouth entrepreneur who wanted to use it in publicising his trading business. But no decision other than that it would have to be dismantled was forthcoming.

Construction of the Douglass tower continued smoothly and at speed, thanks to the two twin-screw steam boats that brought the stone blocks to the work site on the Eddystone from the Oreston workyard. One of the vessels, *Hercules,* had originally been engaged in the building of both Great and Little Basses Rock Lighthouses in Ceylon, but on returning to this country had been seconded by Douglass to help him.

The vessel was specially adapted for lighthouse building and the capability of its

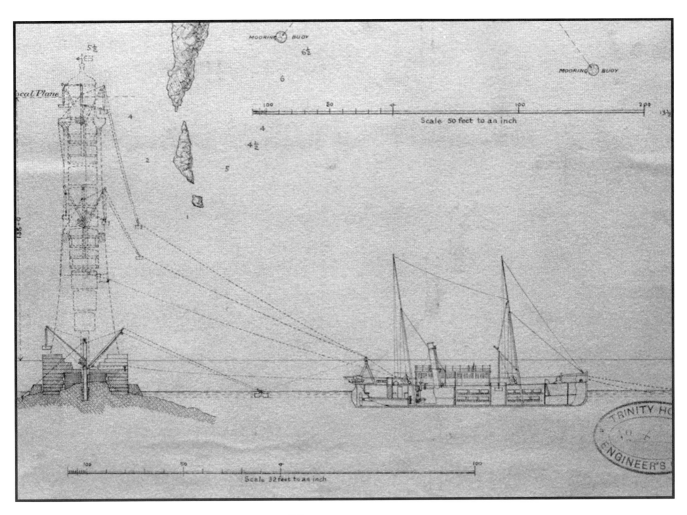

A DRAWING OF THE STEAM-DRIVEN VESSEL *HERCULES* IN THE PROCESS OF MOVING THE STONE BLOCKS
BY KIND PERMISSION OF THE CORPORATION OF TRINITY HOUSE

own steam power provided the driving force to operate all the equipment employed in the work. Her ability in providing the workforce with all the equipment needed made the task much easier and her flexibility in working close to the reef was phenomenal, as she could be moored extremely near to the rocks, in just 30 feet of water. The mighty vessel could also anchor up and sit out the fiercest of the storms, or simply steam back to her Plymouth base within an hour. *Hercules* was a remarkable tool to have and her value was obvious to the workers she aided. Technology had certainly improved. *Hercules* even boasted a railway running over her decks which allowed the large winches and cranes greater movement. Douglass had been responsible for the ship's many modifications and it was to his credit that the vessel produced remarkable working performances.

For landing the stone, *Hercules* was moored to the rock by 10-inch coir hawsers which were attached ahead of the vessel to three iron spherical buoys, moored with one-and-a-half-inch open-linked chain, and 40 cwt of cast iron sinkers, and at her stern to iron posts on the other surrounding rocks. The end of each hawser was provided with a chain for fastening to the ring of the buoy, and to this was attached a tripping line, for use in case of rough weather when the hawsers could be released from the vessel without any aid from another boat.

A hollow wrought-iron mast, 25 feet long and 16 inches in diameter, was firmly wedged in a hole at the centre of the tower, sunk five feet into the solid rock and stayed by three-quarter-inch guy-chains. Two jibs were attached to the mast, one of wood for landing the stones and one of iron capable of travelling around the mast for setting. The

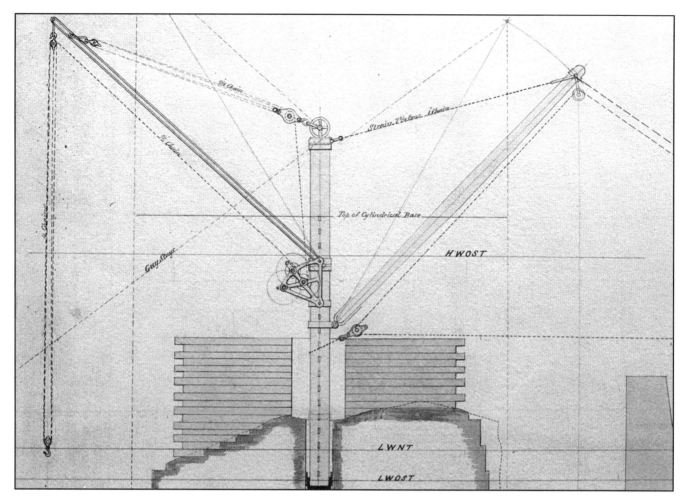

PLAN OF THE DOUGLASS BASE CRANE, SHOWING ITS MOVEMENT FOR THE INTERLOCKING STONE BLOCKS
BY KIND PERMISSION OF THE CORPORATION OF TRINITY HOUSE

wooden jib at the early part of the operations was lowered and taken off at the end of each tide's work to avoid its being damaged by the sea; but the iron jib was lowered and securely lashed to eyebolts on the structure and the winch stowed in the central hole, or removed to the *Hercules* to avoid all risk of being broken or lost.

As the work progressed, the iron mast was lifted by hydraulic jacks and secured to the structure by timbering and chain back-guys. A hollow wrought-iron topmast 19 feet long was fixed to the mast after the second season to cut down on lifting.

By June 1879, the work was sufficiently advanced for the stones to be laid in the foundation courses and a Royal ceremony was arranged for 19 August 1879, when the first foundation block, weighing three-and-a-quarter tons, would be placed by the Master of Trinity House, the Duke of Edinburgh,

who was to be accompanied by his brother, the Prince of Wales.

Originally the ceremony should have taken place on 12 June, but the weather was awful and the event was rearranged for 19 August. Happily, the day arrived with a fresh wind and blue skies and in fair weather the Royal party which included the Prince of Wales landed on the Eddystone to undertake the ritual and declare the stone "well and truly laid".

During the ceremony a bottle containing a parchment scroll with full details of the work was placed in a cavity under the stone and cement bed. It was properly positioned, adjusted and bolted by the Master of Trinity House assisted by the Prince of Wales.

Ten blocks an hour weighing from two-and-a-half to three-and-a-quarter tons could be disgorged from the ships, lifted from their holds by a forward steam-winch and then

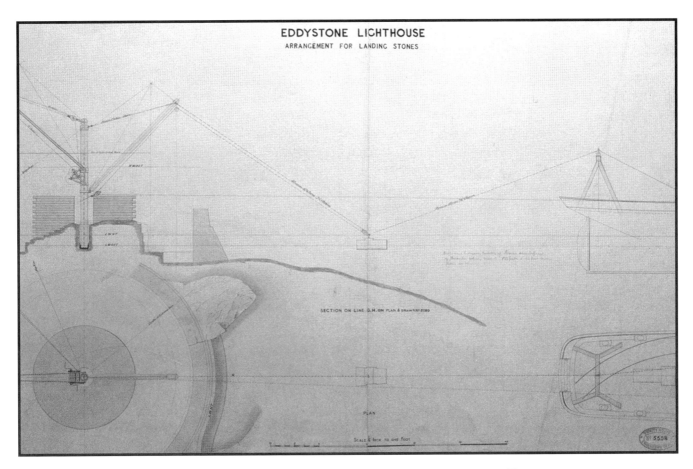

EDDYSTONE LICHTHOUSE
ARRANGEMENT FOR LANDING STONES

A DIAGRAM SHOWING THE PROCESS OF LANDING THE STONE BLOCKS ON THE EDDYSTONE WORK SITE
BY KIND PERMISSION OF THE CORPORATION OF TRINITY HOUSE

deposited on a truck that ran on metal lines to the stern of the ship, where a strong timber gantry was erected. Wooden rollers were also fitted on deck at the stern gangway to carry the stones clear of the vessel. A double barrel winch lifted the blocks above the deck and the stones were hauled onto the Eddystone site, then eased into position and finally cemented into place. The time taken to achieve the single manoeuvre took Douglass and his men under three minutes and every stone in the building, together with the required cement, sand and water, etc, was landed and hoisted onto the work site in one lifting movement from the *Hercules*. It was the first application of floating steam machinery in the erection of a structure at sea.

Sharp sand grit composed of hard quartz was obtained locally from the river Plym at Plympton, with the cement for the building being supplied by Francis & Co of Nine Elms.

Foot upon foot of the lighthouse rose upwards as the dressed and jointed stones were laid together.

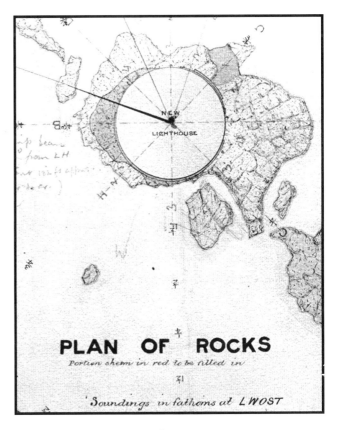

PLAN OF ROCKS
Portion shewn in red to be filled in

Soundings in fathoms at LWOST

A DIAGRAM OF THE NEW HOUSE ROCK
THE AUTHOR'S COLLECTION

After the Royal visit the builders continued to work until the end of December. One hundred and fourteen stones had been set in courses, 1, 2, 3, 4, 5, 6 and 7, which averaged 3.95 hours of work at each landing.

The mighty construction commenced once more in the March of the following year, 1880, and rapid progress was made. On 17 July, two years after the outset of operations, the whole of the cylindrical base was completed and early in November, the end of that season's effort, the 38th course of masonry had been set. During that season 110 landings had been made with 657 hours spent in work and 1,437 stones set, which averaged 5.97 per landing.

In 1881 work started in the middle of January and as soon as the sixth room had been completed the workmen were able to lodge in the tower, which further facilitated progress.

THE TOWER NEARING COMPLETION
BY KIND PERMISSION OF THE CORPORATION OF TRINITY HOUSE

Within just three years, 2,171 units of granite stone had been taken out to the reef and locked into position.

The interior was being completed and the construction schedule had so far been a smooth venture for Douglass to oversee. Occasionally, the work became hazardous, especially during unsettled periods, when judging the weather was difficult.

Later that year a severe storm brought up from the bottom of the ocean an iron cannon, six feet long and three feet in bore, weighing 10 cwt. It was found by builders at the base of the new lighthouse and was thought to have been from the *Winchelsea* which sank at the Eddystone reef on Sunday 28 November 1703, 178 years earlier.

The final stages of work during the autumn of 1881 were almost completed and Douglass's tower waited silently in readiness for its occupants. From a distance, the building resembled a stone finger rising out of the tide and for the moment it was just a lifeless column, an empty hollow structure waiting to be brought to life.

Satisfied with his achievement, Douglass felt his efforts should also be acknowledged as a fitting monument to the pioneers of the previous four Eddystone lighthouses.

On 1 June 1881 everything was ready for the grand ceremony of the setting of the last stone. That season, only 40 landings had been made, work carried on for 294 hours and 620 stones set, an average of 7.35 hours of work on each landing.

Again the stone was laid by the Duke of Edinburgh, who landed on the rock from his ship HMS *Lively*. It was the Duke's second visit to the site and he would return for another special occasion – the lighting of the new Douglass lighthouse on 18 May 1882.

A supply of food was sent out on the day before the lighting ceremony was to take place, the men's rations for their period of duty. The food and other stores had been supplied by Blights of Millbay, who were the long-standing provisioners of the Eddystone lighthouse, engaged by Trinity House.

The final pieces had been put together in the tower and the fittings and fixtures were ready and secured.

THE TWO EDDYSTONE TOWERS IN 1882
THE AUTHOR'S COLLECTION

The design of the building was remarkably straightforward, with its floors arranged for the benefit of those who worked and lived there.

The tower was a concave elliptical frustum, the generating curve having a semi-transverse axis of 173 feet, and a semi-conjugate by the fresh-water tanks, holding 4,700 gallons, which constituted a year's supply. With the exception of the space occupied by the tanks, the tower was solid for 25ft 6in above high-water spring-tide level. At the top of the solid portion the wall was 8ft 6in in thickness, diminishing to 2ft 3in, the thinnest part of the service room.

All the blocks were dovetailed both horizontally and vertically, while each stone in the foundation courses was sunk to a depth of not less, at any part, than one foot below the surface of the surrounding rock, and was further secured by two Muntz metal bolts, one-and-a-half inches in diameter, passing through the stone and nine inches into the

rock below, the top and bottom of each bolt being fox-wedged.

From the lighthouse's cylindrical base, the bond between rock and tower, were 22 gunmetal dog steps, set into a recess of the outer stone shaft, which allowed sea-level access upward to the "set-off" or landing platform, a width of four feet eight inches all the way around the structure. On the outer edge of the surface were evenly spaced depressions which acted as anchor points for metal stakes, where a rope was attached to their tops, acting as a fence rail.

Immediately above the solid mass and fixed into the outer wall of the building were several eye bolts. The small steel hoops allowed for a safety rope to be passed through, around the building, so as to give a secure hold should the keeper experience a problem from a high-rolling wave or some other unfortunate situation.

Above the set-off was the entrance room to the lighthouse's interior and a further 25 dog steps or cleats (positioned on two sides, opposite each other at the north-east and south-west of the building). Either of the "ladders" needed to be climbed to gain access into the building itself from sea level.

Two sets of strong black gun-metal doors weighing a ton each were situated on both sides of the building and faced north-east and south-west of the tower to protect the entrance room's interior from outside forces. The doors had a small window in them which allowed a beam of natural light to penetrate. The doors were also strengthened by thick bracing bars embedded in the interior wall. Below the floor of the first room were the

fresh-water tanks, protected by two manhole covers, to prevent sea water from seeping through on the occasions when the room was flooded by high sea levels.

The lighthouse interior consisted of nine rooms, with the seven uppermost having a diameter of 14 feet and a height of 10 feet.

Moving up into the tower from the entrance, you climbed a winding cast-iron stairway which curved upwards, hugging the sides of the wall to the very top of the building.

The next two levels were oil and battery stores which originally contained nine months' supply of parrafin oil, approximately 4,300 gallons, in 18 wrought-iron cisterns. It was where fog charges and tonite would later be housed.

Above that level was the winch room and main store area of the lighthouse. Further large gun-metal doors placed opposite and positioned north and south acted as the store entrance for the relief boats and maintenance craft which transferred equipment when rough seas prevented them from anchoring to the rocks. The keepers would receive all of their provisions by winching the gear by hand from the decks of the craft bobbing below them.

The room, in the days before helicopter relief, was the normal route of entry to and from the lighthouse, especially during bad weather, when the men were unable to alight on the dog steps and go up into the lower entrance from the surface of the reef.

On some occasions, an individual keeper would be hand-winched by his colleagues into and out of the lighthouse. An arriving keeper would first be strapped into a safety harness on board the relief boat and then taken out of the rolling vessel by rope towards the winch-room entrance opening. The boat's crew would keep hold of the rope and feed it up to the winching gear, where the incoming keeper would be pulled into the building by those inside. The opposite procedure would occur for the outgoing lightkeepers; it is interesting to hear from ex-keepers who served in the rock towers that the descent from the lighthouse always appeared much worse, due to the fact that they were very aware of the

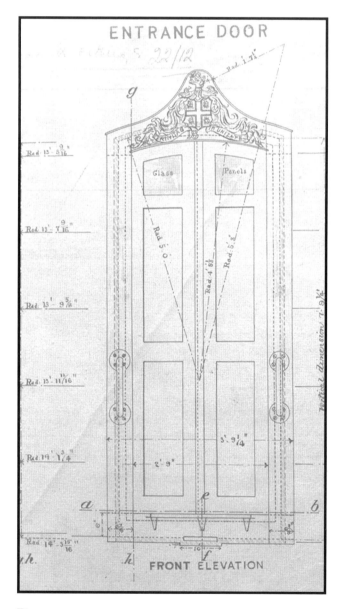

DIAGRAM OF THE LOWER ENTRANCE DOORS
BY KIND PERMISSION OF THE CORPORATION OF TRINITY HOUSE

sea's state and constantly had in view the small boat waiting to take them homeward.

On level 5 was a crane room and dry store area. The apparatus comprised a horizontal girder rack-and-pinion mechanism used for exchanging heavy equipment. The stanchions were fed through holes in the wall to the outside and situated immediately above the winch-room doors below.

Next, the kitchen cum living room originally had a massive granite range that was continuously burning and used for cooking and baking. The impressive fixture faced the one wooden doorway, leading to the stairs. It was the compartment most used by the keepers and was the social area where they could while away spare time together in a cosy and relaxed atmosphere, sitting around an open coal fire.

A large oval copper tank sat on top of the stove and provided the men with hot water for washing, etc. A kitchen dresser full of plates, cups and utensils was placed next to the window recess, above which was attached a cistern of drinking water. One small stone

THE RELIEF BOAT AT THE EDDYSTONE
THE AUTHOR'S COLLECTION

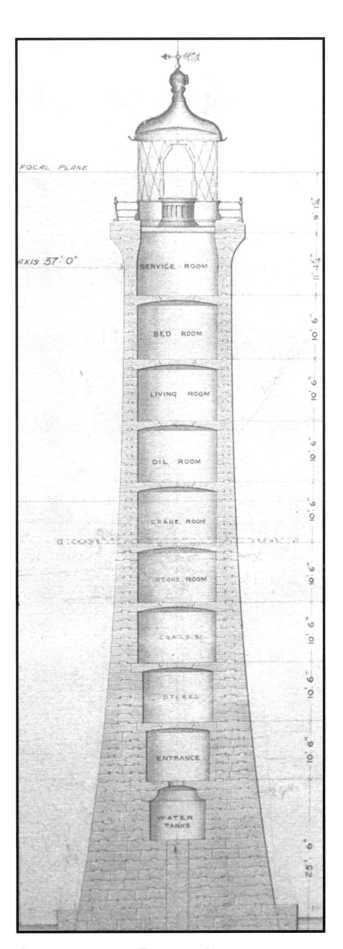

CROSS-SECTION OF DOUGLASS'S TOWER
THE AUTHOR'S COLLECTION

sink with a wooden draining board was situated next to a curved seat and above this was a locker for the various foodstuffs and dry items.

A further cupboard and smaller dresser was placed around the empty wall space. In the middle of the room was a circular wooden table with a small round shelf above, just wide enough to place a glass or cup.

In the middle and running from the domed ceiling through the grey slate slabs on the floor ran a tube-like support which was hollow and contained the chain weight mechanism for the revolving lens in the

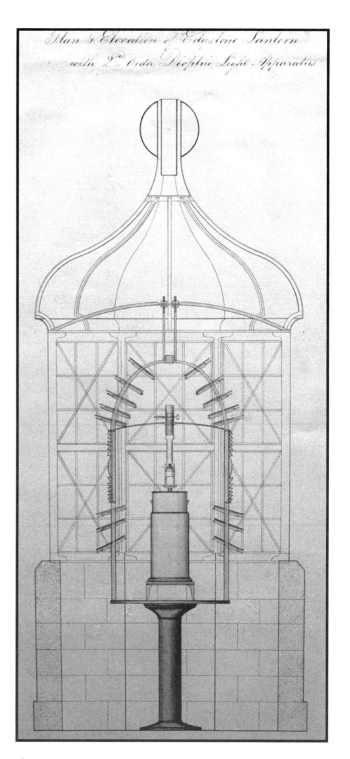

AN EARLY DRAWING OF THE DIOPTRIC LIGHT
BY KIND PERMISSION OF THE CORPORATION OF TRINITY HOUSE

PREPARING TO BAKE A PIE AT THE EDDYSTONE
THE AUTHOR'S COLLECTION

lantern. There were also two armchairs and another table in the room.

On the seventh floor came the low light room where originally two Argand lamps would have cast their fixed subsidiary beam to mark a submerged rocky danger, known as Hands Deep, three-and-a-half miles away. There was also a chair and table. It was an important area for the keepers and where they

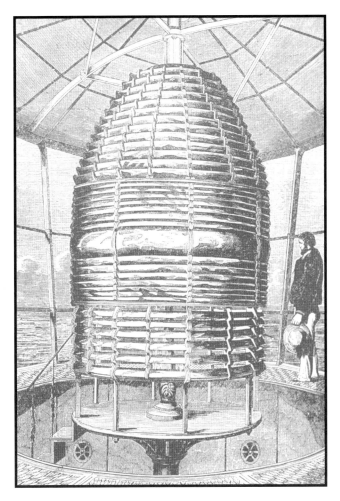

THE LENS KNOWN AS THE BEEHIVE
THE AUTHOR'S COLLECTION

which in the 20th century was used for radio communications between the keepers at the Eddystone and workmates on land.

The room was linked by a short iron staircase to the lantern area. 140 steps separated the room from the entrance to the tower nine floors below. The glazed dome was surrounded on the outside by a gallery, accessed through a small metal doorway.

The walkway surrounded the entire lantern and was itself fenced by metal railings. At opposite sides of the tower below the gallery hung two large fog bells weighing 40 cwt apiece, although they were replaced in 1891 by a fog signal system.

Inside the thick glass and metalwork wall sat the lens, "the eye of the lighthouse", the most important piece of all the equipment used. The wonderfully engineered apparatus had been made by the renowned English firm of Chance Brothers & Co of Birmingham, the only British firm to specialise in that field of optics.

filled in their weather log book every three hours, as well as other records. It was also a quiet place to read or to sit in peace, away from their colleagues.

Above, on the eighth floor, was the keepers' bedroom with its three built-in curved bunks hugging the sides of the wall, with a further two beds above. The higher bunks were reserved for visitors to the lighthouse. For the keepers, their own bunk space boasted a window, panelled partition, curtain and shelves. A wash basin occupied the area next to the fourth window.

On the next floor was the service room. Engraved into its granite wall are the words of the 127th Psalm – "Except the Lord build the house, They labour in vain that build it"– the same words Smeaton used in his tower.

The area was the operational centre of the lighthouse. It contained paraffin tanks and spare parts for use in the lantern; a cupboard, chair and table dotted the compartment,

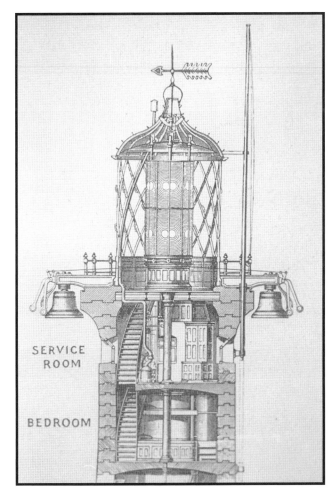

A SECTION OF THE ORIGINAL UPPER TOWER
BY KIND PERMISSION OF THE CORPORATION OF TRINITY HOUSE

In the Eddystone lantern room of 1882, the apparatus was producing a very substantial intensity of light.

In good visibility, the lighthouse could do its job with only the lower burner in operation. Its 450 candlepower would be magnified to 37,800 candlepower by the lenses.

But when the weather was so poor that you couldn't see the Breakwater Lighthouse 10 miles away, both burners would be put into action, producing 1,900 candlepower which was magnified to 159,600 candles. The light was 23.3 times more powerful than Smeaton's and 2,382 times more powerful than Winstanley's tallow candles.

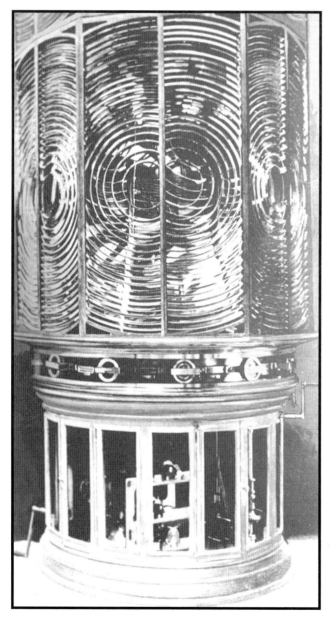

THE LOWER SECTION OF THE DOUBLE LENS
THE AUTHOR'S COLLECTION

The intensity of the light produced at the Eddystone during its first years of operation was the highest that had yet been achieved from oil in coastal illumination and the remarkable lens apparatus which had exhibited that bright light was seen as a piece of engineering brilliance.

It stood more than 10 feet tall and was a sparkling sight, weighing over seven tons and sitting majestically in the centre of the lantern room, mounted on a sturdy plinth, panelled in heavy glass to shield the mechanical mechanism below.

Each keeper knew that careful attention to the delicate system was a vital task and many hours of hard work were required to maintain its brightness and total effectiveness. Being a clockwork weighted apparatus, a chain hung from the lens's base and through each floor of the lighthouse to the lower store room, where a lead of nearly half a ton would rise and fall continuously through the hours of darkness approximately 15 feet between the entrance room and the oil store. To rotate the large lens, which rested on 12 horizontal rollers, and to engage the wheels, gently rotating the lens around the light source, the duty lightkeeper would be next to the lens equipment, winding on the winch handle, turning the handle more than 400 times every hour to bring up the falling weight that was attached to the chain. It ensured there was no interruption to the smooth movement of the turning glass structure above.

Looking after such equipment was a continuous job for the lightkeepers, and cleaning each piece of glass of the lens could take several hours to complete. During the daytime it was common to draw heavy curtains together and surround the lantern, protecting the apparatus from the sun's rays.

From an item written by Robin Allen, the Secretary of Trinity House London, dated 1889, comes his account of the new Lighthouse, entitled *Deep Sea Lamp Posts*:

A fresh platform of rock was of course chosen, one about 100 feet from Smeaton's and, so far as present condition and geological solidarity go, one that seems better fitted for the purpose; the form of the lighthouse, too, presents more of a

AERIAL VIEW OF THE EDDYSTONE IN THE 1960S
BY KIND PERMISSION OF THE CORPORATION OF TRINITY HOUSE

free transmission of the light; and thus again the Eddystone, although it is still a fixed light, and therefore far from the most powerful possible, has been renewed with many modern appliances, including a subsidiary light to mark a special danger, and may be said again to hold its own among the pattern light-houses of the world...

But stations like the Eddystone are now furnished, in addition to bells, with rockets, especially made to explode with a loud noise; and these, even when fired up the wind, burst at sufficient distance from the structure not to shake or crack the lenses, and are of some use to the sailor when befogged; but at such times it behoves him to remember that he has only one safe guide – his lead!

breaking line than a guiding curve to the waves. The height from the bottom of the foundation course to the centre of the lantern-vane is rather more that 170 feet, showing the light at about 135 feet above high water, and thus giving a much greater command over the curve of the earth for distant visibility; and the diameter of the tower now admits of illuminating and optical apparatus of the first order.

The construction of the lantern too with helical or spiral framing and panes of glass slightly curved outwards to accord with the curve of the cylinder, and so as to receive the light radially upon their inner surfaces, offers much less obstruction to the

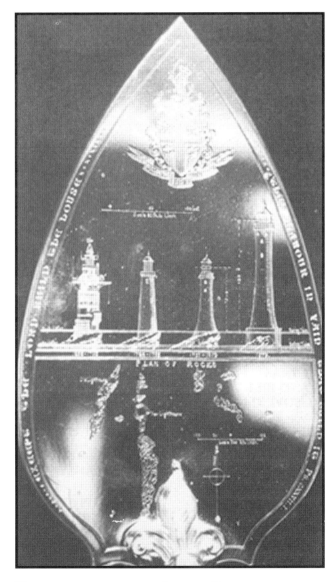

THE TROWEL USED BY ALFRED DOUGLASS
BY KIND PERMISSION OF THE CORPORATION OF TRINITY HOUSE

The poem, *Eddystone,* by Mr Kenward:

> We build on firmer base, with loftier hope;
> The granite shell sits broader on the rock;
> The light will search the sea with larger scope
> And tenfold beam.
> All mists that veil and mock,
> All winds and tides that baffle, shoals that shock,
> Must yield them to the giant lenses might,
> Which, drawn from stores the passing hours
>   unlock.
> Instinct with central flame serenely bright,
> Will flash their splendours soon across the waste
>   of night

The light from Smeaton's old lighthouse was discontinued on 3 February 1882. Its replacement stood proud and had been completed in four years, a year ahead of schedule.

The Prime Minister of the day, Gladstone, wrote informing the builder that he was to be given a knighthood for his services "on the occasion of the completion of the Eddystone Lighthouse, with which your name is so honourably connected".

R H Brunton, an authority on lighthouse matters, speaking at a gathering of the Institution of Civil Engineers, stated:

> It has been said that the green seas rushed up Smeaton's Tower to the cornice and considerably above, and that in the case of the present tower, the circular base breaks the waves, which rush around to the opposite side. If that be so, it would appear that the energy expended in projecting the volume of water, say 50 or a 100 tons so many feet into the air, is now expended directly against the circular base.

THE REMAINING STUMP OF SMEATON'S TOWER AS IT IS TODAY, SHOWING THE INTRICATE BLOCKWORK
PHOTOGRAPHED BY THE AUTHOR

The strong vertical base of Douglass's tower enabled greater resistance to the ocean about it and provided the lighthouse with added protection from the gales and storms it would constantly have to withstand.

The entire work had also been completed without the loss of life or limb and was finished at a cost considerably under the estimate given. The total bill for the work had been £59,255 – £18,745 below the figure Douglass had quoted.

He achieved that mainly due to the successful operation of the various mechanical appliances he introduced to save manual labour.

Publicity for the new lighthouse was such that everyone became interested once more in the Eddystone story, so much so that the people of Plymouth insisted Smeaton's old structure, then without its lantern gallery and in some decay, should be rebuilt in a place of honour on Plymouth Hoe. They set up a fund to finance the work.

Douglass, who lived in Plymouth, was approached to undertake the task of dismantling Smeaton's work. So with his son William at his side, he began to take down "Father" Smeaton's great structure, which proved hard work.

Tragedy nearly overshadowed the undertaking as William fell from the top of Smeaton's Tower, a height of 70 feet, towards the jagged rocks below. He looked certain to be falling to his death, but a large Atlantic roller cushioned his fall as it crashed against the base of the old lighthouse.

In a letter sent by Douglass from the Trinity Works in Oreston, Plymouth, dated 15 April 1882, to his old schoolfriend Price Williams, we read:

My dear Williams,
You have probably ere this heard of the accident to my dear boy Willie at the Eddystone last Monday and his miraculous escape from a terrible death. He had taken down Smeaton's tower to the level of the lantern gallery and had a pair of sheers rigged on it for landing the central crane for taking down and shipping the masonry. On landing the crane however there was some ground swell which caused a heavy surge on the tackle and the chain back guy of the sheers parted, when Willie was struck by one of the legs and flung several feet upwards into the air and thence fell about 70 feet as it was thought at the moment on to the rocks below, but most providentially, a wave rose over the rocks at that very moment, and he fell on to it, when fortunately he recovered sufficient consciousness and strength to strike out and swim ashore.
I am thankful to state that not a bone has been broken and so far no internal injury appears to have been sustained. He has most marvellously escaped with a few cuts and bruises, which we hope will be all right again in a few days. The Doctors recommend him perfect quiet for a week to recover the shock there from. I have taken his place temporarily, which I am only too thankful to do under the circumstances.

Immediately after completing his work at the Eddystone, William boarded the steam boat *Hercules* and with his team of men sailed to their next appointment at the Bishop Rock Lighthouse, where rebuilding work was about to take place. William had been promoted to the position of Resident Engineer and that honour resulted in the distinction that three generations of the Douglass family had been employed there.

William continued to work for Trinity House and went on to construct another lighthouse on Round Island, before becoming an independent engineer. Sadly during the summer of 1913 while on a boating trip with his own son, tragedy befell the party when the vessel capsized. William died in the accident but the young boy survived and was saved by a passing steamer off the coast of Dartmouth.

James Douglass became a member of the Institution of Civil Engineers in 1861 and was still working for Trinity House well into his sixties, until he suffered an attack of paralysis during 1892 which incapacitated him. With this he felt unable to continue in his work and so left the service in the autumn. He spent the rest of his life happy with his wife and children around him. He enjoyed his retirement and loved the simple pleasures of life like gardening, keeping pets and writing letters. The family moved from Dulwich to their country home in Bonchurch on the Isle of Wight where he lived out his final days.

In a warm letter to a friend, just before his death, he wrote:

> I presume that you have heard of my last pet, a baby grey parrot from the Congo, carefully selected by a friend for talking qualities, only two months old. So far it is a very sweet-tempered creature and promises to talk soon. I have now plenty of company, Rollo the dog, 27 fowls, 3 canaries, 2 parrots and a very prettily marked and sweet tempered cat. I fancy you can not boast of such a family.

Days before his death, he wrote a letter to his young son Alfred:

> Do your best as before and let no one be able to say that better could be done. Do not be in any hurry to make money for money's sake, but strive to make yourself useful in this world as your duty lies.

Alfred Edward Douglass was also trained by his father to be a lighthouse engineer and lived at Tresithick House in Devoran for many years. He would often give talks about his family's building achievements to Cornish audiences and was a well-loved figure within the community. A story he would always recount was of his first appointment in 1879, when as a small boy he was asked to be present at the laying of the foundation stone on the Eddystone:

> Many people were present, having come out from Plymouth in steamers, but I cannot remember much about it, except that my father asked me to fetch the silver trowel from the Trinity House steamer and to hand it to him to present to the Master of Trinity House, the Duke of Edinburgh; The Duke would also lay the last stone on June 1st. 1881. In 1882 my father was knighted by Queen Victoria and Trinity House presented him with a beautifully-illuminated testimonial in consideration of the completion of the Eddystone Lighthouse, built under the direction of Sir James N. Douglass in succession to that erected by John Smeaton and also to the many valuable and important services rendered by him in the improvement of lanterns, burners, and apparatus, afloat and on shore, as well as in the building of

lighthouses in many difficult and dangerous positions at home and abroad.

James Douglass's eventual death resulted from another attack of paralysis on 19 June 1898. He was aged 71, and buried in the village cemetery of Bonchurch. Tributes came in from all corners of the country and his name would always be associated with lighthouse building.

In correspondence from James's daughter Alice, relating to her late father, we read:

> My mother who was very delicate for a long time, was always his first thought and he was never really happy away from her. She accompanied him sometimes in his visits to the lighthouses and when he was absent alone, the morning letter never failed, nor did he ever return without some little trifle.
>
> I never recollect my father out of temper or even moody and self occupied. Little time as he had to devote himself to his children, has managed to be completely one with them. No hours of our day were quite so full of fun and happiness as those he spent with us. When we came down in the morning, till he left for town, he was not allowed a moment alone. Breakfast was a ceaseless merry chatter, chiefly about our doings. He entered thoroughly into all our fun, able to sympathise as fully with the children in the nursery as with the elder ones, and although never checking our talk, yet making us, unconsciously, be at our best, for we knew that quarrels or unkind judgements, would hurt him.
>
> Little time as he had before leaving for London, he always read prayers and sang a hymn with us. In order to allow for this, breakfast was at 7 in the summer and at half past in the winter. Sunday was our especial holiday, for then we had him to ourselves, except for one hour in the afternoon, when our mother would insist on his taking a short rest. When fine, we spent as much time as possible in the garden; but wherever we were, he would always keep us merry or interested. During the day he liked us all to repeat to him the collect for that Sunday and a hymn; This was done even by the big sons, home from college, because father liked it. Prizes played a great part in his educational system, but they were not promised, so the work was not done for them, but were only

given at any time that no one should feel jealousy. Improvement in some branch or other was generally discovered in each of us, so that all would feel equally cheered. I remember my mother often looking up from her book, herself laughing, to say "James, you are really worse than the children", and certainly none of us entered into games with more zest. Perhaps the secret of it was that whatever he was doing, that for the moment, completely absorbed him. This probably accounted for the love he won from us all. He would listen to his companion for the time being, with great interest and if there was any way in which he could render assistance, it would be done, even at the sacrifice of his valuable time.

Over a hundred years have now passed since the Douglass lighthouse was first lit, when its achievement was acknowledged around the world. Through all that time, the granite structure has withstood the endless pounding of the mighty ocean.

Douglass would have been proud of his lasting creation, even though many changes to the original lighthouse, both inside and out, have taken place throughout the years in the name of progress and safety. Unfortunately, it seems that while the improvements have continued, other factors including those of working practices in the lighthouse service have changed forever the status of the famous tower.

Its worth to the mariner has also diminished in the face of satellite navigational aids, radar etc, and like the parts which have disappeared from it, the once proud tower is but a sad reflection of its former self.

The original double lens, once a magnificent piece of Victorian engineering, had remained in use on the Eddystone for nearly 70 years although the drive mechanism had been upgraded several times.

New designs to the rollers and a mercury bath system were invented which enabled the lens housing to rotate more effectively on its base. Paraffin and vapour burners were soon installed at the Eddystone, producing a light of 292,000 candlepower. Then electricity arrived in 1956, bringing a big change in the working environment and giving the keepers a better life than they had previously enjoyed.

The tiresome job of winding the weights up the chain every hour ceased as technology advanced. The burners too were redesigned, making the mighty lens redundant.

This wonderful apparatus had given good service during its years at the Eddystone, but was to many people unnecessarily dismantled. As it was an important engineering structure in its own right, a member of Trinity House approached Plymouth City Council with a view that it should be placed in the City Museum. Smeaton's Tower had after all been given pride of place on Plymouth Hoe. The building surely represented the city's genuine affection for the Eddystone's history. So with this opportunity available to the city, a new home for the lens seemed a foregone conclusion. However, no-one at the council wanted the lens for display nor seemed remotely interested in its true importance and so, regrettably, another venue was then sought.

Finally, the city of Southampton asked for the Eddystone lens to be shown in their newly proposed maritime museum and so Trinity House obliged and dispatched the lens to its new home. The massive glass monster was first taken to a temporary venue, that of the pier, where it was exhibited during the 1970s.

Unfortunately, as the years passed, its value seemed to be eroded by more popular tastes and when this venue was condemned, the lens found its way into the background and was eventually lost.

Later, however, this wonderful structure unexpectedly resurfaced, discovered by workmen in the 1980s. Sadly by then it had been destroyed by vandals, smashed to pieces, and lying under debris in a small council yard.

In the final years of the manned Eddystone, its keepers saw continuous changes. No longer was their lifestyle one of complete isolation, as radio and later television had been a constant link with happenings ashore. Indeed modern technology had already spread its hand over the Eddystone as far back as 1903, when the keepers were provided with their first battery radio telephone set, which allowed direct communication with the Trinity House land-based operations. Electricity arrived at the Eddystone in 1956 and revolutionised the working environment,

THE EDDYSTONE LIGHTHOUSE IN 1990 WITH A MAINTENANCE CREW ON TOP OF THE HELIDECK
PHOTOGRAPHED BY THE AUTHOR

providing the lighthouse keepers with a higher standard in their living conditions, life at "the stone" had become a very comfortable one. Fridges and freezers soon arrived at the tower, enabling the keepers to preserve meats, fish and other food. Until then the keepers had been restricted to tinned and salted items which were usually stored with fruit on window shelves between the thick wall of the tower, or otherwise in the dark and cool entrance room at the base of the lighthouse. A

valve radio soon followed, bringing news and music from the BBC to the men and by the 1970s the keepers were enjoying the benefits of television! Progress it seemed meant that isolation was a thing of the past for those on the Eddystone. Pleasure craft too frequently sailed out from Plymouth, bringing passengers close to the house rock itself, so close to the tower in fact that even daily newspapers and mail found their way into the building on a regular basis. Indeed, improvements continued at pace throughout the entire lighthouse service, but with these new advances, some believed that this new technology would bring a real threat of redundancy for many employed by the Corporation of Trinity House.

Traditional working practices were quickly being lost, the old ways and unique hobbies of the lightkeepers were also fading away. In the late 1960s and 1970s it was rare to find any of the men making wooden models, or engaged in marquetry or rope and knot tying. The past was dead and life on the Eddystone would never be the same again. Decline too in the shipping industry had also translated itself upon the ocean and as air travel for business and pleasure became more accessible, the dark clouds started to appear on the horizon for all of those employed as lighthouse keepers.

Over the years the tower too has changed and each floor modernised, although the original bedroom still remains even if the oak furniture has been painted, yet the wooden panelled bunkbeds still offer a glimpse into a romantically imagined yesteryear on the rock.

Looking at the outside of the lighthouse, there appears to be only one obvious difference - that of the helipad, constructed in 1980 for the remarkably quick and efficient light helicopter exchanges, with its steel superstructure bolted together, crisscrossing and anchored around the glass lantern gallery.

The lighthouse's once-proud voice, that of the old fog bells, has long gone, replaced by an explosive sound system which has since evolved to an electric sound emitter.

Eddystone's strong heart was indeed ripped from its strong frame and the life-blood that once gave the beacon its unique place in maritime history has been drained from this grand sentinel of the sea.

In 1982 the last lightkeepers bade farewell to their beloved Eddystone, it was the first rock station in the country to be automated. On completion of the process, the light was reintroduced on 18 May 1982, exactly 100 years to the day after the Douglass tower was first opened by the Duke of Edinburgh. Sadly, its glorious past had been lost to time and the famous building has now become just another lifeless automated skeleton, to be observed at a distance in an ocean setting.

In such a short period of time the human and traditional face of the lighthouse service had been condemned. Automation became the key word for many traditional industries during the 1980s. It was either seen as progress and technical advancement, or a cheaper option for the employer. Many of the old keepers believed that it was simply economics which drove the corporation to change its working practices.

In the 1990s all the remaining rock lighthouses were automated, and by the end of 1998, 300 years after the light first shone from Eddystone Rock, the service was changed for ever.

FISHING FROM THE SET-OFF
THE AUTHOR'S COLLECTION

Many ex-lightkeepers still rue the day when automation was introduced to their service. It did as many predicted deliver the final blow to a unique maritime tradition. A few lucky men remained employed by the Trinity House Lighthouse service, working as custodians of the remaining land lighthouses.

The majority of these sites and countless numbers of Trinity House properties have also completely changed. As the value of land and buildings rose throughout the 1990s the corporation realised their financial assets and began selling off much of what they owned. Today, the old keepers' cottages remain a good source of revenue in so much that many buildings have been sold off for individual developments or are now rented to private companies as holiday homes and the like.

Sadly, all of the rock lighthouse keepers have long gone, no more do they sit around the kitchen table playing cards, singing, or are to be found reading within the low light room. Their traditional hobbies of rug making, marquetry, knot making and modelling have also died out, leaving only memories of a past way of life, that will no doubt soon be forgotten. No man will ever again bake bread and cakes within the tower's kitchen nor catch fish from the set-off or lantern rail.

The tales of these keepers' own unique experiences will surely also fade in time, but perhaps through imagination and storytelling their remarkable tales will live on and be passed down for other generations to marvel at.

THE AUTHOR IN THE TOWER'S KITCHEN IN 1990
THE AUTHOR'S COLLECTION

But for those ex-keepers and last remaining Trinity House men, who are by now in the year 2005 nearing retirement, it must seem quite amusing for them to remember their first communication from the authority, which usually included a sheet of paper advising "suitable candidates for possible employment within the service".

It read as follows:

Candidates for appointment as Light keepers must be of British nationality, medically fit, have full normal vision with or without spectacles, and be between the ages of 18 and 32 years. No technical knowledge is required as preliminary training is given in how to operate and maintain different types of equipment for lighting, fog signalling and radio, and in weather reporting. Thereafter a successful candidate enters the Service as a Supernumerary Assistant Keeper (SAK) for a period of approximately twelve months' probation, during which he will serve at a number of different lighthouses to gain practical experience and, when necessary, be posted as Relief for keepers absent through sickness or on leave. In addition to pay an SAK receives a daily allowance for quarters, and is entitled to seventeen days' paid holiday a year plus one week for each month of service on a rock station. On satisfactory completion of the probationary period, he will then be promoted to Assistant Keeper (AK), and be appointed to a particular lighthouse: rent free married quarters are provided or a housing allowance is paid in lieu. An AK's salary increases by annual increments for seven years after appointment. As and when vacancies occur, promotion to the position of Principal Keeper (PK) on a higher salary scale will follow, with annual increments for a further five years. All posts as Assistant Keeper and Principal Keeper are permanent, and pensionable at current Civil Service Rates. Uniform clothing is provided free each year; and in addition to basic pay and rent free accommodation or housing allowance in lieu, for keepers appointed to rock stations a daily rock-money allowance and daily victualling allowance is paid while the keeper is resident on the station. AK's and PK's appointed to shore lighthouses have twenty-eight days' leave a year; those at rock stations are granted four weeks free from duty on completion of each period of eight weeks on the lighthouse.

THE EDDYSTONE LIGHTHOUSE AND LIGHTSHIP
BY KIND PERMISSION OF THE CORPORATION OF TRINITY HOUSE

THE BEDROOM IN THE LIGHTHOUSE IN 1990
PHOTOGRAPHED BY THE AUTHOR

Most lighthouses worked with a four-man complement, comprising of one PK and three AKs, which might include an SAK.

Watch-keeping and working times revolved around a three-day 24-hour cycle, with four hours on duty and four hours off, except for the morning watch of 0400 to 1200hrs. The breakdown of these timings were: 1200 to 1600hrs; 1600 to 2000hrs; 2000 to 2400hrs; and 2400 to 0400hrs.

The Eddystone Lighthouse has during its lifetime given immense security to every nationality of seafarer passing by and all through the ages generations of romantics and ordinary people have found a unique fascination in this remarkable but isolated structure.

THE PRESENT EDDYSTONE LIGHTHOUSE WITH WATER BAGS UPON THE HELIDECK - AS SEEN IN 1990
PHOTOGRAPHED BY THE AUTHOR

Certainly its fame was at a zenith in Victorian times when its importance was fully understood and when the Eddystone's incredible story was known throughout the world, when songs were written and sung about it.

In one early popular music-hall piece, the Eddystone lighthouse was brought to life and people throughout the land felt something special inside when they sang the song :

THE EDDYSTONE LIGHT

Oh, me father was the keeper of the Eddystone
  Light,
And he married a mermaid one fine night.
From this union there came three.
Two little fishes and the third was me,
Chorus:
Singing yo-ho-ho, the wind blows free,
Oh, for the life on the rolling sea! rolling sea!

One night as I was a-trimming of the glim,
Singing a verse from the evening hymn,
A voice on the starboard shouted "Ahoy!"
And there was my mother sitting on a buoy.
Chorus

Oh, where are the rest of my children three?
My mother then asked me.
One was exhibited as a talking fish,
The other was served from a chafing dish.
Chorus

Then the phosphorous flashed in her seaweed
  hair,
I looked again and my mother wasn't there.
But her voice came echoing back from the night,
To Hell with the keeper of the Eddystone Light!

LOOKING DOWN FROM THE TOP OF THE TOWER
PHOTOGRAPHED BY THE AUTHOR

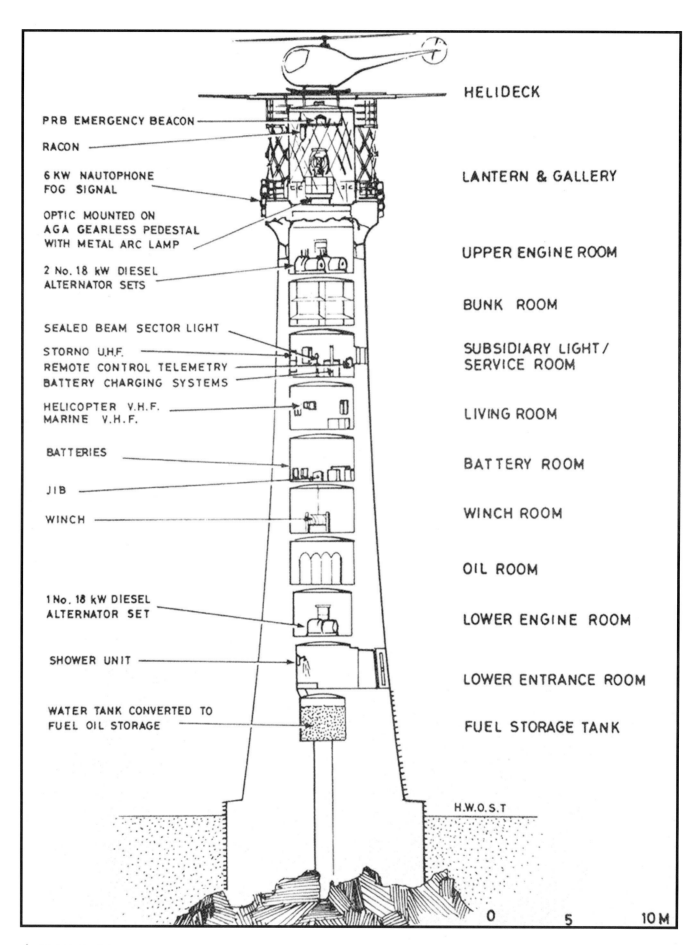

HELIDECK

PRB EMERGENCY BEACON

RACON

6 KW NAUTOPHONE
FOG SIGNAL

LANTERN & GALLERY

OPTIC MOUNTED ON
AGA GEARLESS PEDESTAL
WITH METAL ARC LAMP

UPPER ENGINE ROOM

2 No. 18 kW DIESEL
ALTERNATOR SETS

BUNK ROOM

SEALED BEAM SECTOR LIGHT

STORNO U.H.F.
REMOTE CONTROL TELEMETRY
BATTERY CHARGING SYSTEMS

SUBSIDIARY LIGHT/
SERVICE ROOM

HELICOPTER V.H.F.
MARINE V.H.F.

LIVING ROOM

BATTERIES

BATTERY ROOM

JIB

WINCH

WINCH ROOM

OIL ROOM

1 No. 18 kW DIESEL
ALTERNATOR SET

LOWER ENGINE ROOM

SHOWER UNIT

LOWER ENTRANCE ROOM

WATER TANK CONVERTED TO
FUEL OIL STORAGE

FUEL STORAGE TANK

H.W.O.S.T

0   5   10 M

A CROSS-SECTIONAL PLAN OF THE PRESENT INTERIOR OF THE LIGHTHOUSE
BY KIND PERMISSION OF THE CORPORATION OF TRINITY HOUSE

The Eddystone rock lighthouse is surely the most famous of all the world's lighthouses.

Over the centuries it has been celebrated in paintings and in literature, appearing on postage stamps and coinage all over the world.

And today in the 21st century, the Douglass tower still stands proud upon the English channel, providing seafarers even now with a visual aid for their safety.

Perhaps it is true that the lighthouse itself is now of less importance to the mariner than it once was, as virtually every vessel carries its own radar or remarkable satellite navagation device onboard, but nonetheless lighthouses worldwide still have a role and place within the modern world. Technology, like time, has moved on and the lighting system in particular at the Eddystone lighthouse has been transformed and reinvented many times throughout its long history.

Changes in technology continue to shape the internal workings of this famous lighthouse, and as the 21st century takes its course, new inventions slowly find their way to the Eddystone reef.

During 1999 solarisation was undertaken at the 72 metre high lighthouse, an undertaking which cost Trinity House £350,000. The work was the largest of its type to be attempted and it was only the second rock light to be converted by the authority. This system offered an opportunity for the lighthouse service to save substantially on its maintenance and running costs and the practice of solar conversion proved economically very successful, which was extended to all the other lighthouses, lightships and beacons controlled by the Authority. The costs of this installation created a financial 5 year debit for the service, but this sum has already been paid back by the new technology, which still has a ten year life span, as virtually no professional technical maintenance is now required, so very few visits to the tower are required. The only apparent downside to the conversion programme is an increase in seabird numbers resting on the tower's superstructure, which is creating greater mess on the glass panes and fittings.

At the Eddystone during the first years of the new millennium, the main navigational lighting equipment consists of a 35 watt Philips Mastercolour CDM-T lamp, equipped with a photocell for nighttime operation which gives a range of 17 nautical miles. Also, a standard Lumen Technology two-position lampcharger is fitted to provide a second lamp.

The previous optic, a four panel 4th Order rotating glass unit mounted on an AGA PRB gearless pedestal, remains. Outside, fitted around the complete circumference of the tower are 90 Solar Nova 50D modules with a rating of 50W each and these produce the necessary energy for the new solar powered system. Within the "low light" room, the emergency lighting is provided by two synchronised ML300 lanterns which provide a ten nautical mile range and a 3 watt lamp in a Tideland RL355 range lantern which produces an eight mile nominal range red light.

The fog signal equipment has been altered to a DC powered fog signal, controlled by a HSS VF500 - 11O T visibility monitor, with its emitters mounted off the helideck superstructure, and the operation of this device is linked to the main light. Finally in the lower engine/store room, a Lister TS3 diesel alternator with remote start facility is provided for emergency uses.

The transfer to solar power represents self-sufficiency and environmental improvement and these technical advances continue to change the internal organs of the lighthouse, although from the outside very little has altered since the 1980s when the helipad was fitted.

The Eddystone Lighthouse is constantly monitored from the Trinity House Central Monitoring and Control Centre at Harwich. It is a modern rock station, a vacuum of microswitches, computers and relays, with its own built-in sensing and monitoring gadgets that allow for continuous operation. Further developments at the Eddystone will surely follow in the coming years and Trinity House will continue to maintain their reputation and tradition as a leader in lighthouse management.

THE MAIN EDDYSTONE LIGHT IN 1990, SURROUNDED BY THE HELIDECK SUPERSTRUCTURE
PHOTOGRAPHED BY THE AUTHOR

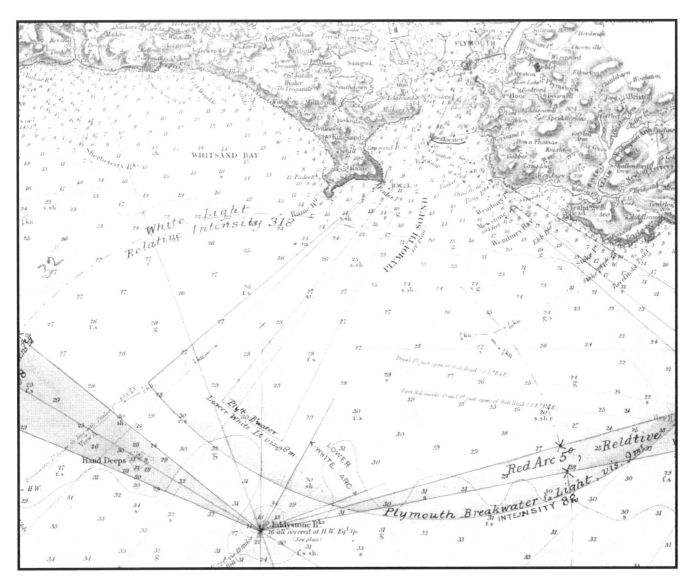

THE EDDYSTONE LIGHTHOUSE AND THE COASTLINE OF DEVON AND CORNWALL
BY KIND PERMISSION OF THE CORPORATION OF TRINITY HOUSE

The Eddystone reef and its lighthouse still remains a focal point for locals and visitors alike, especially when looking out to sea from the high and spectacular vantage point of the historic Plymouth Hoe. Old Smeaton's Tower, sitting majestically on top of this cliff, has also become a massive tourist attraction for the city. Although the structure itself had been in decline for many years, the importance of the tower was not truly recognised until August 2000, when Plymouth city council was awarded a large financial package and grant for major restoration work to begin on the building, which also included the setting up of a permanent Eddystone exhibition near by.

This undertaking enabled the team involved an opportunity of recreating the lighthouse as it would have been in the early 19th century. Conservation demands and sympathetic working practices have transformed the lighthouse to its former glory with the added bonus of wooden shutters being once again attached to the windows. It is now defined by English Heritage as a Grade 1 listed building, this status should hopefully ensure that Smeaton's Tower will never again fall into disrepair and so continue to offer the visitors and generations to come a glimpse into its past and a reminder of the days when men lived and worked in lighthouses.

UPDATED RESEARCH 2005 - JOHN RUDYARD

Further exhaustive investigations concerning the facts about John Rudyerd, correctly spelt Rudyard, have produced overwhelming evidence to prove beyond doubt that he was indeed born in Staffordshire and did not, as many people believed, come from Cornwall.

John Rudyard was born in the village of Leek, Staffordshire during 1650 and baptised on 22 April of that year. He was born into a large family, produced from the second marriage by his father Anthony Rudyard of Delacres Abbey, County Stafford.

The Rudyard family were at that time wealthy landowners who were regarded highly by the gentry of the day. They also owned a respectable and important silk trading business, with mills that employed many people of the local area. These business interests were supported by influential figures, the fashion-conscious high-society elite, besides well-known celebrities, who were all happy to associate themselves with the Rudyard "silk" family, throughout the 1600s.

John Rudyard came from a background of grandeur and importance and was obviously a well-educated child who grew up with Lords and Ladies of the land being family friends. Meeting famous and well-to-do people was an occurrence of his everyday life, so he was well groomed as a young adult to entertain the likes of Edward Stubbs, the painter, who stayed with the family at Abbey Farm during 1666, prior to John's own departure for London.

There can be no doubt that the traditional account of the Cornish lad, a runaway who lived in poverty, is just pure fiction, an inspired version of a colourful and romantic myth which has been handed down by generations, invented perhaps, solely to complete the full Eddystone story.

As a 16-year-old, John Rudyard moved from his Staffordshire home to London, where his new associates and friends came from the same high class of people that he belonged to. Indeed he already knew many people there, acquaintences and family members who would help him to begin his new life as an apprentice. For the next 7 years John Rudyard, as stated on page 30, worked for a Robert Morris, where he learned the import and tailoring business of furs, cottons and silks.

Soon the young man had established himself within the environment and company of the London silk-trading community. It was an obvious conclusion therefore for him to befriend like-minded professionals. Certainly it did him no harm to count as family friends the likes of the Lord and Lady Shirley who would provide him with countless contacts and clients in the years which followed. It wasn't long before he also found a bride, the very eligible Sarah Jackman, a young woman who too came from a good family of wealthy silk mercers, who were living in the smart district of Holborn. Sarah's father and family appear to have taken to their future son-in-law, as they gave him much financial support in setting up his own business, on completion of his apprenticeship, although there is some confusion as to the correct date listed within records at the Skinners Company.

Nevertheless, it is correct to say that John Rudyard aged 24 years and Sarah Jackman were married on 14 December 1674 at St Andrew's Church in Holborn, London. After their union the two worked for her family business, later taking charge of the Ludgate Hill shop, given to them by Thomas Jackman, Sarah's father. Three years later a daughter, also named Sarah, was born, although I have found no evidence to suggest that they had other children and there is no mention of offspring in Mrs Sarah Rudyard's will.

Throughout the late 1600s records show us that John Rudyard was in a variety of legal partnerships with Sarah's father, mainly relating to land deals in and around London. But we can also see that such arrangements were not always straightforward.

We read:-

Lease and release 24/25 June 1686
1. John Rudyard citizen and skinner of London
   and Thomas Jackman of the parish of St
   Brides, London, Gent, brother and heir of
   Francis Jackman, Gent, deceased.
2. John Gurney of Stewkley, Gent. Property in
   D/DU/2/594-594 with la, ar. laid in Potten
   Sands shooting upon Parsonage Close.
   Consideration £107.
Assignment 25 June 1686
1. John Rudyard citizen and skinner of London.
2. John Gurney of Stewkley, Gent.
Judgement in Court of Common Pleas in Hilary
   term against Francis Jackman, for debt of
   £200.

Whether John Rudyard and the Jackman family fell out over such matters is unclear and I feel sad that we know so little about him as a person. I do believe however that he was a hard and experienced businessman who took all the opportunities that came his way. But in later years we read that the special relationship he had developed with his long-time friend and lighthouse partner John Lovett came to a disastrous end. So bad was the situation that a few day's before Lovett's death, his wife Mary writes to her father in criticism of Rudyard, complaining of the "meanness of his character".

The legal documents between Lovett and Rudyard make interesting reading, especially the original contract they had drawn up for their lighthouse venture.

We read:-

1. John Lovett - 2. John Rudyard citizen and
   skinner of London reciting an act for building
   the new Edystone lighthouse; 2. has devised
   and built a model of the proposed new
   lighthouse - He is to have sole management of
   the building thereof for £50 pa and is to
   receive £250 pa from the dues for his life and
   that of his wife Sarah - 19 June 1706.

In another account dated 11 December 1708 we read:-

1. John Lovett. 2. John Rudyard - similar to
   previous agreement - Endorsed.
Surrender of all claims by 2 - 17 November 1709.

References relating to Rudyard during this period are few and far between. He and Sarah continued to live in Holborn, London, although other addresses are mentioned in various sources.

On 24 April 1710 John Lovett died in the knowledge that many financial difficulties remained unresolved within the lighthouse operation. Rudyard himself was with his old friend at Epsom in the hours before Lovett's demise and we can only imagine the strain between Lovett's family and the man who was to Mary now an unwelcome visitor. Although Rudyard and Mary Lovett had little involvement with one another after this time, it is of interest to learn that Mary travelled to meet Sarah Rudyard at a Litchfield address in 1713, a date some have acknowledged as the year of Rudyard's own death. However, we could assume that Rudyard was alive in 1716, from the fact that he was a named lease owner of the syndicate headed by Robert Harcourt Weston, who purchased the Lovett Eddystone lease at auction in 1716 for £8000, when Mary concluded that the purchasers had a "great bargain" and that she was glad to be rid of it. Unfortunately, from sketchy records I can only add that I believe it is possible that John Rudyard died on 20 November 1718 and his widow in May of the following year, and that both were buried in the crypt at St Andrew's Church in Holborn, London. Sadly those buried there were gathered together and reinterred in a new mass grave during 2001.

EDDYSTONE LITERARY FORMS BEFORE 1800

Over the centuries many names have been
used for the EDDYSTONE and the main
variations are listed here :-

YDY-STONE – Earliest references 1453,
1478.

EDE-STONE – 1478, William of Worcester;
1590, Ryther's Discourse; 1759, Tablet at St
George's Church, Stonehouse (destroyed
World War 2).

IDE-STONE – 1586, 1587, 1590, 1594,
1607, 1695, 1722, Camden's Britannia; 1590,
Mariner's Mirrour; 1640, Canalis inter Angl.
et Gallioe; 1646, Arcano del Mare; 1676, De
Nieuve Water Wevelt, Amsterdam; 1789,
Gough's Camden.

IDY-STONE – 1599, Hakluyt's Voyages.

EDI-STONE – 1604, Barker's Of Headlands;
1623, Letter of Sir William Monson; 1646,
Arcano del Mare; 1660, Burston's Portolano;
1670, Comberford's Portolano; 1707, Beaux
Stratagem, act v. sc. 4; Burchett's Complete
Naval History; 1750, Universal Mag., and
Pocock's Travels; 1755, Wyatt's Adventures;
1764, Atlas Maritime; 1768, Ellis's Map;
1774 Postlethwayt's Dictionary of
Commerce; 1778, Brooke's Gazetteer; 1791,
Beaux Stratagem.

EDDI-STONE – 1623, Letter of Sir William
Monson; 1710, Willdey's Devon; 1720,
Burchett's Naval History; 1724, 1731, 1736
Moll's Map; 1742, Badeslade and Toms;
1748, Universal Magazine; 1757, Martin's
Magazine; 1799, Lipscomb's Journey into
Cornwall.

EDIE-STONE – 1584, Norman's Safeguard
for Sailors; 1590, Ubaldino's Expeditionis.

EDY-STONE – 1590, Ubaldino's
Expeditionis; 1699, Winstanley's Print; 1704,
Defoe's Storm; 1705, Act of Queen Anne;
1706, Petition from Winstanley's widow;
1709, Act of Queen Anne; 1713, Bickham's
British Monarchy; 1722, Camden's Britannia;
1724, Moll's Map; 1729, Diary of Pentecost
Barker; 1733, Sailmaker's Print of Edystone
Lighthouse; 1745, Description of England
and Wales; 1748, Bickham's British
Monarchy; 1755, Beaumont and Disney's
Tour; 1756, Brice's Gazetteer; 1762, Letter,
Dr. Mudge; 1791, Gilpin's Observations on
West of England; 1791, Smeaton's Narrative.

EDYN-STONE – 1625, Sir John Glanville,
Voyage to Cadiz.

EDYE-STONE – 1636, Letter from the Lord
Mayor of Plymouth.

EDDY-STONE – 1664, Trinity House, report
on Petition; 1693, Collin's Coasting Pilot;
1694, Patent for the first lighthouse; 1701-2,
Bateson's Petition; 1704, Defoe's Storm;
1706, 1707, 1708, Letter, Trinity House;
1708-9, Hovenden Walker's Diary; 1716,
1720, Gay's Trivia; 1724, Defoe's Tour; 1730-
31, 1737, 1745, 1770, 1776-9, Gray's Poems;
1739, Morant's Defeat of Spanish Armada;
1755, London Magazine; 1755, 1757,
Gentleman's Magazine; 1756, Patent for
Floating Light; 1758, Borlase's Natural
History of Cornwall; 1759, Brice's Gazetteer;
1764, Mortimer's History of England; 1769,
Borlase's Antiquities of Cornwall; 1774,
British Museum, Copy of Letter by Lieut.
McKenzie; 1781, Great Britain's Coasting
Pilot; 1788, England Delineated; 1797,
Encyclopedia Britannica.

THE EDDYSTONE LIGHT IN FIGURES

The Eddystone Rock Lighthouse is monitored and controlled from the Trinity House Operations Centre in Harwich, Essex.

- Position 50 degrees 10'.80 north and 04 degrees 15'.90 west.
- Established in 1698, it is 49 metres high with its light 41 metres above mean high water. The 250 mm rotating optic is of the 4th order, and its character consists of a group of white lights flashing twice every 10 seconds. It has a 70-watt lamp with an intensity of 199,000 candela and a range of 22 sea miles.
- The fog signal character is three blasts every 60 seconds.

Information supplied by the Corporation of Trinity House website 2005

THE BEAUFORT SCALE

WIND SPEED (KNOTS)	FORCE	DESCRIPTION OF AIR AND SEA
Nil	0	Calm. Like a mirror
1–3	1	Light air. Gentle ripple
4–6	2	Light breeze. Small wavelets
7–10	3	Gentle breeze. Wavelets with crests
11–16	4	Moderate breeze. Small waves and white horses
17–21	5	Fresh breeze. Moderate waves, many white horses
22–27	6	Strong breeze. Large waves with some spray
28–33	7	Near gale. Waves heap up and foam
34–40	8	Gale. Waves crests break into spindrift
41–47	9	Strong gale. High toppling waves and spray
48–55	10	Storm. Surface broken up and tumbling
56–63	11	Violent storm. Chaotic; rarely experienced
Over 64	12	Hurricane. Chaotic; rarely experienced

The equivalent on land is:

0	Smoke rises straight up in the air
1	Smoke drifts slightly
2	Rustling of leaves in the trees
3	Small twigs move on a tree
4	Paper blown about
5	Trees with leaves sway
6	Hear the noise of the wind
7	A little difficulty in walking against it
8	Twigs break from trees
9	Some structural damage
10	Find shelter
11–12	Life-threatening

As a final tribute to those who have worked on and at the Eddystone over the last 300 years, I felt it would be a fitting to offer the poem by Longfellow:

THE LIGHTHOUSE

The rocky ledge runs far into the sea,
And on its outer point, some miles away,
The Lighthouse lifts its massive masonry,
A pillar of fire by night, of cloud by day.

Even at this distance I can see the tides,
Upheaving, break unheard along its base,
A speechless wrath, that rises and subsides
In the white lip and tremor of the face.

And as the evening darkens, lo! how bright,
Through the deep purple of the twilight air,
Beams forth the sudden radiance of its light
With strange, unearthly splendour in the glare!

Not one alone; from each projecting cape
And perilous reef along the ocean's verge,
Starts into life a dim, gigantic shape,
Holding its lantern o'er the restless surge.

Like the great giant Christopher it stands
Upon the brink of the tempestuous wave,
Wading far out among the rocks and sands,
The night-o'ertaken mariner to save.

And the great ships sail outward and return,
Bending and bowing o'er the billowy swells,
And ever joyful, as they see it burn,
They wave their silent welcomes and farewells,

They come forth from the darkness and their sails
Gleam for a moment only in the blaze,
And eager faces, as the light unveils,
Gaze at the tower, and vanish while they gaze.

The mariner remembers when a child,
On his first voyage, he saw it fade and sink;
And when, returning from adventures wild,
He saw it rise again o'er ocean's brink.

Steadfast, serene, immovable, the same
Year after year, through all the silent night
Burns on for evermore that quenchless flame,
Shines on that inextinguishable light!

It sees the ocean to its bosom clasp
The rocks and sea sand with the kiss of peace;
It sees the wild winds lift it in their grasp,
And hold it up, and shake it like a fleece.

The startled waves leap over it; the storm
Smites it with all the scourges of the rain,
And steadily against its solid form

Press the great shoulders of the hurricane.
The sea bird wheeling round it, with a din
Of wings and winds and solitary cries,
Blinded and maddened by the light within
Dashes himself against the glare, and dies.

A new Prometheus, chained upon the rock,
Still grasping in his hand the fire of Jove,
It does not hear the cry, nor heed the shock,
But hails the mariner with words of love.

"Sail on!" it says, "sail on, ye stately ships!
And with your floating bridge the ocean span;
Be mine to guard this light from all eclipse,
Be yours to bring man nearer unto man!"

— HENRY W LONGFELLOW

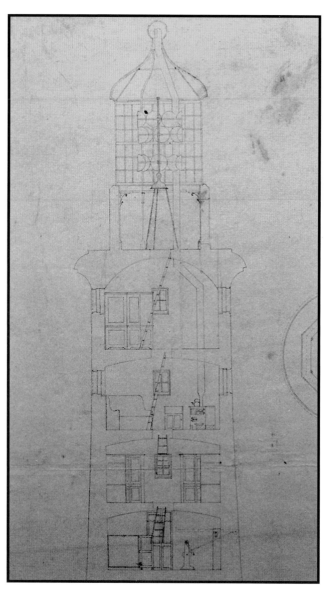

AN ORIGINAL DRAWING OF SMEATON'S TOWER
BY KIND PERMISSION OF THE CORPORATION OF TRINITY HOUSE

ACKNOWLEDGEMENTS

Special thanks to all those who helped during my research for this book:

Breda Wall, Jane Wilson, Frank Celano, Jon Sim
TRINITY HOUSE

Helene Mitchell
THE NATIONAL MARITIME MUSEUM

Bill Torrens
THE COUNTY RECORDS OFFICE, AYLESBURY, BUCKS

Dr Alison Morrison-Low
THE NATIONAL MUSEUMS OF SCOTLAND

Edmund Verney
CLAYDON HOUSE, BUCKS

Mrs S R Ranson
CLAYDON HOUSE TRUST, BUCKS

Victoria Manning
THE CITY OF WESTMINSTER ARCHIVES, LONDON

Ursula S Carlyle
THE MERCERS' COMPANY, LONDON

Stuart O Seanoir
TRINITY COLLEGE LIBRARY, DUBLIN, IRELAND

Stephen Freeth
GUILDHALL LIBRARIES, LONDON

Aideen M Ireland
THE IRISH NATIONAL ARCHIVES, DUBLIN, IRELAND

Les Douch, Dr Michael Nix, Martin Boyle, Dr A Q Morton, Stephen D Snobelen, Christine Allison, Gareth Hughes

Trinity House Archives, Cowes, I O W

The Public Records Office, Kew

The National Register of Archives, London

Leeds Industrial Museum, Yorkshire

West Yorkshire Archive Service, Yorkshire

The Saffron Walden Museum, Essex

The Skinners' Company, London

Cornwall Records Office, Cornwall

The University of Reading Library

The British Library Reference Dept, London

The National Library of Ireland, Dublin

West Devon Records Office, Devon

The William Salt Library, Staffordshire

Salisbury Library and Galleries, Wiltshire

Plymouth City Museum and Art Gallery

Plymouth City Library

English Heritage Photographic Library, London

The Royal Commission on Historical Manuscripts, London

Staffordshire, Stoke on Trent Archive Service, Staffs

The United Kingdom Hydrographic Office, Somerset

With my grateful acknowledgement to:

Patricia Eve
Louis Mackay
Hugh Brazier
Chris and Ros Evans
Nigel Overton
Maureen Attrill
Mike and Michelle at E J Rickard

Also to my wife Jan and daughter Lara for their understanding during my absences - Thank you all.

BIBLIOGRAPHY AND REFERENCES

DOCUMENTATION and serious literature relating to the Eddystone Lighthouse, which has proven to be useful in my research:

N LUTTRELL
A Brief Relation (1697)

H WINSTANLEY
Edystone Lighthouse, Narrative of the Building (1699)

DANIEL DEFOE
The Storm (1704)
The Spectator (1712)

W MAITLAND
The History of London (1739)

H WALPOLE
Catalogue of Engravers (1786)

JOHN SMEATON
Narrative of the Building and a Description of the Construction of the Edystone Lighthouse with stone (1791)

ROBERT HARCOURT WESTON
Letters and Important Documents relative to the Eddystone Lighthouse, selected from the correspondence of the late Robert Weston (1811)

R STEVENSON
English Lighthouse Tours (1801, 1813, 1818)

BRAYBROOK
History of Audley End (1836)

A STEVENSON
A Rudimentary Treatise on the History, Construction and Illumination of Lighthouses (1850)

S SMILES
Lives of the Engineers (1862)

D STEVENSON
Lighthouses (1864)

ALPHONSE ESQUIROS
Cornwall and its Coasts (1865)

J POLSUE
Lake's Parochial History of the County of Cornwall (1867–72)

W H DAVENPORT ADAMS
Lighthouses and Lightships (1870)

E L HERVEY
The Rock Light (1870)

T NELSON & SON PUBLISHER
The Story of John Smeaton and the Eddystone Lighthouse (1876)

T STEVENSON
Lighthouse Construction and Illumination (1881)

E PRICE EDWARDS
The Eddystone Lighthouses (1882)

R N WORTH
Calendar of the Plymouth Municipal Records, Plymouth for Rame Head (1893)

EMMA MARSHALL
The First Light on the Eddystone (1894)

D P HEAP
Ancient and Modern Lighthouses (1889)

C R B BARRET
The Trinity House of Deptford Strond (1893)

THOMAS WILLIAMS
Life of Sir James Douglass (1900)

H F WHITFIELD
Plymouth and Devonport (1900)

PARTHENOPE & MARY VERNEY
The Verney Memoirs (1907)

SAXBY J WRYDE
British Lighthouses (1913)

F A TALBOT
Lighthouses and Lightships (1913)

L G CARR LAUGHTON & V HEDDON
Great Storms (1927)

LADY MARGARET M VERNEY
Verney Letters of the 18th Century (1930)

W H McCormick
The Modern Book of Lighthouses (1936)

J P Bowen
British Lighthouses (1946)

D A Stevenson
English Lighthouse Tours (1946)

Hilary P Mead
Trinity House (1947)

R A J Walling
The Story of Plymouth (1950)

J Fernand Lanoire
La Phare de Cordouan (1953)

Fred Majdalany
The Red Rocks of The Eddystone (1959)

D A Stevenson
The World's Lighthouses Before 1820 (1959)

M Oppenheim
The Maritime History of Devon (1968)

Cyril Noall
Cornish Lights and Shipwrecks (1968)

Lee Chadwick
Lighthouses and Lightships (1971)

Douglas B Hauge & Rosemary Christie
Lighthouses (1975)

Kenneth Sutton-Jones
Pharos (1985)

Michael Tarrant
Cornwall's Lighthouse Heritage (1990)

F Ross Holland
Lighthouses (1995)

Alison Barnes
Artist, Inventor and Lighthouse-builder
Henry Winstanley. Plymouth City Museum
& Art Gallery (2003)

Further Reading

Henry Winstanley's papers
Saffron Walden Museum, Essex

**Royal Society of London Philosophical
Transactions – Vol 49, pt 2** (1756)

Captain Chaplin's papers
The Guildhall Reference Library, London

Eddystone papers
Plymouth City Reference Library, Devon

A Week on the Eddystone
Arthur O Cooke

Genealogical Abstracts
Sir William Betham

The Eddystone: Facts and Fictions
Woodhouse

**Celebrated Mechanics and Their
Achievements**
F Holmes

The Hastings Papers - Vol 1 (1928)
Reginald Rawdon Hastings

**Dictionary of National Biography: Missing
Persons** (1993)
James Hodge

The Lighthouses of England and Wales
Martin Boyle

THE RESTORED SMEATON'S TOWER ON PLYMOUTH HOE 2005

PHOTOGRAPHED BY THE AUTHOR